# Loving Big Brother

Constant sc... v surveillance cameras is usually seen as, at best, a necessary invasion of privacy and, at worst, an infringement of human rights. But in this radical new account of the uses of surveillance in art, performance and popular culture, John E. McGrath sets out a surprising alternative: a world in which we have much to gain from the experience of being watched.

In *Loving Big Brother*, the author tackles head on the overstated claims of the crime-prevention and anti-terrorism lobbies. But he also argues that we can and do desire and enjoy surveillance, and that if we can understand why this is we may transform the effect it has on our lives.

*Loving Big Brother* looks at a wide range of performance and visual artists, at popular television shows and movies, and at our day-to-day encounters with surveillance. Rooting its arguments in an accessible reading of cultural theory, this iconoclastic book develops a notion of surveillance space – somewhere beyond the public and the private, somewhere we will all soon live. It's a place we're just beginning to understand.

**John E. McGrath** is Artistic Director of Manchester's groundbreaking Contact Theatre, which brings bold new performance to diverse young audiences. He has directed work by Lemn Sissay, Jeff Noon and others. In both theatre and theoretical work he focuses on the intersections of space, media and language.

For Tom and Margaret McGrath,
who have always watched over me!

JOHN E. McGRATH

# Loving Big Brother

Performance, privacy and surveillance space

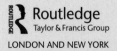

Routledge
Taylor & Francis Group

LONDON AND NEW YORK

First published 2004
by Routledge
11 New Fetter Lane, London EC4P 4EE

Simultaneously published in the USA and Canada
by Routledge
29 West 35th Street, New York, NY 10001

*Routledge is an imprint of the Taylor & Francis Group*

Typeset in Rotis by Prepress Projects Ltd, Perth, Scotland
Printed and bound in Great Britain by TJ International Ltd, Padstow

*British Library Cataloguing in Publication Data*
A catalogue record for this book is available from the British Library

*Library of Congress Cataloging in Publication Data*
McGrath, John E. (John Edward), 1962–
   Loving big brother : performance, privacy, and surveillance space /
John E. McGrath.
      p. cm.
   Includes bibliographical references and index.
   1. Electronic surveillance – Social aspects. 2. Electronics in crime
prevention – Social aspects. 3. Privacy, Right of. 4. Technology and the
arts. 5. Video recording in the theater. 6. Popular culture. I.
Title.
HM846.M34 2004
306.4–dc21

                                                     2003014202

ISBN 0-415-27537-7 (hbk)
ISBN 0-415-27538-5 (pbk)

# Contents

# Preface

A body throws itself out of a burning tower, diving through the air in the agonizing moments before the impact of concrete below will smash the life out of it. We are watching live on network television. There is nothing we can do.

A group of unremarkable people are locked in a house for two months, bored and bickering; cameras record their every mundane move. We watch in our millions, interrupting busy schedules to catch up on the ins and outs of lives restricted to the entirely inconsequential.

If two experiences have defined my relationship to the recorded image in recent years they are the footage of September 11, 2001 and an addictive viewing of the UK version of television show *Big Brother*. I am undoubtedly far from alone. These two events – and particularly the World Trade Center attacks of course – shocked in a wide variety of ways; but in a world in which the average city dweller is caught on camera hundreds of times a day, part of our response to these images related to the daily surveillance of ourselves. In both cases, we obsessively viewed footage when it was clear that, in the case of the World Trade Center, nothing new was about to emerge since we were watching the same shots, perhaps occasionally from a different angle, again and again, and in the case of *Big Brother* – well, nothing much new was going to emerge there either. Yet this obsessive viewing, I believe, revealed not that we had all suddenly taken leave of our senses, but rather that we were in the process of realizing, of taking in the fact, that our world had been changed forever, not just by terrorism or television, but by surveillance itself.

Not so long ago, the words 'Big Brother' conjured in the public mind not the image of annoying, lovable or devious day-to-day people suddenly elevated to stardom by a television game show, but *Nineteen Eighty-Four*, the book by George Orwell, which, although perhaps not as widely read as it was referenced, had entered the popular consciousness as a representation of the repressive nature of an all-seeing state. It was pretty clear what everyone meant by the phrase 'Big Brother' – they meant invasion of privacy. Winston Smith's closing epiphany in the book – 'He loved Big Brother' – was interpreted, when it was remembered, as a chilling prophecy of the complete destruction of self by the surveying state. Now we find ourselves in a society in which watching ordinary people do not much on television has become a popular pastime, and in which there is significant public support for massive extension of state surveillance powers.

I have said that I was not alone in my intensive, regular viewings of both *Big Brother* and the events of September 11. However, I did bring a particular viewpoint and experience (as we each do) to my watching, in that for some time I had been developing the ideas on surveillance that form the backbone of this book. Within this work, two strands of thought had unexpectedly emerged as key: first, the idea that surveillance has proliferated not least because we desire it – we enjoy it, play with it, use it for comfort; and, secondly, more surprisingly, and initially perhaps seemingly contradictorily, the thought that, at root, all of our experiences of surveillance are structured by the expectation of death.

Spending many summer evenings watching the *Big Brother* housemates doing not much, and then, in September 2001, spending all night every night for days on end watching footage of the World Trade Center attacks (I had lived in New York for many years and found it difficult to be reconciled to my safety and distance from a place in which I had spent so much time and knew so many people), theories of why we want to watch and be watched by the surveillance machine were very much at the front of my mind. And yet, while ideas about the desire for surveillance, and about the structuring role of death in our experience of surveillance, were both justified and complexified by these two periods of watching, such understanding was of little help in freeing me from my obsessive viewing. In the end I had to reconcile myself to the fact that sometimes, in this surveyed, imaged, recorded world, we need not only to discuss and develop ideas about surveillance, but also to encounter the results of this recording again and again. Through repeated viewing we reposition ourselves, our psyches, in relation to what I have come to call in this study surveillance space.

# Preface

My work on surveillance has involved the review of a great deal of, and the making of some, performance and art work which explores the issues, ideas and pleasures of this field of experience. It has also involved an analysis of the ways in which our encounters with surveillance are organized by, but exceed, ideologies based on concepts of crime prevention and of privacy. Out of these analyses I have developed ideas about the ways in which we experience surveillance, and ourselves within surveillance, that are quite different from the common ideological understandings. When I was first working on this study, the idea of surveillance as a new space – with different possibilities for communication and behaviour – became a very liberating one for me. And I continue to believe that our evolving relationship to space – our participation in the evolution of surveillance space – opens up new prospects for society. However, my hours watching the trivia of *Big Brother* and the horrors of the World Trade Center attack – my obsessive repetitive viewing of this footage – reminded me very viscerally of the fact that the products of surveillance in our society are largely not the questioning, productive art works which I have explored throughout this study, but instead the abandoned, unsatisfying, addictive bits of footage and data which the surveillance system routinely produces. While art and theatre work responding to surveillance society can help us exist productively in this world, it is still the banal experience of day-to-day footage and data that defines our encounter with surveillance. In my almost endless viewings of the World Trade Center images, death was not transcended in the way that theatre and poetry can promise. What I experienced instead was a repetition of the emptiness, the perpetually unsatisfying nature of any approach to death. I left my viewing, eventually, exhausted, not enlightened. However, the opportunity to view this footage again and again was perhaps more crucial than any other factor– any art, or commentary, or eventual visit back to New York – in allowing me to approach my most disturbed, disturbing feelings about the event. It was only in these addictive viewings that I could find something which expressed the dirty, useless, selfish, distant closeness that I felt to the World Trade Center deaths. Of course, my own adjustment to the events is of little use to anyone else, but my point is that the degraded, obscured, remnant relationship to death which surveillance-type footage can bring us towards is, in fact, an appropriate and sensitive way to understand death in our society.

# Preface

As for *Big Brother*, it continues series by series, and I continue watching. A part of me hopes that this addiction, too, will eventually wear itself out, that I will come to see the dreary day-to-day activities and bickering as just the sort of thing I try to avoid in my own life and reach for the remote control. However, another part of me hopes that the series will run and run, and that I will always make time to watch these ordinary people being watched by cameras. Because,my viewing of *Big Brother* reminds me, on a felt rather than a theorizing plane, of the space in which I move and live. I would never want to be a contestant in the *Big Brother* house; there are too many other things that I want to do in my day (though I have a certain respect for those who take on this existential experiment). However, the trashiness, the repetitiveness and the occasional unexpectedness of this game show reminds us that, unlike Orwell's totalitarian eye, the many Big Brothers of our society can be submitted to partially and conditionally, can be played with and perverted. Unlike Winston Smith, we are not necessarily conceding defeat or loss of self when we admit to loving Big Brother.

# Acknowledgements

This book began life as I balanced academic explorations at New York University's Department of Performance Studies with work for theatre company Mabou Mines. My thanks first and foremost go to my dissertation advisor, Peggy Phelan, who guided me in a way that was both supportive and challenging. Many of the ideas in this book arose in response to her thought and provocations during my time at NYU. At the same time, the mad, marvellous world of the Mabou family, and particularly the guidance of my friend and mentor, Ruth Maleczech, provided me with a confidence and inspiration that allowed me to think creatively and boldly. My friends and fellow students at NYU have been my source of strength and intellectual nourishment. In particular, Jennifer Fink, Richard Green and Ed Miller were (and are) my academic family. In New York, Frances Sorensen provided a second home and much support and laughter. And designer Paul Clay was, throughout, a constant source of questions and inspiration. In England, Mandy Colleran provided invaluable input on disability politics and always encouraged ideas, ideals and a sense of the ridiculous. Caroline Cowie and Richard Thomas provided a home when I was homeless and a retreat into peace on many occasions. Declan Buckley provided me with shelter, innumerable fine meals and much support as the book developed. Margaret McGrath scoured newspaper, television and radio for mention of surveillance; many of my examples and references were her discoveries. The enthusiasm and support of these friends and colleagues was and is invaluable.

# Introduction

## Thinking surveillance

Surveillance – the word comes pre-loaded with imagery and emotions. George Orwell and Big Brother, the FBI and the KGB, private detectives and James Bond devices, real-life television and grainy images of criminals, a lone vulnerable human targeted by the resources of the state, a space-age future in which implanted chips monitor our thoughts – few of the connotations of surveillance are positive. And yet, in contemporary Western society we have largely embraced surveillance; while we worry about the limits of privacy and about things getting into 'the wrong hands', in general a burgeoning of electronic surveillance is accepted as a means of making our world safer.

In the academic world, the mention of surveillance almost always raises the ghost of Michel Foucault, whose equation of the practice of centralized surveillance with the emergence of the 'disciplined' individual in the eighteenth century forms an inevitable starting point for any subsequent study. In Foucault's terms, humanist society from the late eighteenth century on could be said to have been formed in relation to a culture of surveillance. Foucault's theories of surveillance, and his citation of the 'panopticon' prison designs of the English utilitarian Jeremy Bentham, have achieved a cross-disciplinary ubiquity, and are quoted as much by social scientists and journalists as they are by the cultural theorists who are the more usual audiences for Foucault's ideas. In fact, for a considerable period of time there seemed to be a consensus that Foucault had pretty much had the last word on surveillance in terms of academic critique.

For a field which has such a vast range of imagery and ideas associated with it, the practice of surveillance had, for several years until very recently, undergone profound and massive growth with relatively little critical engagement. While privacy campaigners have raised their arms in despair and politicians have chosen to believe that there is nothing controversial to discuss, cameras and data banks have proliferated throughout the dimensional and virtual spaces in which we move and live.

Since the late 1990s, however, the subject of surveillance has been reinvigorated as an area of discussion. Social scientists, activists and cultural theorists have started to respond to the fact of comprehensive surveillance in a variety of surveys, studies and texts. While a range of disciplines and references are brought to these discussions, certain themes inevitably prevail. Specifically, discussion of surveillance is almost always framed in terms of issues of crime prevention (now very much extended to terrorism prevention) and privacy rights.

While this study addresses both of these questions in some depth, it does so without assuming that they are in fact the appropriate frameworks in which to view surveillance. Rather, I have taken as my starting point the belief that these ways of looking at surveillance are simply ideologies – means of addressing the issue that seem natural only because they are the conventional structures through which we have been encouraged to understand the profound changes that surveillance is making in our lives. Like all ideologies, the discourses of privacy and crime are as important for what they hide about our surveillance society as for what they reveal.

As a different way in to thinking about surveillance, I have developed the idea of 'surveillance space'. Drawing on a range of thinkers including Foucault, but as diverse as Kant, Lefebvre, Benjamin and Butler, I have focused on the lived experience of surveillance and the cultural products that reveal our lives under surveillance to us. I hope that this different approach to thinking about surveillance may help us to deal in new and complex ways with the fact that the relevant question about surveillance today is not whether we should live in a surveillance society, but how.

## The absent eye

My interest in surveillance, and my instinct to analyse the phenomenon in spatial terms, grew out of my work as a theatre director. At a certain point several years ago I found myself incorporating video imagery into most shows that I directed, and live video into many. Increasingly, also, I would use microphones to amplify a mutter into a roar, or to hear the breath of an actor resound across the playing space. Such use of technology was, by that time (the late 1980s and early 1990s), far from unusual; rather it was in danger of becoming a cliché of downtown New York theatre. Nonetheless, the urge remained for me – an obsessive tendency to think through the performed potentials of a script or idea in terms of the relations between audience, performers, the space of the event and the pervasion of that space by representational technologies.

At the same time, I was developing a debilitating horror at the role of the theatre director. Increasingly, it seemed to me that the link between the various forms of theatre that I loved was provided by a fetishization of the figure of an absent but despotically controlling eye. From the political energy of Brecht to the visual feasts of Robert Wilson, from the quasi-rituals of Grotowski, Kantor, Bogart to the sly confessionalism of The Wooster Group and Mabou Mines, engaged, enquiring theatre was judged a success, *felt like* a success, when it projected back to us the figure of an absolutely controlling director, masterminding every inch, every second, of the spectacle.

The dominant cultural fantasies of surveillance – the protecting eye or controlling Big Brother – equate in many ways with the fetishized figure of the twentieth-century theatre director, controlling events from which he or she is absent through the creation of a structure that necessitates and depends upon continued obedience. And yet the incorporation of representational technologies into the stage space does not necessarily support this fetishization of the director figure. At the simplest level, the failure of most theatrical uses of video, the tendency of the technology to negate the theatrical frame, to appear much like an ill-thought-out visual aid in a shoddily constructed lecture, tends to expose the inability of the director to control anything beyond the illusory movements of play acting. The directors most accomplished in the use of on-stage video are very aware of the destruction of stage illusion that video equipment can enact, and are often actively engaged in the exploration of how this destruction relates to and undermines the production of directorial control. The Wooster Group's Liz LeCompte has perhaps the longest and most consistent record in this area. While LeCompte certainly could not be described as a director who eschews the pleasures of creating and witnessing an almost impossibly well-controlled and complex stage environment, her introduction of video teases and undercuts the fantasy of such control. When video monitors are used to introduce actors who cannot perform owing to illness or other commitments, LeCompte refers us out of the frame, away from the domain of the director's eye and towards the compromises and omissions involved in the actual making of a theatre work.

It seemed to me that, perhaps surprisingly, rather than replicating the fantasy of a controlling absent figure, the use of video in theatre – and particularly uses that incorporated either live feed of performance or audience, or, as in LeCompte's work, rough footage of absent figures – tended to emphasize the incompletions, the edges, the obscurities of the theatrical space. Introducing surveillance-like moments into theatre pieces myself – sequences in which the audience appeared, through video, on stage, or where the stage space itself was interrogated by its reappearance on screen – I found that the audience reaction was often quite gleeful, very different from the reluctant response that accompanies attempts to bring the audience bodily on stage, or to expose stage illusion through other means. Whereas these last strategies often intensify the fantasy of directorial control by seeming to undercut it, the incorporation of surveillance-like imagery into the theatre space, which might be expected to demonstrate the increasing reach of the controlling eye, in fact playfully exposed its entirely fantastical status. In one production, in which the audience was informed that it was under surveillance and instructed to 'act realistically', an extraordinary sense of improvisation took over among audience members, who used the opportunity of the instructions to play at acting.

The introduction of surveillance technology in theatrical space could, it seemed, re-enliven that space with a sense of agency and choice. Such agency and choice asserted themselves in the gap between two systems of seeming knowledge and control, between the surveillance representation and the theatrical space. I began to wonder whether the reverse proposition might not also be true, whether the introduction of theatrical understandings, above all of the spatiality that distinguishes theatre from film and video, might open up an equivalent agency in relation to surveillance.

For a director who had always been interested in the physical engagement of the audience with the theatre space, this subject was inevitably interesting. Given that surveillance also seemed to reflect yet distort the idea that most worried me in theatre, the idea of the director's controlling eye, I could hardly fail to look into the subject more thoroughly. So, I started to research the phenomenon of surveillance technology in contemporary life, with the instinct that theatrical space was a strange but productive place to start.

And so, much of the key evidence in this study is theatrical, from the art of The Wooster Group to the performances of New York's gay go-go boys to the theoretical texts of Bertolt Brecht, Antonin Artaud and Elin Diamond. Indeed, the key Brechtian idea of the self-aware spectator and the central Artaudian image of the 'double' were immediately relevant tools with which to start rethinking surveillance – ways to get outside of the seemingly self-evident ideologies via which surveillance was almost always seen and discussed. Theatre – and crucially the sense of space that it inevitably introduced – catapulted me into different ways of thinking about our experience of surveillance.

My approach to surveillance via theatre also had the benefit of keeping me away from an easy and lazy cliché of commentary on surveillance – the idea that surveillance is turning the whole of life into a public performance. In the case of my experiments with surveillance technology in theatrical space, it was the non-equivalence of surveillance and theatrical systems which had opened the theatre space to new possibilities, and disrupted the sense of total representational control. Equivalently, the elements of performance which can no doubt be introduced to surveillance systems do not so much theatricalize our lived experience under surveillance as open our understanding of surveillance to encompass a recognition of its productive omissions and contradictions. A sense of this interesting gap, this productive tension between theatre and surveillance made me cautious of any attempts to explain surveillance simply in terms of the way in which it puts life on show – in terms of specularization.

## Space versus spectacle

However, theories of the spectacle have inevitably informed the discussion of surveillance. After Michel Foucault, the two theorists who are probably most often referred to in analyses of surveillance are Guy Debord and Jean Baudrillard. While these theorists pursue very different arguments, they both deal with the ways in which the image has become the predominant mode of experience in our society, and discussions of surveillance often blend these critiques into some version of a paranoid world in which surveillance technology has coercively devalued our lived experiences by converting them into imagery. The theorists invoked are more complex than the invocation, but an analysis of surveillance as spectacle can appear tautological: if contemporary culture has already become the realm of simulation, as Debord and Baudrillard argue, then the recirculation of our images again thorough surveillance hardly carries any loss or danger.

Moreover, the behaviour and use of the surveillance image in our society does not necessarily cohere with that of other images. For example, Debord argues that specularization involves the commodification of experience. Although there are undoubtedly examples of the surveillance image circulating as a commodity, and a highly fetishized one at that (examples are discussed throughout the following chapters), commodification is a process happening to the surveillance recording in a manner entirely at odds with Debord's assumption that specularization enacts commodification per se. Unlike the movie, television or magazine image, which has such a high value in our society, the surveillance image is almost a by-product, a trashy residue of the surveillance system.

Likewise, Baudrillard's hyper-real world of simulations provides few tools to explain the current eruption of surveillance in an already entirely mediated world. A Baudrillardian reading can see surveillance only as symptomatic of hyper-real society, of the need to repeat obsessively the mediation of our already mediated selves and experiences. While there is undoubtedly validity to this reading, it can find nothing unique, nothing different, in surveillance. I am interested not only in reading surveillance as yet another proof of the mediation of experience, but in exploring whether, within our mediated world, the current proliferation of surveillance practices provides any indications of new understandings and consciousnesses.[1]

It seemed to me that it may be more useful to separate surveillance from spectacle, or perhaps to understand the practice of surveillance as a surprisingly productive perversion of spectacle. Central to this reading is the analysis of surveillance as space.

Given the fact that surveillance technology routinely reduces dimensional space to flat imagery, the idea of space as the key paradigm in exploring contemporary surveillance might initially seem absurd. However, the process is initiated by Foucault in his seminal book *Discipline and Punish*. Foucault used the example of a prison design by philosopher Jeremy Bentham (1748–1832) – the much-discussed panopticon – in which, from a central tower, a prison guard could look out at every movement of the prisoners arranged in a circle of cells surrounding him. This model of discipline, Foucault suggested, emblematized a key shift in consciousness in the Enlightenment – a shift from a view of morality that involved graphic punishments for wrongdoing, to a sense of a self that is always subject to viewing by authority – and which therefore must forever engage in the measuring, grading and censoring of behaviour. In Foucault's reading of Bentham, the panopticon symbolizes a society thoroughly pervaded by the disciplining view. As such, for many years Foucault was considered in the academic establishment to have said all that needed to be said about surveillance, and his work in the area, while very different, with its historical basis, from that of Debord and Baudrillard, was subsumed into a general understanding that surveillance was a symptom of the specularizaton of society. However, the panopticon is, of course, irreducibly three-dimensional, and Foucault is quite definite about the distinction between surveillance and spectacle: 'Our society is not one of spectacle, but of surveillance; under the surface of images, one invests bodies in depth . . .' (Foucault, 1991: 217). The historical trajectory described by Foucault in *Discipline and Punish* in fact moves away from the effects of pre-humanist display – a world of public hangings and displays of the body – towards a naturalized discipline of the self – a world in which individuals police themselves. The inhabitants of the Foucauldian prison are imprisoned and watched precisely because they have failed adequately to internalize the process of self-discipline, or self-surveillance, which is demanded of humanist man. So, Foucault's vision of a disciplined society points us towards a view of surveillance according to which the all-seeing eye may cause many things to be repressed, hidden within – where depth and questions of space are the results of the very processes of specularization.

However, the contemporary eruption of surveillance also has features which contradict the progress and process of disciplinarity found in Foucault's history. While the much vaunted capabilities of surveillance systems to identify criminal bodies could be said to maintain and extend the Foucauldian policing of the insufficiently self-disciplining subject, the technology does little to instil the kinds of normalization centralized in Foucault's account. Instead, under contemporary surveillance, we see (and we will discuss throughout the upcoming chapters) a proliferation of excess – of crimes, deaths and sexual exhibitionism.

A spatial reading of surveillance addresses this contradictory return to excessive display by asking primarily not about the effects of images, but about the lived environments produced by our inter-actions with surveillance recordings. With Foucault I have followed the idea that the discourse of surveillance has bodily effects, bodily products. Reading one Foucault in response to another, however, I have not assumed that these effects are necessarily normalizing, but have looked also for the possibility of heterotopias (other, alterna-tive worlds) produced in the excess of surveillance (Foucault, 1986: 25–7).

Today's cities are not panopticons; there is no single guard in a central tower spying upon urban populations. Yet many people con-tinue to imagine and fear one. The popular version of this figure is the Orwellian 'Big Brother'. Some authors have argued that, although Big Brother has actually never appeared, a myriad of 'Little Brothers' actually make the Foucauldian dispersal of disciplinarity throughout our surveillance society all the more complete.[2] Throughout this study, however, I underline the restrictive, even destructive, nature of the 'Orwellian' critique of surveillance. To the extent that Foucault's historicized analysis can be equated with this popular fear, my approach, while very indebted to Foucault, is in some ways anti-Foucauldian.

## Surveillance sociology

The other primary writers on the subject of surveillance are sociolo-gists and social scientists, a growing band, among whom Gary T. Marx and David Lyon are perhaps the most influential and longstanding. It was writers such as Marx and Lyon who first documented the actual reach of surveillance systems into Western society. For many years they were voices crying in the wilderness, alerting us to the escalation in surveillance capabilities during a period in the late 1980s and early 1990s when the humanities in general, having accepted that surveillance was universalized, assumed therefore that there was little more to say on the matter (particularly as Foucault's academic star waned). Books such as Marx's *Undercover: Police Surveillance in America* (1988) and Lyon's *The Electronic Eye: The Rise of Surveillance Society* (1994) detailed the extraordinary proliferation of surveillance technologies and documented the ways in which such new manifestations of surveillance in turn produced new effects. Perhaps inevitably, this prophetic role fell primarily to those social analysts who were deeply worried about surveillance – particularly about the implied threat to civil liberties. Newer sociological work has sometimes taken a more open attitude to the potential cultural consequences of surveillance proliferation (see Norris et al. (1998) for a variety of perspectives). However, a reinvigorated journalism of surveillance, which has emerged after years of very limited coverage, tends to draw on the established critical sociological voices, Gary T. Marx in particular, in asserting academic justification for its concerns – recirculating the civil liberties critique at a popular level.[3] In recent years, both journalists such as John Parker (2000) and campaigners such as Simon Davies (1996) have produced books which have a lot of the factual depth of the sociological work, but develop fairly simple, urgent arguments of the 'wake up and smell the surveillance' kind.

My own starting point, my engagement with the spatial productivities of surveillance, has led me to avoid the value judgements about surveillance's threat to privacy that inform and drive much of this sociological and political work. Nonetheless, my analysis owes a considerable debt to the exhaustive work done by Marx, Lyon, Norris and Armstrong and others in documenting the growth of citizen surveillance by government, police and corporate bodies in the past twenty years, and to their insistence that such proliferation has consequences far beyond the rubric under which the systems have been initiated and justified.

Unlike the sociologists of surveillance, however, I do not deal primarily with the statistics, or even the commercial/governmental/ policing uses of the new systems. I am interested primarily in studying the cultural effects of these systems, effects which may or may not equate with the intentions of surveying institutions. To this end, I make extensive use throughout my investigation of analyses of cultural artefacts (both 'popular' and 'artistic', and without subscribing to a hierarchy or strict delineation between these categories) which engage with the materials and meanings of surveillance. It is in the analysis of such products of surveyed society that the heart of my study lies – an attempt to understand the various developments of experience, understanding and consciousness within surveyed society as evidenced by cultural activity.

## Surveying space

My spatial understanding of surveillance is developed from a reading of Kant. As the canonical philosopher who most centralized space as an organizing principle – 'Space is nothing other than the form of all appearances of the external sense, that is, the subjective condition of sensibility, under which alone external intuition is possible' (Kant, 1993: 52) – Kant maintains a defining position in relation to both common sense and theoretical understandings of space and perception. Obviously, a theoretically informed study written at the start of the twenty-first century is not going to take Kant's categories of intuition as immutable laws; however, the proposition that space is the fundamental *subjective* condition of perception, of knowing and understanding the external world, underlies my thinking. I have consistently returned to the question of space in analysing our understanding and experience of surveillance phenomena that may at first seem to be non-spatial by definition.

However, to discuss sound recordings, data and two-dimensional imagery – the materials of surveillance – in terms of space necessitates a complex analysis of the very areas of perception most marginalized in Kant's system. At times, particularly with respect to the key question of surveillance sound and its relations to interiority, I have teased at the edges of Kant's thought, looking for ways in which a productive contradiction between his organization of perception and the experiences of surveillance may help us understand surveillance's unexpected effects. More often, I have used subsequent thinkers as guides to a post-Kantian understanding of space as a mode of experience and knowledge.

A key figure here is Henri Lefebvre, perhaps the theorist who most thoroughly, and most unmetaphorically, extends spatial analysis beyond its relegation to the specifics of the familiar three dimensions in the post-Hegelian philosophical environment. In his typology of space – perceived space, conceived space, lived space and a hoped-for differential space – Lefebvre refuses a hierarchy between the space through which we move and the understandings of space we carry. In fact, he asserts that a dichotomy between these ways of knowing space involves and propagates a fundamental misunderstanding of the ways in which space structures our lives. His three primary categories of space, also described as spatial practice (perceived), representations of space (conceived) and representational spaces (lived), reconfigure the ways in which representation functions in our experience of space. In Lefebvre's system, representation pervades all spatial experience. Extending Kant's proposition that space is a means of structuring perception rather than a quality of the realm of noumena, of things-in-themselves, Lefebvre proposes that the secondary representations of space, marginalized in Kant's system, are intrinsic to the form of space itself. The third type of space in Lefebvre's system – lived space – is particularly employed in this study to explore the idea that our experience of space is as involved in representation as it is in dimensions.

Lefebvre's grounding in economic and social theory, and his insistence that spatial organization is not a product of economic forces but a fundamental social principle, also contributes to my analysis of the spatial effects of surveillance and to an underlying expectation that practices and products arising from a spatial understanding of surveillance may in turn influence the socio-economic structures of today's surveillance society. A reading of Walter Benjamin which emphasizes the inter-relation of image reproduction and spatial experience in twentieth-century culture interacts productively with this use of Lefebvre: Benjamin's notion of an architectural, 'distracted' cultural experience (he examines the way in which we experience and appreciate the architecture of a building – wandering through it, not staring at it) adds a resonant psychological/behavioural dimension to Lefebvre's representational space.

However, the theoretical understanding of space upon which I have most relied is something I have described as 'performative space'. The ideas behind this notion are discussed in detail towards the end of Chapter 1, but it is important to introduce the background to this concept right away.

As I have described, my focus on surveillance grew out of my use of it in the inhabited, fantastical space of theatre. In beginning to think about surveillance as a space, I was able to draw upon thinkers, such as Foucault and Lefebvre, who explore the dynamic relation between psychological/representational structures and the world thorough which we move. However, my key experience of using surveillance technology in theatre was of the way in which the presence of the technology could – immediately it was switched on, revealed or noticed – alter the very feel, the mood, the dimensions even, of the space that we were in: our lived experience of space changed as soon as the space became surveyed. It was to explore and explain the active change in space brought about by surveillance that I turned to ideas of performativity.

It is important here to emphasize the difference between performativity and theatre performance. Although my interest in surveillance and my spatial understandings of it have their roots in theatre, the notion of performativity has its origins not in theatre but in language.

My use of the term 'performative' grows out of a now canonical sequence of work by J.L. Austin, Jacques Derrida and Judith Butler. Austin's theory of performativity examined how 'speech acts', e.g. phrases such as 'I bet you', 'I promise you', actually do the thing their words reference – they perform rather than just describe. In her groundbreaking studies, *Gender Trouble* (1990) and *Bodies that Matter* (1993), Butler not only extended the notion of performativity to an understanding of how gender is constituted, but opened up the possibility that performativity could be a key tool in a wide variety of cultural analyses. In essence, Butler argued that the apparent fact of gender is created for the child in its articulation. The moment of announcement – 'It's a boy/girl' – is not the description but the enactment of gender. However, and this is crucial for an understanding of 'performative space', the speech act is not actually necessary to this enactment of gender: the socio-cultural environment can produce performative effects without the intention of a 'speaker' and without the conscious understanding of an 'auditor'. Butler's analysis demonstrates that performativity is independent of a subject: 'gender proves to be performative – that is, constituting the identity it is purported to be. In this sense, gender is always a doing, though not a doing by a subject who might be said to preexist the deed' (Butler, 1990, 25; see also Butler 1997, 24).

Butler's reading of Austin is, in turn, indebted to that of Derrida, and particularly his essay 'Signature/Event/Context' (1977). While Derrida's text does not open up a vista of cultural performativity in the way that Butler's does (not least because, in Derrida, the thinking of culture other than as language is nonsensical – a characteristic of Derrida's thinking of which Lefebvre is particularly critical – Lefebvre, 1991: 5), 'Signature/Event/Context' is extremely important for the way in which it thinks through Austin's position on language performativity. Austin's own argument develops from an initial description of the performative (as opposed to the constative or descriptive) utterance – 'in which *by* saying or *in* saying something we are doing something' (Austin, 1976: 12) – to a point of view according to which performativity is discovered to be a defining aspect of all language – 'there can hardly be any longer a possibility of not seeing that stating is performing an act' (ibid.: 139). Derrida develops this argument further, arguing that language does something regardless of the presence or absence of a speaker/writer, and that part of what it does is produce effects beyond any present intention:

> What holds for the receiver also holds, for the same reasons, for the sender or the producer. To write is to produce a mark that will constitute a sort of machine which is productive in turn, and which my future disappearance will not, in principle, hinder in its functioning, offering things and itself to be read and rewritten.
>
> (Derrida, 1977: 8)

The coherence and reach of the insight into writing summarized by Derrida in this essay and developed throughout his work also allows other areas of his thought, notably his discussion of death in *Aporias* (1993), to be very usefully employed in thinking about the performative space of surveillance. The citation of Derrida's arguments always draws us back to the notion of performativity, to the productivity of a system which is in no way pre-dated or produced by presence.

For an understanding of surveillance as something other than simple representation of an event and place, the concept of performativity is crucial. Whereas Lefebvre complicates our view of space, allowing us to see the degree to which space is representational, the theorists of performativity enable us to separate surveillance from representational self-evidence, and to understand the degree to which it is spatially productive.

It is a distance from performativity to performance. For some (Austin and Butler) there is an irreducible gap, even a dichotomy, between the two terms. However, while the distinction is important, the relations between performative space and theatrical space in a surveillance context are also significant. Eventually, in my analysis, these two understandings of space meet in a concept of 'weakness'. Whereas performativity is often seen as having the 'force' of a doing, the stage act is famously dismissed as 'etiolated' by Austin (1976: 22), a dismissal that Butler echoes in her rebuttal of readings of gender performativity as voluntaristic (Butler, 1993: x). However, in pursuing a theatrical analysis of surveillance space alongside the theoretical development of the concept of spatial performativity, we begin to see how the two can exist alongside each other productively, the 'weakness' of performance contributing a questioning openness to the experience of performative surveillance space.

## From crime to agency

The first half of this book focuses on the ways in which surveillance technology developed and proliferated in British and US society in the past two decades, with an emphasis not on an exhaustive history or sociology, but on the ways of thinking about surveillance that allowed for and were encouraged by this growth. In Chapter 1, I examine the 'ideology of crime prevention' that has largely justified the proliferation of surveillance technology. I look at the ways in which this ideology is circulated via television shows that use surveillance footage, emphasizing the degree to which these programmes are constructed to compensate for the social unease caused by the experience of being repeatedly recorded. I suggest, however, that this unease breaks out nonetheless, showing itself particularly in a discontinuity between the reception of sound and video recordings, in the concept of 'encodedness' and in the 'misuse' of surveillance footage. I examine the concept of 'surveillance space', and look at the ways in which this space could be described as performative, introducing ideas of uptake and suspense in relation to performativity as tools for understanding our various experiences of and feelings about surveillance.

In Chapter 2, I specifically undertake a critique of privacy arguments in relation to surveillance, emphasizing the degree to which these concepts are based upon a public/private binary that prioritizes a very particular set of values. Using examples from gay popular culture, media interpretations of lesbianism and disabled people's art activism, I assess the ways in which groups excluded from the public/private binary are engaging in surveillance-related practices as a means to achieve sexual and political agency. Returning to the concept of surveillance space, I use these examples to help analyse its characteristics, finding that its borders, its temporal disruptions, its separation of image from sound are defining aspects of this space.

In Chapter 3, I use the extreme example of death recorded on surveillance to push further into an examination of the characteristics of surveillance space, particularly as regards its relation to performativity. Starting with the observation that surveillance allows death to be recorded 'accidentally', I explore the ways in which the ever-present expectation of the sight of death in surveillance society is radically altering our relation to what Derrida calls this 'possibility of impossibility' (Derrida, 1993: 72). Derrida's essay *Aporias* is used here as a theoretical context for a discussion of how the expectation of an encounter with imagery of death structures surveillance culture.

In Chapters 4 and 5, I move on to a more detailed discussion of art and performance works which deal with or refer to surveillance technology. These art works are used as means to help us understand the possibilities and complexities of surveillance space. In Chapter 4, I focus on art works which are to a degree self-contained, that is to say they do not rely upon the image of the audience member or viewer for completion. I introduce the terminology of Henri Lefebvre, particularly his concept of 'lived space', space that results from the representations, associations and bodily relations structuring our lives, and I examine works by Bruce Nauman, Mona Hatoum, The Wooster Group and others, analysing the ways in which the surveillance (or surveillance-like) imagery in these works exceeds representational reference, creating instead unique spatial experiences. These experiences are also related here to the phenomenon of data surveillance, which is analysed as the creation of non-visible versions of ourselves. The ways in which these data selves haunt us from across the border of visibility is closely related to the art works discussed.

In Chapter 5, I focus upon works of art and performance which in some way incorporate imagery of the audience or viewer. Focusing particularly on the work of artist Julia Scher and on the feminist–Brechtian theories developed by Elin Diamond, I examine the ways in which surveillance art works use audience imagery as a means to structure space. Referring to Walter Benjamin's discussion of 'modern man's legitimate claim to being reproduced' (Benjamin, 1969: 232), I examine the ways in which the desire for auto-reproduction functions in surveillance art works, and explore the complex and contradictory matrices of desire and identification which can be created in these works. In relation to these questions of desire and identification, I stress the importance of separating the fantasized Big Brother figures of our surveillance imaginings from the actual operatives of surveillance systems. Finally, I suggest that surveillance art works may even begin to indicate the possibility of love in surveillance space.

In the sixth chapter, I return to an examination of the social processes of surveillance, emphasizing the history of counter-surveillance and looking in this history for clues as to how agency may be achieved in surveillance culture. A variety of counter-surveillance practices are discussed. Each of these practices provides indications as to how we may make choices and have effects within surveillance space. Returning to the paradigm of spatial performativity, we see that our responses to surveillance space, our lives within it, while never fully volitional, are nonetheless uncontrollable by any single source of surveillance. Finally, I return to the question of encodedness, the ways in which surveillance produces discontinuities, excesses needing constant reinterpretation. I suggest that, rather than ignoring the reproduced selves that populate the data banks and recordings of surveillance culture, we should embrace them as aspects of a new consciousness: selves producing selves, prostheti-cized and discontinuous, communicating in a proliferation of codes and secret languages, replacing the containment of privacy with the productivity of surveillance space.

## Already dead

The biggest surprise to me in exploring our responses to technologies of surveillance has been the importance of the idea, the thought, the 'impossible possibility' of death in reaching an understanding of our lives in a surveillance-saturated society. In the final chapter of my investigation I suggest that even the most protective of counter-surveillance practices ultimately presents to us an image of ourselves so separated from our consciousness that it is as though we see ourselves 'already dead'.

In embarking on this study, death was the last thing that I expected to find lurking in the constant rewinds of surveillance recordings. Clearly, the case of surveillance imagery of death would need to be discussed, but I expected it to function as a limit point of the analy-sis, the point at which the desires and productivities of surveillance culture ceased to function.

To have found death inhabiting surveillance space so thoroughly was a strangely liberating discovery. Technological development of-ten manifests as a means to avoid once and for all this modern taboo, and much cultural analysis of technology is underpinned either by an obsessive cyber-fetishism or by the kind of doom-laden conservatism that even as sharp a critic as Paul Virilio has fallen into in his recent work (Virilio, 1994, 1997). By contrast, the importance of death in an analysis of surveillance suggests the possibility that some values or cultural touchstones marginalized in modernity may return, albeit in much changed forms and relations, in an emerging surveillance society. The values via which surveillance culture was created may not be the values with which it is lived.

# 1

# An ideology of crime

Videos are watching me
But dat is not stopping me
Let dem cum wid dem authority
An dem science and technology,
But
Dem can't get de Reggae out me head.

(Zephaniah, 1996: 20)

You are under surveillance. Not many years ago, this statement could not have been made in a generalized form to an unknown addressee. Today, assuming that you are an urban dweller in a developed country, to be 'under surveillance' is a general condition. Cameras watch over you as you journey to work, registering your number plates or recording your behaviour on the underground train platform. Your image is recorded by every ATM you use, in almost every convenience store you enter, and many times on virtually every street you walk along. Vast commercial data banks assess your shopping habits and your credit history. Intergovernmental networks analyse your phone conversations, searching for key words as indicators of subversion.[1] Your boss is probably recording you too.[2] Your neighbours can now buy satellite pictures of your back yard.[3] In New York, even the police dogs carry cameras.[4] 'You are under surveillance' is no longer an announcement made to a selected individual – it is a description of our culture.

While it is difficult to give a precise figure, the general consensus is that currently the average city dweller in the UK is captured on CCTV 300 times a day;[5] the USA and many other Western countries are fast catching up. In London, capital of the world's most surveyed country, the figure may be far higher. And the cameras are only the tip of the surveillance iceberg. Writers such as John Parker (2000) and David Lyon (1994, 2001) have exhaustively documented the quite extraordinary degree to which the average citizen in Western society is documented by government and commercial data banks, and the comprehensive reach of phone and email monitoring systems such as the US-controlled Echelon.[6]

In the wake of September 11, US, UK and European governments have enacted sweeping legislation in the name of anti-terrorism that will further strengthen the right of a variety of security and other government bodies to gather and store information on residents. The Bush administration's proposed Total Information Awareness programme (renamed the Terrorist Information Awareness System after congressional and public protests) has the potential to take data surveillance of citizens to previously unimagined levels in an attempt to identify terrorist behaviour traits in evidence ranging from educational and medical records to purchasing and travel patterns.

A belated rearguard action is emerging in some instances to limit the more over-reaching powers of government,[7] and on the web in particular there is a sophisticated group of core users who continue to work to undermine the claim of nation states to control this medium. However, even with the efforts of organizations such as Privacy International, the Omega Foundation, the American Civil Liberties Union (ACLU) and UK civil liberties group Liberty, there seems virtually no chance at this point that these vast systems of surveillance will be rolled back. The battlegrounds that remain for campaigners are primarily in relation to the areas of privacy that an individual may be allowed by law to create (a key example here being the ongoing argument over encryption on the web, with the US and UK governments in a war of attrition with web users over whether encryption technologies for which national security services do not have the key may legally be used on the international medium of the Internet – see Perri 6, 1998: 116–21) and the nature of a citizen's rights regarding disclosure of and access to the information held on him or her.

My purpose in this book is not to add my bit to a discussion of the legal limits appropriate in a high-surveillance society, although I will document some of the arguments and refer to several of them. In the last few years, many books examining the growth of surveillance in the UK and in the USA have been published, and it is right that such an important development in our society is finally being analysed widely and in depth. The point of this book, however, is to explore the experience of surveillance – how we feel and live within what we might call surveillance space, and how we respond creatively. I have chosen Benjamin Zephaniah's poem as my starting point, because, as an artist who addresses the black male experience, Zephaniah is responding directly to the lived condition of surveillance and can, I hope, help to keep us grounded in the fact that surveillance is a reality that we must think and feel our way through. Zephaniah also provides us with a couple of good clues on how to proceed. He indicates that surveillance space is deeply politicized – that science and technology are inevitably about authority; and he reminds us that, while much of contemporary surveillance may function outside the realm of the visual, the issue of the surveillance image is as vital a place as ever to start.

Zephaniah's poem also issues a more obscure challenge. In proposing the space of the Reggae Head, a space filled with complex systems of rhythm and language, Zephaniah suggests a role for some kind of interiority, for coded, cultural, non-dimensional spaces which challenge surveillance authority in ways that it can never fully address. As we disentangle the maze of fears, philosophies and interests that constitute the ideology of crime under which surveillance has proliferated, we will also begin to see the many ways in which these other kinds of space can emerge.

## Hey you!

In the face of the degree of covert or undisclosed surveillance of the average citizen by government and corporations reported by Parker, Lyon and others, it might be easy to become almost sanguine about the CCTV cameras that point down at us from every street or shop corner. And, indeed, the kinds of worries about privacy that many of these writers and campaigners focus on as their core approach to the issue may seem to be of limited relevance in the case of street surveillance. After all, few of us would claim a right to privacy in the street or shopping mall. However, CCTV remains the most public and discussed form of surveillance. As a visual medium in a visually oriented society, its characteristics are of particular relevance in discussing the cultural impacts of surveillance, and an analysis of CCTV may in fact help us separate the wider question of surveillance from an argument about privacy that has, to all intents and purposes, already been lost.[8]

In general, our relations to street surveillance are largely determined by our relationship to crime and policing. It is important in this respect not to underestimate the role of policing in constructing who we are and how we behave. Althusser (1984: 48) identified the voice of the policeman – 'Hey you there!' – as a quintessential moment of 'interpellation' into the contemporary state. It is in this naming as potential wrongdoers that we become aware of our status as citizens. However, the impact of this policing voice is not felt evenly; certain bodies can more confidently expect to believed when they protest their innocence in response to the policing voice: 'Who me, officer? I live here!' While there are important gaps (which will be discussed below) between Althusser's vocal police presence and the removed gaze of the CCTV camera, it is not hard also to see the links between the two moments – the police voice, and the camera's eye – 'You are under surveillance.'

As a Rastafarian poet living in east London, Benjamin Zephaniah has for many years written about the Black British experience of policing – of, for example, the notorious 'sus' laws, which in the 1980s allowed police to detain individuals on 'suspicion' of an intent to commit crime.[9] Zephaniah's work documents an experience in which suspicion is often dependent upon skin colour.

Equivalent examples exist in the experiences of racial minority groups in any developed Western society. (New York's zero tolerance campaign is one of the most recent and notorious cases.) In the poem Reggae Head, Zephaniah highlights the likelihood that the systematic spread of CCTV will in fact extend this culture of suspicion, so that every camera functions within a field of power and prejudice structured by visual markers. His poem acts as a challenge to any analysis of surveillance – a challenge to understand the ways in which generalizations about surveillance experience, about the statement 'You are under surveillance', must be opened out into an examination of the various and specific experiences that this sentence may signify.

The street surveillance camera, far from being a neutral tool of crime prevention, basically works, one way or another, by targeting groups that the employers of the systems deem likely to commit crimes. Operators of surveillance systems routinely use the systems to watch, zoom in on and follow the members of the public they judge likely to display criminal behaviour. Overwhelmingly, these individuals are young and male, and very often they are black (Norris and Armstrong, 1999: 108–10; see also McCahill in Norris et al., 1998: 51). The introduction of automated systems that will identify criminals through use of records and algorithms will hardly be less prejudiced.[10] Automated face-recognition programs, such as the Visionics FaceIt system (pioneered in the London borough of Newham, and touted aggressively for business in the wake of September 11), are advertised as identifying criminals known to the police, but there is very mixed evidence of their ability to identify individual faces. What is far more likely is that such systems will be used – as current manual systems are – to identify 'criminal types' based on age, behaviour patterns, location and, perhaps, skin colour. On an anecdotal level, when I visited Manchester City Council's new Urbis Museum – a museum focusing on urban life (Manchester is, like Newham, one of the UK local councils most aggressively implementing CCTV) – I tried out the interactive surveillance face recognition systems available to the public. The system that was meant to recognize me as I wandered around the museum identified ten matches – all of them different people and none of them me. My niece, who wears glasses, was matched with a window! In another display, I was encouraged to try and find a criminal in a crowd on a computer screen by asking a range of questions of the 'male or female?', 'bearded or clean-shaven?' variety. I identified the criminal. He was a young black male!

While surveillance is routinely justified in terms of crime prevention and routinely criticized as an invasion of privacy, an accommodation between these two universalizing viewpoints will do nothing to affect the experience of the black man under surveillance in the streets of New York or London. Protection of privacy is not relevant to the ways in which the camera targets him. The terms in which surveillance is routinely critiqued obscure his experiences, and those of many others, in the name of a 'privacy' fantasized as a universal right.

For these reasons, I am starting this study exactly where most studies of surveillance start, by tracing the growth of CCTV. In following this history, I want to focus on the way in which an 'ideology of crime' creates a narrative not only for the deployment of surveillance cameras (a story told by well already by Norris and Armstrong

(1999), Cummings (1997) and several others) but also for our psychic processing of the experience of surveillance – a processing that is most clearly revealed at the moments when the ideology of crime lets us down.

## Kicking off

It is generally agreed that, while most Western and many other countries now have pretty comprehensive surveillance camera networks in place, the UK led the world in mass surveillance of public space.[11] A number of factors contributed to this phenomenon – the nature of the British government in the 1980s, the relationship of that government and its policing policies to the press and, most significantly, the lack of any constitutional limits on public surveillance in British law. The earliest newspaper articles on the uses of CCTV to trap criminals seem to have been in *The Times* and *The Sunday Times* in November 1978 (Cummings, 1997; see also Moran in Norris et al., 1998: 277). However, it was in the mid-1980s, and specifically in relation to government programmes to eliminate football hooliganism, that the CCTV camera really took off.

> There's nothing we can do and we're just sitting back playing it calm. We don't know if the old bill have got specific information about the meeting, or just know something's being planned. It's a bit worrying. Like you're being watched and your conversations taped. Seems you can't do anything these days without spies recording the event. If it's not a video camera watching you it's some undercover cunt keeping his head down passing on information. It's like being in a South American dictatorship or something.
>
> (King, 1996: 127)

John King's novel *The Football Factory* follows the experience of an English football hooligan in the early 1990s. It portrays a culture in crisis. While the book makes graphically clear that the 'firms' of young(ish) men who engage in elaborate rivalries and street battles organized around support for particular football teams are part of a long tradition with its own heroes and histories, it also demonstrates a growing desperation in that tradition, as policing techniques and resources make it increasingly difficult for these rituals of violence to take place in their traditional venues in and around the football ground.

> The camera under the roof records our sins and it's only kids and pissheads who step out of line. You've got to be daft to do anything else, though occasionally things boil over and then the papers are clocking faces and running witch-hunts. It's hard to believe there was a time when you could go on the rampage inside the ground and get away with it week after week.
>
> (Ibid.: 9)

The history of the surveillance camera in the UK is inextricably tied up with the football hooligan and the various cultural responses to that phenomenon. Surveillance cameras were first introduced to grounds in the mid-1980s as part of a Thatcherite attempt to curb a perceived crisis in football-related violence. In 1985, at the Heysel Stadium in Brussels, where Liverpool were playing Juventus in the European Cup final, Liverpool fans were held responsible for a wall collapse that resulted in the deaths of thirty-nine people, an event that represented a watershed in the public perception of football violence. The issue was perceived, at least in the media, to have reached epidemic proportions, and Margaret Thatcher pledged to act. Television camera footage and press photography had already played a part in locating the perpetrators of violence at matches and, with video technology affordable for department store crime detection, the use of the technology in football grounds was an obvious and popular measure. By the end of the 1980s, crowd surveillance at football matches was routine. (A comprehensive history of football hooliganism and the security and surveillance measures employed to overcome it is given by Gary Armstrong and Richard Giulianotti in their essay 'From another angle: police surveillance and football supporters', in Norris et al., 1998.)

The extraordinary rapidity with which Britain achieved its status as the advanced nation with the highest level of public video surveillance followed on from the perceived success of the programme to eliminate hooliganism from football grounds. In fact, the cameras could almost be said to have followed the hooligans out of the ground through the transport systems and into the town centres: 'We wait for the next train a couple of minutes later, watched by London

Underground lenses . . . . London's turning into a surveillance arcade' (King, 1996: 25).[12]

King's novel is a useful source, because it traces the evolution of the CCTV camera from the viewpoint not of the police or criminologist, but of the young men whom the cameras were specifically installed to target. King catches the degree to which this history creates a change in consciousness in the narrator; not a wish to change behaviour, or a repentance for the error of his ways, but a changed relationship to the spaces through which he moves and the forces which act upon him. Surveillance, King viscerally demonstrates, changes the ways we feel and behave within the spaces that are surveyed. We might even say that it changes the spaces themselves.

The basic argument in favour of CCTV usually goes along the lines of 'if you've done nothing wrong, then you've nothing to fear'. But the CCTV camera creates its own rules and structures as to what is and isn't wrongdoing. A dramatic example of this – and an example that richly demonstrates the multisidedness of the arguments around CCTV – was provided by one of the worst ever UK footballing tragedies.

## In the pen

In April 1989, public perception of the relationship between assertive policing and surveillance in the UK entered into a new and more complex phase as the result of a second disaster involving Liverpool fans. At an FA Cup match between Liverpool and Nottingham Forest at the Hillsborough ground in Sheffield, ninety-six Liverpool fans were killed when overassertive policing led to panic as one of the spectator pens was unnecessarily overfilled. A crowd control operation had gone seriously wrong. With football supporters in general, and arguably, since Heysel, Liverpool supporters in particular, demonized as potential troublemakers and criminals, the police had created a system for crowd flow at the event focused entirely on keeping potentially warring groups of supporters separated from each other. When error led to one of the pens being dangerously overfilled, the simple measures (opening the gates) that could have solved the problem were completely counterintuitive to the police. A policing operation entirely primed to deal with violence lacked the flexibility to respond to the very different needs emerging from a panic partly created by its own overaggressive tactics.[13] Ambulances were kept waiting outside the ground as people died, and gates that could have been opened to ease the crowd pressure were left locked. The disaster was caused and exacerbated by policing itself. A description of the events and the police response is given by Armstrong and Giulianotti (in Norris et al., 1998: 128–9). They describe the gap in perceptions that occurred:

> Cameras were trained on the ensuing tragedy, as scores of fans were slowly crushed, fatally injuring 96 in total. For the commanding police officers, however, the meaning of the CCTV images was something rather different. Fearing a seemingly more offensive scenario, such as an organised pitch invasion and potential violence, the gates remained closed; police with Alsatian dogs were ordered to stand in front of the terracing to prevent fans from trying to enter the field of play.
>
> (Norris et al., 1998: 129)

The crowd were being policed as criminals, and the policing machine was unable to shift to protect them as victims.

Moreover, this criminalization of the victims did not end with the deaths. Police attempted a cover-up, blaming drunken fans for the disastrous surge, and initially the press followed suit with entirely unfounded stories of fans urinating on dying bodies and blocking police rescue attempts.

Ironically, while the situation was partly created by a police operation using CCTV cameras to identify hooliganism and unable to interpret behaviour that was actually due to legitimate panic as anything other than a potential symptom of violence, the initial media-encouraged police version of events would perhaps never have been publicly contradicted if it were not for the evidence of cameras. Both television and security camera footage were used to trace the events that led to the disaster. The cameras were instruments both of the problem and of its uncovering.

This example indicates that the marriage of police and video technology is not entirely seamless and cautions us against both utopian and dystopian views of surveillance cameras in relation to policing. While the destination of surveillance images is not automatically some 'public realm' (if indeed such a realm exists), there remains a possibility that the workings of police repression will appear in public view not only through citizen surveillance incidents such as the Rodney King video, but also through the very cameras installed for purposes of law enforcement. This possibility emphasizes a question around the ownership and distribution of surveillance imagery which is obscured by the smooth transition of some imagery to television: the policing shows that we will discuss below.

In the 1996 television 'docu-drama' reconstruction of the events by Liverpool writer Jimmy McGovern, families sit at home horrified as they watch the disaster occur live on television, trying to locate the faces of loved ones on the screen and astounded that apparently nothing is being done to prevent the carnage that the cameras are revealing (*Hillsborough*, Granada TV, Manchester, 5 December 1996). This image emphasizes the general point that in very many cases cameras will increase our horror at crimes – bring them more forcefully into our lives – but have no power to interrupt the rapidly unfolding events they are relaying. Armstrong and Giulianotti suggest, following Bogard (1996: 148), that this 'sense of strangeness' introduced by the culture of visual surveillance – the experience of being both 'near and far' to the events depicted on the screen – was precisely what paralysed the police response in the first place (Norris et al., 1998: 128). The strange space we inhabit in relation to surveillance may not only radically alter our felt experience of disaster and death, it may actually be a life and death issue.

Perhaps more than anything, though, the example of Hillsborough demonstrates the force of the identities that surveillance can create. Whatever the ambiguities and delays that the cameras introduced to the scene, whatever the evidence ultimately created to contradict police versions of events, the cameras, watched carefully by police for outbreaks of violence, helped to structure a scene in which the Liverpool supporters were cast as potential wrongdoers. This structuring surveillance was nothing less than the cause of their deaths. If you have done nothing wrong you may have an awful lot to fear.

Are all of us susceptible to this fear?

## Crimewatching

One of the most high-profile crimes in Britain in the last few years was the murder of television presenter Jill Dando. Dando was the presenter of *Crimewatch UK*, the first major network television show in the UK to use CCTV footage as key material in a programme structured around the idea that the public would identify criminals shown or described on television and phone in to help the police in their enquiries. That Dando, the blonde, middle-class, caring female face of the show, would be brutally murdered was a national shock. One of the symptoms of the shock was the frequent replay on television news programmes of CCTV footage of Dando in a store just before her murder. The footage was of no apparent value in locating Dando's killer, but somehow it seemed as though it was necessary to address Dando's murder via the form of television watching that she had helped to pioneer. I suspect that the public dismay over Dando's death and the impotent replay of her final CCTV image indicated a real anxiety that Dando's murder would put in danger the psychic work that *Crimewatch* was doing for the British public.

The tone of the *Crimewatch UK* is earnest, busy, occasionally reassuring: on a set filled with researchers, phone receptionists and real-life police officers, the presenters introduce cases where the police need the public's help, using descriptions, crime reconstructions and surveillance camera footage. They intersperse their appeals with information on cases solved with the help of the public's phone calls. There is an emphasis on success: a follow-up bulletin in the late evening after each monthly show catalogues calls made in response to that evening's footage. Police officers solemnly thank viewers for their help in bringing criminals to justice. The whole show is based upon the recognition of criminality: 'Do you recognize this man?' is its constantly repeated refrain.

*Crimewatch* is one of many programmes which have enacted a hybrid of the television cop show, the consumer watchdog programme and the news to involve the public in a visceral engagement with the complexities and sometimes the brutalities of modern policing. Other UK examples have included *Crimestoppers*, a more direct series of five-minute slots focusing on specific CCTV-recorded cases, and *Crime Beat* (which is more documentary in style); they all in some way involve the videotaping of members of the public by surveillance cameras. The material is ultimately grim, petty or violent, and repetitive.[14] Yet the earnest presenters and voiceovers rarely comment on the degradation being witnessed; instead they urge us to phone in with clues or simply to empathize with the men and women in uniform who protect us from all this.

Given the commercial imperative of television, while we may suspect an ideological function to this outpouring of police fetishization, there can be no doubt that the stuff is popular. One of the reasons for this popularity may be that these shows provide a seemingly appropriate narrative for an experience that otherwise might be worryingly inconclusive – the daily capturing of our images on video cameras.

It has been feasibly suggested that CCTV cameras are a fitting, or even necessary, response to worries about crime that are largely fuelled not by direct experience, but by crime portrayed on television. According to this argument we need cameras to protect us from television crime. The English town of King's Lynn, which was one of the first towns in the world to install a comprehensive CCTV system, despite never having had a significant crime rate, provides an example of how the 'worry factor', particularly among elderly populations, drives the perceived need for surveillance (Davies, 1996: 177). Studies such as Richard Sparks's *Television and the Drama of Crime* complexify these arguments, suggesting, for example, that there is no justification for claiming that there is an 'appropriate' ratio between fear and incidence of crime (Sparks, 1992: 11). Sparks points to the many factors influencing both television viewing and feelings about crime and cautions against drawing simplified causative links. On the other hand, he also points to the complex interdependence of our narratives of crime:

> It is not a trivial matter that 'crime scarers' such as *Crimewatch UK* do in a very real and particular sense employ the same syntax of depiction, narration and editing as crime fictions do, nor that newspaper reports similarly use television fiction as a point of reference in their narration of real events.
>
> (Sparks 1992: 156)

Bearing in mind Sparks' arguments, it is worth tracing the reverse trajectory to that which sees CCTV cameras as a response to television crime and asking in what ways the appearance of CCTV on our television screens processes the 'rhetorical and emotional nature' (Sparks, 1992: 151) of our daily CCTV experiences.[15]

On the streets, at ATM machines, in the lobbies of our workplaces, in convenience stores and in shopping malls, video cameras watch us, but where do the images go? We know that these cameras are 'crime prevention' devices. Once again we tell ourselves – if we have done nothing wrong we have nothing to fear. Yet the experience of being continually photographed is a potentially stressful one. Do we need now to be on some special code of behaviour? What if we show up as a bystander in someone else's crime? One successful lawyer friend of mine worries when she sees a camera pointing at her in a store that some hidden demon will emerge from within, causing her to steal right in front of the camera's eye, destroying her career. She is perhaps not so much more sensitive to the camera's presence than most of us, but rather more able to articulate the psychic effects of constantly being spied upon. Could the obsessive repetition of CCTV imagery on television be, in some way, a means of narrativizing, of making sense of, the daily experience of being watched and recorded?

## Surveillance interpellation

If video cameras provide chief inspectors with dozens of extra pairs of eyes, what happens to the policing voice? As we noted above, Althusser identified the voice of the police officer – 'Hey you there!' – as the quintessential moment of interpellation into the contemporary state. It is not difficult to see the degree to which the inability of the camera to name, to command, the subject leaves a disconcerting hole in our experience.

The interpellating voice of the policeman not only restricts us within the behavioural and rational framework of the state, it also makes sense of our relationship to the power of the state and its police. It carries the promise that if we are in a position to answer politely – 'Who me, officer? I live here.' – we will not be arbitrarily crushed by the state's power. Yet with the policing camera we are offered no such opportunity to respond. The failure of the camera to engage in ideologically grounding language exchange reintroduces the possibility of arbitrary power displays by the state, of an irrational totalitarianism, unaware of and unrestricted by our good citizen status. (The emerging evidence of mistaken identity convictions in cases in which CCTV is used as evidence can only add to our anxiety: *Dispatches,* Channel 4, London, 25 March 1999.)

The links between the social experience of ideological interpellation and Lacanian psychoanalytic concepts of the symbolic order have been persuasively examined by Slavoj Žižek in *The Sublime Object of Ideology* (1989) and other works. Žižek's achievement is to demonstrate the degree to which ideological experience – the sense made of society in order for society's power structures to be sustained – is not only parallel with the psychosexual development of the individual subject, but is in perpetual exchange with this process.[16] In Žižek's work we get a sense that the way in which the policeman interpellates us may have profound effects on our psychic structuring.

The lawyer who fears the onset of kleptomania in response to in-store cameras attests to the possibility of such a confusion of psychic and social boundaries when the individual is faced with the failure of interpellation under the camera's gaze. Television shows such as *Crimewatch UK* suture our psyches and cameras back into a familiar social fabric by re-joining the policeman's voice to his watchful eye.

As Žižek has also pointed out, however, moments of social insecurity are particularly likely to lead to the re-employment of regressive ideologies. In Žižek's analysis of contemporary European culture, the 'sublime object' of admiring hatred returns again in the figure of the Jew. In the policing television programmes of US/UK surveillance society, it is the criminal (and quintessentially the young black male criminal) who is the abject figure of our desire/fear. By providing an object – the criminal – understood to be other than 'ourselves', the ideology enacted by video-crime shows explains the disappearance of 'our own' images. 'We' do not appear because 'we' are not the criminal object. By additionally marking the criminal as a young black male, the programmes also perform a satisfying ideological self-contradiction. The object is racially marked as other than the presumed viewer, and at the same time is made ideologically difficult to identify by this viewer, who will conflate all young black males under this same criminal mark. (I, for one, have had the misfortune to hear a young white male watching *Crimewatch UK* comment that surveillance footage of black criminals is next to useless since it is so difficult to 'tell them apart'.) In this way the programmes demonstrate video surveillance's importance (identifying a menace) and impotence (the menace is unidentifiable). We are allowed to wander the streets fully interpellated once more, and also have a handy rationale available if all these cameras make no difference to the crime rate.[17]

The 'ideology of criminality' which the television programmes so satisfyingly express relies on a very basic assumption: I am not seen by the camera because the camera sees only criminals and I *do not look like* a criminal. The argument made is ultimately one of visual representation – the camera only sees and therefore what I look like must separate me from the abject object. Underlying this formula is its brutally prejudiced form – I do not look like a criminal because I am not a young black male. (My friend, the lawyer's, psychic dilemma is probably initiated by the fact that, as a lawyer, she would know that a middle-class white woman in Woolworth's is the demographic archetype of the kleptomaniac. Shopping for knick knacks, my friend 'looks like' a criminal and therefore no longer has the ideological support to prevent her from acting like one.) By contrast, the vast amount of crime related to data, perpetrated by criminals ranging from white middle-class teenage hackers to tax-evading corporate executives, does not appear in the visual realm of *Crimewatch UK*.

The parade of television shows aligning video recording with the policing of undesirable individuals provides a narrative conclusion to an otherwise disturbingly inconclusive experience. The programmes reassure us that the images of us have been reviewed and have passed the test of good citizenship. We have passed the test so well that the police now require our help, or at least our viewing support, in locating and dealing with those who have trespassed against video normalcy. As the primary medium for our reception of public video imagery, perhaps only television is in a position to give this reassurance. On *Crimewatch UK* we see that all these images of us *are* being collected and assessed and dealt with by the appropriate authorities. And, very importantly, we get to be the viewers of the appropriately sorted footage.

## Misreading murder

In the Jill Dando murder, the public was particularly traumatized because the suturing figure, the reassuring female presence who convinced us that things were, ultimately, safe and sane in the surveillance world, had become victim of the very sort of random violent crime from which she and the cameras were supposed to separate us. Perhaps more worryingly, the impotent imagery of Dando shopping just before her murder potentially reminded us that there will always be a mass of surveillance footage available of each of us, but very little of it is doing its ostensible job of protecting us from anything. It potentially opens our eyes to the open secret so clearly articulated by Norris and Armstrong:

> The message [of *Crimewatch*] is complete: CCTV works because it deters crime, if it does not deter crime it enables police to be deployed and apprehend a suspect, and if it does not result in immediate apprehension, in the absence of the police knowing the identity of the culprit, then the public can provide it. And the proof is there before the viewers' very own eyes. For all the words and scripted statements in praise of CCTV, it is perhaps the continuous repetition of the visual narrative structure of success which makes such programmes so seductively powerful in promoting CCTV. But of course this narrative structure tells us almost nothing of the routine operation of CCTV hour by hour, day by day, week by week. What is shown is just a minuscule fraction of what is in excess of 17 million hours of video footage recorded on camera [in the UK] each week. The footage shown has been carefully selected by the police or local authority, mindful of the public relations implications of broadcasting footage from CCTV systems. Thus the extracts show only the morally unambiguous interventions in line with public and police conceptions of 'real police work'. The more contentious, yet routine, aspects such as the surveillance of political prisoners, the deployment of police officers to move on 'troublesome' youth, or the use of the system by private security guards to exclude children from shopping malls are of course not shown.
>
> (1999: 69–70)

Another potential trauma in the pact we make with television to interpellate us into surveillance society occurs when the footage itself is unreadable or misread. Again, Norris and Armstrong (1999), in their comprehensive observations of CCTV control rooms have documented the routine frequency with which crimes get misread as other activity and legal behaviour is misinterpreted as criminal. Much of this misreading is confined in its results to a camera lingering or not lingering on an individual for a few minutes. However, on occasion, the effects of the gap between what seems to be happening and what transpires can be far more public and distressing.

The most famous and dramatic case of a gap between the apparent video image and the events that occurred again involves the city of Liverpool. In February 1993, two-year-old James Bulger disappeared while his mother was shopping in a shopping mall in the deprived Bootle area of the city. His dead body was found on the tracks of a railway line. Within days, surveillance footage from a mall security camera emerged, showing two other young boys leading James away by the hand. This footage was widely shown on television, including *Crimewatch UK*, in a version enhanced by Ministry of Defence experts.

The video of James Bulger being quietly abducted by Robert Thompson and Jon Venables, both aged ten, was shocking not only for what it showed, but for what it failed to show. The action recorded, in fact, seems surprisingly tender – two small boys caringly taking a smaller boy by the hand: the clip contradicts the kind of action that the camera is presumably awaiting – vandalism or mugging. (When Denise Bulger, James's mother, initially saw the video, the day after the disappearance and before the body was found, she was reassured by it – assuming that it meant that her son was safe.) The violent act of kidnapping, much loved by Hollywood for its dramatic bursts of action, here does not look violent at all, and hence is not noticed. This unreadability of the image contributed to a public sense of trauma, of helplessness, in relation to the case. As Dr Susan Bailey, consultant adolescent forensic psychologist, commented, talking about the public reaction in a BBC documentary on the case:

> I think it was triggered by a very unusual visceral image of the offence starting, and I think it was that that was in people's heads and it was that that made this take on a life of its own. The video perpetuates the sense

An ideology of crime

of helplessness, powerlessness and inability as an adult to intervene in the start of what was a pathway to a young child dying.

*(Children of Crime: A Riddle Wrapped Inside an Enigma,*
BBC, 7 April 1998)

Blake Morrison has described the case from a very personal, subjective stance:

It was the video footage from a security camera, jumpy and poignant as a cine film, that made the case famous.

(Morrison, 1997: 21)

And now, in court and on the news, the video compilation of security stills plays in endless detail for us all. 15:38:55, James alone outside the butchers. 15:40:24, Denise searching. 15:41:29, James on the upper floor, close to two other boys. 15:42:10, Denise still searching. 15:42:32, the still that froze a million hearts, James's hand – raised in trust – in the hand of Jon Venables, Robert Thompson leading the way. 15:43:08, the three boys leaving the precinct. Forward and back, stop, rewind, review, pause, freeze. Forward and back, forward and back, as if we watched it often enough the picture might change and James be there again, safe by Denise's side.

(Ibid.: 46)

## Cameras and compensation

At the heart of the public trauma of the Bulger video (and here the case relates closely to the Hillsborough disaster) was the realization that the camera was powerless to intervene in what it was witnessing. Whereas in Hillsborough, however, this intervention was due to the incapacity of the policing machine to recognize and respond to visual evidence clear to other witnesses, in the case of the Bulger video every viewer shares in the dilemma of witnessing without recognizing the crime. The surveillance scene, which becomes horrific once the fate of James Bulger is known, is otherwise recognizable as, at worst, boyish naughtiness, at best, child-like kindness. The information that could cue prevention is available only after the event – as a result of the event. The case introduces a doubt which continues to trouble the smooth surfaces of the *Crimewatch* world – the possibility

36

that in prioritizing visual surveillance we have in fact become blind to something.

A range of political responses to the Bulger case attempted to compensate for this doubt on a visual level, with the presiding judge pointing to the potential influence of horror videos on the crime, and the British Home Secretary seemingly intent on locking the boys themselves away from sight for as long as possible. One particularly interesting response occurred when artist James Wagg's art works (two pieces, *History Painting: Shopping Mall 15:42:32* and *History Painting: Railway Line*) were shown at the Whitechapel Open exhibition. The canvases showed digitally enhanced photos of the scenes of James Bulger's abduction and murder. They seem to have been thoughtful and fairly subdued responses by an artist to some very public imagery. However, the tabloid newspapers, having themselves shown the original images many times, seemed to find their representation as art rather than journalism repulsive (Morrison, 1997: 235). Interviewed afterwards by Alesandro Imperato, Wagg commented:

> The image itself was highly problematic, but it was never put forward as problematic. It was 'clear and simple' . . . the image is in fact two young boys walking hand in hand or one young boy leading a baby hand in hand. It could quite easily be a sentimental picture postcard. It is so 'benign'. It is so 'wonderful', little boys are walking hand in hand, 'ah how sweet' . . . but actually it isn't because we're always looking at the image in the past . . . before anyone had actually seen that image, that baby was already dead . . . So there is a total disjuncture in time, a displacement of event and image. Whereas when it was presented in the newspapers with all the text explaining how evil the boys were, this disjuncture was hidden.
>
> (Wagg, quoted in Friedlander, 1998: 13)

Jennifer Friedlander argues that Wagg's artwork 'retraumatizes' the event for us by making this image soft and sweet and unexplained again (Friedlander, 1998: 13), by reawakening us to visual discontinuity. Wagg reminds us that, whatever visual compensations have been made by journalists and politicians, the CCTV realm is producing images that do not make sense in the narratives of crime with which we soothe ourselves.

Friedlander points out the ideological falsities underlying the idea that these video images were ever intended to prevent crimes such as the death of James Bulger. CCTV cameras in shopping malls, she emphasizes, are installed not with murder in mind, but to prevent theft. The installers of the cameras, the businesses that paid for them, and the security guards who watched them were on the lookout not for abduction, but for theft and damage to property. The subsequent police and press use of the video images are heavily contextualized to separate us from this fact.[18]

Friedlander also argues that the public space of adulthood is contrasted in our culture with a childhood 'interiority, privacy, the deepest place inside' (Steedman, 1993, quoted in Friedlander, 1998: 3). As well as the search for visual closure and compensation in the case of the Bulger video, there was also a huge outpouring of articles and volumes on the psychology of young criminals. This need to explore the intentions and mind of the perpetrators speaks to a public desire for access to interiority, to a way of identifying the intent of Thompson and Venables, to a translation of the shopping mall recording that reveals the violence, or a cause for the violence, which appears to be missing. This search for interiority takes us outside the simple *Crimewatch* equation of 'Do you recognize this criminal?' and enters us into the more complex questions of how and whether we can recognize the criminal. At this point we are no longer so smoothly interpellated into the ideology of crime but are starting to do our own work of interpretation and narrative.

This contrast between the clear equation of surveillance with crime prevention and a more problematic interiorized relationship to events is often experienced in relation to sound. As Morrison (1997: 128) writes of listening to the taped interrogations of Thomson and Venables: 'Read the transcripts, and Robert sounds clever, confident, precocious. But listen, and you hear the desperate voice of a little boy slowly being caught in the web of his own lies.'

As Friedlander might point out, the encounter with the sound of Thompson's voice allows Morrison to re-establish for himself the child inside the killer, the real sense inside the apparent meaning of Thomson's words. This child-like interiority provides a very different explanation for Morrison to that presented by the narratives of *Crimewatch*. It is not necessarily any more true than the ideology of crime, but it is a break with it. Crucially, this break involves Morrison having to interpret or decode the tone of what he hears.

The appearance of the voice in the realm of surveillance – and specifically the appearance of the bugged voice in the courtroom – has a history of problematizing the clear narratives of surveillance evidence.

## Sound space

In the USA and the UK, two of the most notable incidents of covert audio recordings used as evidence in the judicial system relate to high-profile police cases involving black men – the quintessential criminal bodies in surveillance ideology. In both these cases, the introduction of covert audio recordings was an attempt to expose and undercut a representational logic whereby the policing system could see black men only as criminals. In the O.J. Simpson trial, the audio tapes of telephone conversations in which LAPD (Los Angeles Police Department) detective Mark Fuhrman made a series of racist comments were used by the Simpson defence to imply that Fuhrman was a racist cop who would be motivated to frame Simpson for the murder of his wife and her lover. In the Stephen Lawrence case in England, by contrast, Lawrence was a young black man murdered by a white gang in a case never successfully brought to trial by the police, owing, as was later exhaustively documented in the report of the public enquiry by Sir William Macpherson, to an institutionalized racism that could not properly respond to a violent crime in which a black male was the victim.[19] In an abortive private prosecution, Lawrence's family attempted to use covert recordings of the suspects at home engaging in racist tirades to indicate their racist motivations.[20] However, this evidence was never allowed to be heard in a full trial.[21]

In neither case could it be proved that the tapes were directly linked to actions. They were circumstantial evidence at best. Whereas visual surveillance, particularly in public places, tends to highlight the black male as identifiably criminal, in both these cases the tapes centre on the white male voice as not-quite-proven-to-be-criminal, and do so in relation to the fate of a black male body. Whereas video evidence is gathered with an expectation of direct representational reference, it seems that audio surveillance, which can never quite equate with the criminal deed, evokes a more complex response – a response which is, I would suggest, closely linked to the performative qualities of language and to our spatial understandings of the realms of sound and vision.

In *The Critique of Pure Reason*, Kant (1993: 52) identifies space as the condition upon which intuition of the external world is based:

> Space is nothing else than the form of all appearances of the external sense, that is the subjective condition of sensibility, under which alone external intuition is possible.
>
> ... It is therefore from the human point of view only that we can speak of space, extended objects, etc. If we depart from the subjective condition, under which alone we can obtain external intuition, or, in other words, by means of which we are affected by objects, the representation of space has no meaning whatsoever.

Space is a subjective organizing principle, but an absolutely necessary one.

From a Kantian perspective, is there a space of sound? Kant's imagery is visual, and the phenomenal objects of his sensory world relate to each other in a visual, spatial world of proximity, quantity, etc. His statement, nonetheless, is absolute: space is 'the subjective condition of sensibility under which alone external intuition is possible'.

Consistent with this reasoning, sound is organized in space through its location as a characteristic of an object. Sound does not have the status of an object per se; so, in *The Critique of Judgment*, music 'since it merely plays with sensations, has the lowest place among the fine arts' (Kant, 1987:199).

However, as any musician knows, the primary organizational axis of sound is not spatial but temporal. It is on the axis of time that sound achieves its qualities and variations. Considered temporally, a sound achieves the status of a phenomenon.

Of course, there are many post- (and pre-) Kantian philosophical systems which place music highest among the arts, but the tensions in the Kantian system are useful in exploring how ideas about sound may impact on the externally focused world of legal evidence. Because time, Kant (1993, 56) emphasizes, while underpinning all phenomenal perceptions, is particularly associated with the internal:

> Time is nothing else than the form of the internal sense, that is, of the intuitions of ourselves and of our internal state. For time cannot be any determination of outward appearances. It has to do with neither shape nor position; on the contrary, it determines the relation of representations in our internal state.

For Kant, sound appears externally not as a phenomenon in itself, but as a characteristic of objects. Yet, if we insist on the phenomenal objectivity of sound, it takes us less into the external world's spatial organization than into the internal world's temporal organization.

As a founding thinker of the Enlightenment, Kant's theories still have the force of common sense in our public understanding of the 'natural' organization of the world of phenomena, and hence of closely linked legal structures such as rules of evidence. The non-use of surveillance evidence in the Stephen Lawrence prosecution and the use of the Mark Fuhrman tapes in the O.J. Simpson trial both relate to the Kantian distinction between the spatial/external and the interior realms. Whereas, in legal terms, the tapes were being used to introduce links with subsequent acts or to discredit other testimony, i.e. for their ostensible relation to the spatial world of deeds, in fact the intended effect might have more to do with the disruptive introduction into the courtroom of interiority. The tapes sought to introduce not the direct intent of the speaker to enact certain words, but rather the space inside the speaker's head. The sound of surveillance tapes feels different to other evidence. These sounds reach into the founding 'if only' of the courtroom – 'if only we could get inside the accused's head'.

## Words that wound

One way to investigate the gap between language as evidence, as description, and language as interiority is through the concept of performativity. In J.L. Austin's speech act theory, the ways in which words 'do things' are exhaustively analysed. In brief, Austin argues that, whereas the dominant Anglo-American tradition judges language in terms of its descriptive, or constative, capacities – its ability to tell the truth – one of language's major characteristics is its ability to bring about states or events that did not exist prior to the enunciation. Austin's primary examples are contractual – the marriage vow ('I do'), the wager ('I bet you'), the threat, the dare, the promise. However, once established, this performative quality of language can be seen to be a factor in most, if not all, uses of language.

Other theorists have gone on to explore the relation of performativity to, for example, the legal system, in which a complex system of citationality – of references to prior judgements and laws – allow the words of a judge to have the effect of acts (Cornell, 1992). In her essay 'Burning acts – injurious speech' (1995), Judith Butler assesses the implications of such thinking for hate speech legislation in the United States.[22] Butler rejects the absolute position of 'free speech', but also argues against a literalist politics which implies that violent words in some way enact the violence they describe. Butler's argument is that in their performativity words become other than the representations of things. Their performativity – the ability to act, to wound – is the very site of their difference from their referent.

Referring to Derrida's arguments in 'Signature/Event/Context' (1982), Butler stresses that performative speech has power to act only in so far as it is citational, i.e. draws upon 'a prior and authoritative set of practices' (Butler, 1995: 205). Thus, in so far as the speech act functions, it does so with the approval of the language/social community. For the court to prosecute such speech is, to an extent, for the court to prosecute itself. (Butler has also persuasively demonstrated the connections between Althusserian interpellation and Austinian performativity; Butler, 1997: 24.)

In the case of Mark Fuhrman or Stephen Lawrence's attackers, however, physical, spatial acts by the subjects, rather than the injurious qualities of words, were under examination. The audio surveillance 'feels' like it provides a direct causal link – hence the insistence of the O.J. Simpson defence on playing the audio tapes to the jury. But the link is just that – a feeling. In a spatial exterior world of actions and effects, these audio surveillance tapes show only that this is the kind of person who might undertake the act (a quality attributable, perhaps, to others of the courtroom's inhabitants).

This failure of the interior sound space to make a link with the causal space of deeds can easily seem a frustration, even a tragedy. However, Butler's insight that it is in their very difference from the referent that the injurious power of such words lies helps us to think through this disconnection in a different manner. Following her argument, we can see the ways in which the interior sound space draws attention to what is unfigured in the exterior realm of evidence. The sound space transgressively reintroduces what has been representationally excluded from the visual field. So, in the Simpson and Lawrence cases, these tapes function not really as evidence but as part of a debate about race in society.

## Reggae Head

In his poem 'Reggae Head', quoted at the beginning of this chapter, Benjamin Zephaniah makes an unexpected claim. Speaking from a society (England) where the sound of reggae was for many years the most public sign of the social presence of African-Caribbeans, Zephaniah claims that the reggae in his head is a secret space that cannot be reached through police surveillance tactics. On a common-sense level, Zephaniah's point is straightforward – no amount of force can eliminate the thoughts and rhythms inside the mind. But these thoughts and rhythms are exactly what Zephaniah believes white society wants to eliminate, because they don't stop in the mind. Reggae in the head inevitably means reggae bursting into the streets. The means of this transmission from inner to public may be the, to white ears, coded nature of the Rasta's speech: 'Dem say/Obey yu masta/Stop talk Rasta/But I tek a dub/An jus rock a little fasta . . .' (Zephaniah, 1996: 19). The coded language of the Rasta carries both a secret meaning and the transmission of rhythm.

In surveillance technology there is a discontinuity between sound and representation. The soundtrack to the surveillance camera is usually disconnected from the image; it is the television commentator's voice perhaps, or nothing at all: silence – the strange sensation of watching drastic public events played back, recorded on a system in which microphones are not worth the money. The sound of audio surveillance is one of coded words – words not quite attached to actions, needing interpretation. In a James Bond Hollywood world this may mean strange-sounding gibberish secretly recorded, to be decoded later. In the court room it involves the dilemma of the speech act as evidence: following Butler's argument, to the degree that the recorded language is itself, for example, a violence, it is not the same violence that the court is considering. In Benjamin Zephaniah's words, the sound of surveillance is precisely what eludes surveillance, and travels back through language. To some degree, in each of these cases, the sound of surveillance lives in the time-based interior world, rather than the spatial exterior world of phenomena.

The break between the visual and audio spaces of surveillance, between exteriority and interiority, indicates a reason for the associations of audio surveillance with code. Since surveillance is ideologically supposed to carry a representational, evidential weight, and since covert audio recordings can never achieve the representational self-evidence of video recordings, the difference of language under surveillance from its referent will tend to be emphasized. In this difference, the performative emerges. Such performativity in language may result in hate speech, but it may also, as Zephaniah indicates, create a language of cultural difference, of non-representational rhythmic qualities, or ambiguous messages. Code structures our understanding of the sound of surveillance because the ideology of crime instructs us to interpret audio surveillance's difference, reducing it to equivalence with the field of visual evidence. But once the concept of code has been introduced, it may be used to develop a space of emotions and communications – a performative space – in which an endless expansion of possibilities beyond the evidence of representation can occur.

## Caught in the act

If the sound of audio surveillance performatively creates a space that questions the objective realm to which visual representation refers, are we simply left with a binary between the inevitable suturing ideologies of video surveillance and the potentially radical intimacies of audio bugging? Clearly, such a binary would be highly unstable. While a performative analysis of the sound space of audio surveillance opens the possibility of disruption, particularly in the fields of jurisprudence and policing, there is nonetheless a considerable police investment in audio surveillance, and we can assume that this investment is not entirely intended as a contribution to the development of radical performative sound space. Police investment in audio bugging is, perhaps, partly the result of an understandable desire to play legally with the tools that are an everyday part of organized crime. A certain technophilia operates also, plus the engaging fantasy of James Bond intrigue. There are undoubtedly practical policing uses of the technologies. These uses, however, are easily extended to accumulation of information on individuals which, although it may be innocent, is susceptible to a decoding that may reveal criminal or antisocial potentials undreamed of by the speaker. This accumulation of 'decodable' information about individuals is the reverse side of the desire for access to interiority discussed above. Linked to the practice of data surveillance, the potential for audio evidence to create a body of information about a person which can potentially predict a person's criminal tendencies (or other actions) has obvious attractions for a criminology faced with the paradoxes of innocent-looking boy murderers. The ideologies of encoding and deciphering associated with audio surveillance are far more powerful in relation to such bodies of information than the ideologies of visibly identifiable criminality which function in the case of video surveillance.

One of the most complete fantasies of such prediction is explored in Steven Spielberg's 2002 film based on a Philip K. Dick story, *Minority Report*. In this elaborately realized fantasy, it has become possible for police to predict confidently that an individual is about to murder someone, and to arrest them in advance. The predictive capacity involves an elaborate psychic process using drug-affected mutant humans, but the central question of the movie is one not of technology but of morality. Do we have the right, for the greater good of society, to punish people for things they are about to do? The close relationship of time and interiority comes to the fore again here: things not done in the world of events, or space, nonetheless have a reality – and a complexity – in the interior world. And yet this world's organizing principle, time, has its rules – what has not yet happened can still be changed. (The film's denouement – in which a character has to decide whether to prove the predictive perfection of the system by himself killing – features the dilemma of choice, of free will.) Can the rules of time be ignored in order to preserve the safety and lawfulness of the exterior, spatial world?

The moral conclusion of *Minority Report*, unsurprisingly in a mass market movie, is that our core organizing moral principles should not be subverted for apparent short-term safety gains. The Department of Crime Prediction is disbanded, and in a saccharine epilogue we are shown the ways in which time, left to its traditional workings, heals. However, the movie has also allowed us to inhabit an ethical dilemma in which predictive technologies, based upon knowledge of intent, affect and protect our exterior spatial realm of actions. The interplay of these realms, and the role of surveying technologies in this interplay, has been taken, in a mass fantasy, to one of its limit points.

However, just as the realm of evidence, the exterior, the spatial, will colonize the space of audio surveillance, the interior, the temporal, so, the ambiguities associated with audio surveillance's performative distance from its referent may also be seen to operate in the visual field. Despite the dominance of the 'ideology of crime' in relation to video surveillance, we have already begun to see, in the experiences of the subjects of surveillance, whether football hooligans or worried shoppers, that the fact of being under surveillance can alter our consciousness of the world through which we move. This difference may also be analysed and perhaps mobilized in relation to a concept of 'performative space'.

Just how pervasive the gap between our ideological understanding and our psychic experience of surveillance had become by the mid-1990s was indicated by the release in Britain in 1996 of the video *Caught in the Act*. A compilation of footage purchased from the operators of CCTV systems, *Caught in the Act* featured not only scenes of crime chosen for their drama, violence or comedy rather than any policing results, but also scenes of illicit sex in lifts, stockrooms and cars. As a *Washington Post* article explained from an American perspective: 'Without a bill of rights [in Britain] offering protection from government intrusions on privacy, individuals have no recourse against local government agencies that provide such tapes to producers.' ('The latest from Britain: sex, private lives and videotapes', *Washington Post*, 17 March 1996).

The article's tone of bewildered amusement underlines the difference in the legal situations relating to privacy in the two countries:

The videos ... have prompted modest outrage (but no laws) in parliament ...

'This misuse of material brings CCTV, which is a very valuable tool

46

in the fight against crime, into disrepute; Bruce Gale, a member of Parliament's Media Committee, told Britain's Press Association.

'Anyone can do this; said Duncan Lustig-Prean, a spokesman for the civil liberties group Liberty. 'There are no controls at all. We think it's quite appalling that members of the public can be caught like this.'

(Ibid.)

The language of crime entirely dominated the debate – CCTV is good because it catches criminals, but this means that, if 'members of the public' are 'caught' by the camera, they somehow become criminals too. *Caught in the Act* exposed the glaring inconsistency in surveillance's 'ideology of crime': the cameras themselves do not sort criminal behaviour from the non-criminal, recording only the former, nor is there a system which views and sorts the material. Rather, certain material is rescued from an unsorted mass and used in criminal investigations. The rest remains, at least in the short term, a mess of comings and goings that do not quite add up to the term 'innocent'.

*Caught in the Act* provided an early indication of just how interesting superficially dull material could become once set in the context of surveillance. What is actually depicted on the tapes is mundane at best. We are invited to watch a presumably adulterous assignation in a car park, involving little more than one woman getting in a car to sit while another has left to shop. Some of the crime scenes are dramatic, but of course they are poorly shot. None of the sex would be out of place in a moderately contemporary BBC drama. The appeal of the material must therefore lie in something other than its representational capacity. As the voiceover encourages us to register excitement as 'CCTV records the dark shadows of urban violence', we realize that this commentary is functioning as a reminder of the presence of the cameras. It is through this presence that the scenes become interesting; the tension of watching derives from the fact that we are, by proxy, present in the scenes without the actors knowing it. A scene of a couple having sex in the stationery stockroom at an office party shows a blurred image of male buttocks and a woman's arms grasping at the man's back. The image, obscured and poorly resolved, is not particularly erotic in its own right, nor does it expose any new information about human behaviour. It is

47

interesting precisely because it shows a couple who did not think that they were being watched.

There is a fine but important distinction here. The interest does not lie in finding out what people do when they think they are not being watched. There is very little in the tapes that would surprise. Rather, the interest lies in watching people think that they are not being watched. In playing the tape we are not, in fact, viewing a representation of actions previously performed in front of a passively recording camera; we are participating in a new event in which, by viewing the recording of the scene, we are involved in the creation of another space – a watched space, which prior to our watching did not exist. In this space, a couple who were previously engaged in a secretive office affair become, as video signals, performers of a coy display. A space different to the one experienced by the office lovers is created, a space in which my eye and body are located high in the corner of a black and white room. And yet this space is not created by any act. Simple entrance and exit of the room by the couple would not create the space. It is dependent on engagement in acts that the subjects would not want me to see.

Here, then, is a second 'performative space' of surveillance – a space which happens in being watched. Like the intimate sound space created by the replaying of audio surveillance evidence in the court room, the performative space of *Caught in the Act* comes into being in a contextualized replaying. Again, as with audio bugging, in the *Caught in the Act* tapes, the expectation of privacy by the subject is a base upon which the surveillance space is reliant (in Chapter 2 we will analyse examples in which this is not the case). Unlike the sound space, however, and consistent with the Kantian arguments above, this second surveillance space does not create any impression of interiority. Watching the fuzzy images of people we do not know doing embarrassing or slightly shocking things, we are not engaged in the thought that we have access to the true inner worlds of these people. On the contrary, we are very aware that we know almost nothing about them. Our engagement is not in their interior but in the exterior surrounding them – in the knowledge that we are putting them in a place that they did not intend to be. There is an excitement in watching *Caught in the Act* which draws upon a feeling of power over the video's subjects.

How does this performative space relate to the ideology of crime, which, we have seen, dominates our understanding of video surveillance? Once again, the videos place the viewer in the position of surveyor, not the surveyed. Yet the framing here is very different to that of *Crimewatch*. Instead of viewing alongside the police, helping them solve the case, we are watching, as the cover sleeve to the video puts it, 'footage "they" don't want you to see', material that has been condemned in Parliament. Who, then, is the criminal? The spokesman for Liberty (the civil liberties group) decried the 'appalling' fact that 'members of the public can be caught like this'. The strange implication of his statement is that innocent people have somehow been turned into guilty criminals by the act of being caught on CCTV. In the context of such disapprovals, the watching of *Caught in the Act* becomes a kind of pleasure in criminalizing. By watching, we are turning furtive acts into crimes. We are enjoying the subversive pleasures of bringing crime about while it is others – the subjects of the videos – who actually become the criminals through our watching.

As opposed to accessing some interior world of these subjects, we have become engaged in the creation of new external versions of them – criminal bodies entirely divorced from any internal reasons for or justifications of their actions.

The performative spaces of *Caught in the Act* contrast with the smooth surfaces of *Crimewatch*. Whereas the television programmes imply a consistent process from surveillance recordings through police review of material through broadcast of relevant (criminal) material to arrest of the guilty, *Caught in the Act* reminds us of a mass of unsorted surveillance material available for interpretation and appropriation. It permits the thought that our viewing is not just a late reactive stage in a linear process, but an intervention that may start its own processes.

*Caught in the Act* opens the possibility of a relation between the viewer and the hermeneutics of surveillance, and beyond that to the creation of surveillance spaces. This is a heavy weight of possibility for a money-making scam to carry, and even within its own material the video contains the seeds of its collapse. A footnote on the cover of *Caught in the Act* states: 'In the interest of complying with legal restrictions some of the footage contained in this programme has been reconstructed.' Several of the scenes on the tape, including 'sensational Princess Di' footage, are actually recreations of surveillance footage, shot to look like real CCTV video. Ostensibly, the reconstruction should make no difference. If the producers are honestly recreating actual footage, then any points about privacy or crime prevention or whatever are still being demonstrated. But, of course, the reconstructed footage in fact only works if we forget or do not notice that it is reconstructed (as the placing and tone of disclaimers and introductions on the video encourage us to do). In order for this video to engage, it is reliant upon the formula outlined above, whereby individuals engaged in private acts are brought into criminal space by our gaze. If the bodies on display are actors then the effect does not occur.

The phenomenon of the 'reality television' show *Big Brother* could almost be read as a direct response to the dilemma created by the question of trustworthiness in relation to *Caught in the Act*. The formula of *Caught in the Act* works only when we trust that the situations spied upon are real. If they are in any way staged, they become unwatchably uninteresting. *Big Brother* answers the dilemma of *Caught in the Act* by putting its subjects – the competing housemates – in a controlled environment: we know that they are ordinary people and there is a branded guarantee that they are really doing the things that we watch. The trade-off is, of course, that the competitors in *Big Brother* are no longer, like the subjects of *Caught in the Act*, unaware that they are being filmed. The excitement for the viewer is less a result of a hidden gaze, creating a space that the subjects did not know they were in, and more an engagement with the contestants in creating together, watched and watcher, a unique shared world. (The terms of this world will be discussed in more detail in later chapters.) However, the criminalizing tendencies of surveillance space continue to function: we are forever hoping to catch the contestants off guard, and are never so happy as when we see them trying to get away with something at the expense of the other housemates.

The questions raised about the 'truth' of surveillance space in *Caught in the Act*, and the productivity of responses such as *Big Brother* indicate that the seemingly simple formula of enjoying the act of spying upon others is in fact subject to a huge complexity of responses. To understand this complexity, it is useful to relate our interpretation of the performative space of surveillance to some of the work undertaken on the complexities of performativity in language.

## Spatial suspense

In his essay 'The unhappy performative' (1995), Timothy Gould analyses and expands upon J.L. Austin's concept of 'uptake' in performative speech. 'Uptake' involves the recognition by the auditor that a speech act has occurred. So, for example, it means that in hearing someone say to me, 'I dare you to kick that policeman', I understand that a challenge has been issued – even if it is a challenge that I choose to ignore; even, indeed, if I feel that it is a challenge that expresses nothing other than the appalling character of the speaker. Gould, using Austin's terms, describes a speech act in which uptake occurs as a 'happy' performative, and one in which it does not as an 'unhappy performative'.

Gould's point that performative happiness depends on uptake and not upon the 'force' of the performative (a feeling that I must indeed kick the policeman or forever be less of a man) is used to separate his analysis from what he sees as a tendency in deconstructive criticism to reinvent Austin as a 'Nietzschean' linguist.

Gould locates a second level of 'happiness' in the speech act when the intended effect occurs – when I kick the policeman, or at least feel ashamed of not doing so. Following Austin, Gould labels these two phases of response to the performative, the 'illocutionary' and the 'perlocutionary' (Austin, 1976: 99–102). The gap between uptake, the illocutionary aspect and the second, perlocutionary, level at which uptake actually has an effect in line with the intent of the speaker, Gould dubs 'illocutionary suspense or perlocutionary delay' (Gould, 1995: 28). His point, ultimately, is that such suspense or delay is not a bad thing; in fact, it allows a space 'between the possibility of sense and the possibility of tyranny of sense' (ibid.: 41) which is very different from language philosophy's usual insistence upon the constative truth or falsehood of statements. Gould suggests that Austin's larger project may be to introduce, or rather tease out, this spectre of suspense, or a certain openness, in all language, disrupting the very terms of the true/false binary.

Gould's reading has a particular relevance at a point where we are faced with a dilemma of 'uptake' in relation to surveillance space. His complexifying of the ways in which a performative utterance may generate response indicates that, far from the 'performative space' of surveillance being cancelled out by a sophistication of our responses to footage such as the *Caught in the Act* tapes, the decreasing likelihood of our unquestioningly accepting the producers' intended effects opens new ways in which surveillance space may be experienced and understood.

The ideology of crime in relation to surveillance extends the character of constative speech to the realm of representation. Surveillance footage describes events that happened. Rooted in secure distinctions of outer and inner, action and interpretation, this ideology follows the police officer's edict to 'stick to the facts'. The performative spaces that we have traced as a counter to this discourse can never 'stick to the facts'. They invoke the experience of double meaning, spaces within spaces, transformation of representation by the circumstance of reception. In the Anglo-American positivist tradition in particular, such transformations will tend to be thought of as secondary to the empirical, constative truth.

Gould's point, however, is that such 'truth' is always only a naturalized elimination of illocutionary suspense – a desire to enforce not only the illocutionary uptake of a statement, but also its perlocutionary effect. In spatial/representational terms, this means that the viewer of surveillance footage is expected to relate to the footage as self-evident description of the events recorded. The introduction of responses, emotions, desires or a questioning of the authority of the document, its framing, its interpretive agenda, all reintroduce a perlocutionary delay into the proceedings. Instead of the 'truth' of representation, we have uptake of a performative space, and delay/suspense in relation to this space. In the concept of this delay we begin to see how the doubt introduced by the question of 'reconstructed' surveillance footage may in fact support a counter-discourse to the 'ideology of crime' in surveillance.

## Public uptake

Perhaps inevitably, the first major example of the effects of such delay occurred when the incident was one of 'counter-surveillance' and when it was in the short-term interests of the police to introduce doubt into the self-evidence of representation. The Rodney King beating and trials were the first widely publicized introduction of spatial performativity into the field of evidence. The disparate performative spaces we have analysed were each introduced in the trial in the cause of throwing doubt upon the self-evidence of video images of white police violently beating a black man. Interior spaces were introduced – what were the cops thinking?, what reaction did they fear?, what drugs might King have inside his body which might provide him with superhuman strength and imperviousness to pain? (Koon, 1992). Members of the jury were told that they needed to imagine the interior, intimate spaces which the tape could not show. The transformative capacity of the camera – turning private into public space – was also emphasized. These isolated events might look uncalled for in the public realm, suggested the defence, but the public has no knowledge of the day-to-day pressures of policing in Los Angeles. The tape makes appropriate acts appear to be inappropriate. It criminalizes. Finally, the constative truth value of the tape itself was questioned by appeal to its performative qualities. The tape – which does not show what went before, which was shot from a certain angle and which was recorded by a certain kind of person – has the effect, the defence implied, through mass television broadcast, not of constative description (the police beat Rodney King and I am describing this to you) but of performative uptake. Unlike any reports of a beating, this tape itself, this mass experience of watching the tape, has become a public experience of police violence. In the defence's argument, this public uptake of the performativity of the tape bears no relation to the events of the night itself and must not be allowed to influence the jury's verdict. The tape becomes an event, a space, separated from the beating, the evidence.

If the LAPD's defence team used performativity successfully to separate the Rodney King tape from the beating, and thus achieved the usual verdict in cases of suspected police violence against black men, they also underlined the tape's importance as a shared performative space – where 'uptake' had already been secured. The trial, then, became the scene of illocutionary suspense/perlocutionary delay, with response to the uptake hanging in the balance. A guilty verdict might have sutured the performative space of the tape, however shakily, back onto the surfaces of evidence. The 'not guilty' verdict ensured a mass response appropriate to an experience cut off from any shared ideologies. The public, and particularly black Los Angeles residents, having 'uptaken' the performative space of the tape as an experience of LAPD violence, paused in their response to see whether the legal system was capable of processing their trauma. Once the impossibility of even a partial legal response was revealed, the suspense was over, and the perlocutionary effect emerged as a violent rage against the system of law itself. Following this argument to its conclusion, we can read the criminality of the Los Angeles riots, the looting and destruction of property, as not just a side-effect but a direct consequence of the trial's separation of the public's experience of the tape from the frame of evidence, legality and justice.[23]

## Uptaking surveillance space

I have indicated – particularly in the case of audio surveillance – that there may be instances when the performative spaces of surveillance disrupt the surface of the 'ideology of crime' without necessarily re-sulting in street riots. Indeed, following Gould's reading of Austin (in which the performative introduces a gap, a freedom, into the consta-tive realm in general), we can see ways in which the recognition of performativity in surveillance experience will, per se, have an effect upon representational ideologies.

However, whereas linguistic performativity is initiated by an individual (though, *pace* Derrida, Cornell, Butler, guaranteed by the linguistic power structure, by citationality), the performative spaces of surveillance which we have been tracing bear a closer relation to Butler's (1990) example of gender performativity, in which the citational power structure will tend to impose gender performativity upon the subject regardless of any choice of utterance/behaviour by him/herself. In the case of surveillance, what is 'uptaken' is not simply the happiness of a single performative utterance – I bet you, I dare you, I do (marry you) – but also the possibility of performativ-ity itself: the acceptance that a space is brought into being which is neither the original space nor a self-evident representation of it. Such performative space, in Kantian terms, properly occupies neither external nor internal realms of intuition but is a bleeding of subjectivity into the spatial field.

Lacking the speaker of the speech act, the performative space of surveillance, once 'uptaken', is subject to various attempts at securing effect (by lawyers, newspaper editors, video producers, etc.), but it is free of the authority of the speaker. As such, its illocutionary suspense/perlocutionary delay is perhaps more completely open to variety of effect.

I do not mean to imply, however, that the effects of the performative space of surveillance may be subjectively chosen by the viewer/auditor. Butler's notion of gender performativity is particularly resonant here: Butler herself has had to argue against readings of her work which imply a choice by the subject in relation to the 'performance' of gender (Butler, 1993: x). The intimacies, disruptions and doublings which appear once the performativity of surveillance space is 'uptaken' are not simply pleasurable crises in a representational ideology. They are crises of the relation, the suturing of the self to the objective world.

To negotiate such crises without an exhausted return to ideology and its sublime objects necessitates a fuller understanding of the non-voluntary effects of surveillance space upon the subject, and the consequent potentials for comprehended and to a degree volitional responses. In the third chapter of this study I will return to the subject-as-viewer/auditor of surveillance space, examining in particular the dilemmas introduced by the surveillance recording of death. In the upcoming chapter, however, I will move sideways to the subject-as-surveyed and explore the crisis of subjectivity initiated by the notion that we inhabit surveillance's performative space.

# 2

# Perverting privacy

Talk to anyone about electronic surveillance and they very quickly tell you what's wrong with it. Their privacy is invaded. . . . The sheltering walls of privacy have been digitally dissolved.

(Lyon, 1994: 180)

The concern for privacy is the predominant conceptual framework within which a resistance to, or worry about, surveillance is socially articulated. The idea of privacy as a possession that we need to protect is deeply embedded in our culture. And yet it seems that the notion of privacy is functionally quite weak as a counter to the growth of surveillance. The seemingly legitimate 'public' uses of surveillance can justify most of its intrusions. As we saw in tracing the history of surveillance as a supposed crime-prevention tool, while the gut public reaction to surveillance may be that some notion of privacy has been offended against, in most specific instances of surveillance activity, public consent, or at least passive assent, can be achieved relatively easily because the common perception of the private sphere has not, in fact, been transgressed. While privacy campaigners may warn against the ways in which new technologies can 'snoop' on our lives, the most common uses of the technologies cover behaviour in public or the collation of data that we have freely handed over to commercial or government bodies.

There is something of a gap between the common-sense feeling of what privacy is and any attempts to define it. In his policy discussion for the Demos think tank, *The Future of Privacy*, Perri 6 (1998: 37) notes: 'Privacy, it has rightly been lamented, cannot be defined very satisfactorily.' He chooses A.F. Westin's definition as representing the most straightforward academic consensus:

The claim of individuals, groups or institutions to determine for themselves when, how and to what extent, information about them is communicated to others.

(Perri 6, 1998: 37)

This is still a fairly vibrant definition, pointing towards the importance of data protection legislation in determining our rights in relation to information about ourselves. However, it does not really express the *feel* of privacy as a particular state – a place, a space in which we do certain things. Perri 6 initially outlines a history of privacy that is based not so much on the privacy rights described by Westin as on our experiences of and behaviours in private life. He suggests, though, that a future understanding of privacy will have less to do with this historical/cultural notion of being in a space where organizations and other people are prevented from knowing what we are doing, and more to do with agreements about what can and cannot be done with data. Privacy, he suggests, will not be an absolute right but will remain an important principle (ibid.: 13).

While this viewpoint is consistent with Westin's definition, it abandons the sense of being 'in private' that is central to the common understanding of the term. Whether it is useful to continue to use the word 'privacy' in this situation is debatable. Perri 6 appears to have a political agenda (centre-left pro-technology) which involves attempting to harness the positive ideological associations of 'privacy' to suggest a governmental framework for a society in which the common-sense notion of what it means to be 'in private' no longer functions. (A free market trade in relative privacy will replace any universal right.) However, if we doubt the virtue and value of 'common-sense' privacy, we may have fewer reasons to hold on to the word.

In fact, privacy has never been uniformly available, nor uniformly valued. David Lyon (1994: 182) has noted the fact that 'the private has usually been associated with the domestic'. Lyon suggests that the encroachment of surveillance into the private sphere reveals a fundamental ambiguity in relation to the public/private binary, an ambiguity that is particularly notable in those whose relations to the public sphere is not one of privilege:

> Abused women frequently welcome such attention and, indeed, deplore the lack of seriousness with which issues such as domestic violence and rape are treated by public authorities such as the police. This extends to the era of information technology where surveillance methods such as caller ID may be used to the benefit of just such women.
>
> (Ibid.: 183)

For those without controlling public power, the apparent invasion of privacy can sometimes seem welcome.

Lyon carefully traces a history of privacy, emphasizing both its historical continuities and the very specific ways in which it has developed in the modern state into a public/private binary, with both sides depending upon and shoring up the privilege of property. In modern society, he notes: 'Privacy connects closely with freedom; at least, it does in accounts given by men' (ibid.: 184; see also Lyon, 2001: 20–3).

Because of the association with the domestic, the protection of privacy often becomes equated in public discourse with protection of the weak, of women and children. When the privacy of politicians is 'invaded' by the press, it is the innocence of the 'wife and family' that is routinely defended. Yet this defence is dependent upon the privilege of the man. Single mothers are, of course, much more per-missible targets of government and media attention, as society seeks to protect itself via surveys, databases and newspaper articles from fraudulent welfare families and delinquent fatherless children.

Lyon attempts to build a containing framework for surveillance 'beyond privacy' (ibid.: 196) on a Habermasian notion of public covenant, an understanding of 'personhood' in relation to 'social participation' (ibid.: 218). In his vision, the limits of surveillance would be defined not by a paranoid response to invasion of personal privacy, but by a new understanding of how, in the age of advanced electronic representational technology, differing surveillance prac-tices do or do not build a society of inter-human relations. Such a programme, however, is based upon a coherent, humanist (ultimately, for Lyon, a Christian) concept of individual identity. It relies on a sociological viewpoint that rarely touches upon the contradictions and confusions experienced in the psyche in response to surveil-lance. Once we begin to explore the psychological experience of the subject under surveillance, the critique of privacy as a framework for understanding surveillance, in fact, becomes more wide-reaching in its consequences than Lyon's humanist frame suggests.

## Space for desire

We have seen already that surveillance may be experienced spatially. We also experience privacy very much in spatial terms – to be in private is to be in a special, often domestic, place. To explore in more detail the complex relationship between private space, public space and surveillance space, we could do worse than look at the experience of individuals who, we might say, are on the avant-garde of privacy loss, i.e. some of the many groups who never really had access to privacy in the first place. So if privacy, as Lyon indicates, is intimately tied in with the domestic sphere, and, by extension with the heterosexual married bedroom, how does this affect those whose desire does not fit into that bedroom? Given that sexuality is to a great degree constructed and legislated in relation to a notion of the private, what does a sexuality which has never been allowed full access to privacy have to teach us about a post-private world?

## The hidden photographer

In 'A case of paranoia running counter to the psychoanalytical theory of the disease' Sigmund Freud (1963a: 97–106) describes the story of a woman who believed a hidden photographer to have spied upon her in bed with a man. Freud had earlier posited the rule that paranoia always results from a homosexual wish ('On the mechanism of paranoia', Freud, 1963b: 29–48), and in typical fashion he uses the apparent exception of the hidden photographer to prove his rule. The woman, who appears to be experiencing the delusion of the photographer as a response to the guilt induced by the illicit nature of her involvement with the man, is in fact, Freud suggests, responding to a continuing fixation on the mother figure. Her paranoid fear of the man and his imaginary ally, the hidden photographer, is preceded by and transferred from a fear that a mother-substitute is aware of the affair. It is this mother figure who, Freud suggests, is the initial object of paranoia, and this paranoia results from homosexual desire.

In beginning to explore the position of the surveyed subject, the story of the hidden photographer gathers many of the concerns and analytical tools which may be useful in an assessment of the psychological consequences and possibilities of a surveillance society. Paranoia is clearly related to the fear of 'Big Brother' – paranoid delusions can involve the most futuristic of surveillance technologies. Freud's link between paranoia and homosexuality may seem annoyingly pathologizing to the contemporary gay man or lesbian, but if we remove the assumption that there is something here to be cured, we may find that there is much to explore in the relationship between same-sex desire and fear of being watched – after all, on the most practical level, for hundreds of years, in most societies, to be seen in a homosexual act was and often still is an extremely danger-ous position to be in. Freud's analysis reminds us that these fears and fantasies not only frame our desires socially, they inevitably inform and structure desire itself.

There is also a direct link from Freudian treatment of homosexual-ity to another crucial psychoanalytic concept in the exploration of a society of reproduced selves – narcissism. Homosexuality in Freud's work is always intimately associated with narcissism – the stage in sexual development between 'auto-erotism' and 'object love', at which 'the individual . . . begins by taking himself, his own body, as his love object' (Freud, 1963b: 31). Narcissism is an immensely powerful force in Freud's work and reasserts itself at many stages in human development. Various commendable characteristics, such as concern for the greater social good, either may be appropriate sublimations of residual narcissistic/homosexual libidinal energies subsequent to heterosexual object-choice or, particularly if over-developed, may signify repression of homosexual object-choice. (In a simplified nutshell: unable to focus his desire on an appropriate female object, the homosexual man refocuses on writing a novel, leading an expedition, or founding a religion.)

Narcissism is intimately linked to the fetishes of sight. In 'Instincts and their vicissitudes', Freud (1963b: 96) locates the initial phase of both scopophilia (love of watching) and exhibitionism (love of show-ing) as a 'narcissistic formation' in which 'the subject's own body is the object of the scoptophilia'. Following this Freudian logic, it would seem reasonable to suggest that the paranoid delusion of the hidden photographer also betrays a narcissistic/homosexual desire to be the object of the photograph.[1]

A bunch of clichés about gay people are undoubtedly in operation here – the homosexual as vain, exhibitionist, voyeuristic and para-noid. However, by digging into the Freudian theories of desire that relate to these clichés, we may begin to see how desire is indeed often structured in relation to these forces, not because of some intrinsic homosexual dysfunction, but because desire operates in relation to social rules and ideologies, among which the function of the private sphere has, particularly in post-Enlightenment bourgeois society, been central.

Freud tends to use female homosexuality as a secondary example of male homosexuality in his work (and this is undoubtedly the case in the story of the woman and the hidden photographer) – a contradiction, given his emphasis elsewhere on sexual difference (and a contradiction I don't want to repeat).[2] Later in this chapter, we will look at the very different ways in which female desire is figured and structured in relation to surveillance. However, in beginning to think through the position of the subject under surveillance other than via the criminal, Freudian theory is a rich place to start, precisely because of its conflations of homosexuality, narcissism, paranoia and scopophilia/exhibitionism. In theorizing the relation of desire to the image of one's self, Freud's work introduces us to the possibility that a culture of surveillance may profoundly impact upon the psychosexual experience of the individual.

## Public sex

The story of the hidden photographer indicates a number of potential starting points for an analysis of the psychology of the subject under surveillance. To start with the most emphatic strand of Freud's analysis, the relation of homosexual object choice to paranoia – and by extension to an instability in the public/private binary – has a particular resonance (and one which does not end with a shift from homosexual repression to gay identity).

Gay sexuality occupies an ambivalent and endangered position in relation to the protected sphere of privacy. Most legal campaigns for decriminalization of homosexuality have largely been argued in relation to privacy rights.[3] However, as theorists such as Michael Moon have argued, the social construct of privacy is predicated upon a concept of the domestic sphere that is inherently and conservatively bourgeois and heterosexual.

As the gay rights movement developed, the role of non-private sexuality began to be articulated. Pat Califia (1994: 71) raised the question in her 1982 essay 'Public sex'. She starts with a simple summary of the gay rights agenda:

> Since its inception, the American gay liberation movement has demanded that all sex acts performed in private between consenting adults should be decriminalized.

Califia goes on to examine the problems with that position, asking 'Why is sex supposed to be invisible?' For Califia, a society that could engage openly in consensual acts of public sexuality would be one freed of the repressive terms of the bourgeois domestic sphere:

> Seeing other people having sex is reassuring and enlightening. It calmed the panic I've been carrying around ever since I first heard my parents fucking and thought they must be murdering each other.
>
> (Ibid.: 81)

Besides, she notes, at this point the idea of private sex is a fiction anyway:

> The technology of electronic snooping has become so sophisticated that intimate information can be gathered anywhere, including your bedroom.
>
> (Ibid.: 77)

For Califia, there is a distinction between the openness of public sex, which is liberating, and the menace of surveillance, which is characteristic of the police attack upon non-domesticated sexuality. However, the gay male relation to public sex is often more traumatic than such utopianism would indicate – a combined fethishization and fear of the public space and its policing forces. Likewise, the relation to surveillance technologies may also be sexually complex.

## Steam

As Moon and Califia emphasize, gay sexual practice has long incorporated a significant element of 'public sex'. In the early 1990s, one of the leading forums in the USA for discussion and description of this phenomenon was *Steam*, a quarterly journal dedicated to description and celebration of cruising spots, sex clubs and other opportunities for public and semi-public gay male sex. *Steam* did not only act as a resource for information about public sex, it also had a strong editorial point of view, insisting that liberation from oppressive morality involves pornography, promiscuity and sex in public places.

In *Steam*, as in Califia's essay, surveillance cameras were seen primarily as a threat. One of the magazine's last issues warned about a surveillance camera installed outside a Macy's bathroom and about DC park police who use high-powered binoculars to spot sex acts (*Steam* Vol. 3, Issue 2, summer 1995). However, whereas Califia's theory tends towards a utopian concept of public sex, there was a definite sense in much of the writing of *Steam* that the potentially disapproving public eye generates sexual excitement. That is to say, although *Steam* did propose personal sexual liberation, it did so within an understanding that the structures of desire are inherently conditioned by social structures. The desire for public sex exists not within some other utopian environment, but within the moralities, visual conventions and power structures of contemporary society. This desire is, at least in part, a result of the fact that we think of the private, domestic sphere as heterosexual. Homosexuals are not only forced by social marginalization to look for sexual partners in public places, they are conditioned from an early age, via the public/private binary to expect sexual fulfilment to take place outside the private – to sexualize the public sphere and, by extension, its disapprovals and dangers.

As *Steam's* libertarian but pragmatic agenda historically suc-ceeded Califia's utopianism, so in turn the subversive viewpoint typified by *Steam* was, as the 1990s wore on, increasingly displaced by a commercial gay scene with seemingly little space for discussion of the complexities of desire's relation to spatial politics. However, within this scene, with its aggressive promotion of the idealized gay male body, we very quickly also saw the incorporation of a range of surveillance technologies into the structures of desire.

## Splash

With the easy and cheap availability of surveillance cameras by the early 1990s, it was perhaps inevitable that this technology would fast find its way into the languages of erotic/pornographic display. However, the results of such incorporation point towards much more than just another way of looking at the same old sexual activity.

My own introduction to 'surveillance sex' came in the Manhattan gay bar Splash – a shrine throughout the 1990s to the airbrushed, perfected, 'post'-AIDS commercial gay culture that was colonizing gay male society.

The event occurred at the end of one of the regular go-go boy performances that took place every half-hour or so on a stage behind the main bar area. In keeping with Splash's water theme, this act involved a muscular young guy in a swimsuit dancing under huge spurting showers of water. As he left the stage, we assumed that the act was over, and a curtain lowered in front of the stage area. The curtain had earlier doubled as a projection screen displaying music and soft porn video clips. However, this time, as the video curtain came down, a much grainier, less polished image appeared. Those of us still watching began to realize that we were, in fact, seeing the go-go boy again – now shown on live video, apparently 'off-stage' in a more realistic shower than the vast theatrical spurts that had framed his stage act. The boy was, it appeared, being spied on by a surveillance camera. As we watched, instead of dancing and displaying himself for us, we seemed to see him in a private moment, fondling his own body under the stream of the shower. Of course, we knew that this was as much an act as the previous display; in fact, the boy could vaguely be seen in his 'off-stage' shower behind a glass brick wall to the side of the video screen. However, the erotic language and appeal of this moment were very different. Display was replaced with apparent concealment; the boy's engagement with the audience was replaced by our excitement in feeling that we were spying on him.

Eventually, the boy wandered off-camera and the screen switched to clips of porn and music videos again. The surveillance scene lacked the clear conclusions of related live or recorded performances. It was an unsatisfying but fascinating show, and seemed to me to point to some of the potentially radical effects of surveillance technology.

A number of characteristics emerging in this performance help open up the question of subjectivity under surveillance. On the level of fictional narrative, the gay male audience member is encouraged to enjoy the pretence that the go-go boy is actually being spied upon, that his privacy has been invaded. On the level of performance, we are also encouraged to enjoy the display that the performer makes for the camera – a display different from, more intimate than, the live bar-top dances preceding it. On parallel and contradictory levels we both engage in spying on the boy and enjoy the intimate vanities of his display.

The combination of these contradictory instincts within one scene reflects a very similar conflation of contradictory trajectories in Freud's essay 'On narcissism: an introduction' (Freud, 1963b: 56–82); and while a bearded man in a frock coat might seem out of place among the muscled, hairless bodies of Splash, I think that a conversation between Freud's theorizing of homosexuality and Splash's performance of desire is worth pursuing.

## On narcissism

In 'On narcissism', Freud explores the phenomenon of narcissism and attempts to develop a structure for understanding how the various forms of self-love relate to the development of sexual object-choice and sexual behaviours. Freud initially defines adult narcissism as a turning back upon the self (the ego) of the sexual libido 'normally' focused upon sexual objects (for example, in heterosexual male desire, upon the woman – or some part of the woman). This process of turning back is a secondary narcissism (Freud, 1963b: 57–8), in that it returns to 'an original libidinal cathexis of the ego' (ibid.: 58). In the earlier parts of his essay, it seems as though Freud's example of adult narcissism par excellence is the vain woman – who loves her own image far more than she loves any male suitor, and in fact loves the suitor primarily for his appreciation of her beauty (ibid.: 69–70). However, as the essay progresses, Freud introduces the concept of the 'ego-ideal'[4] – an ideal version of the self – which provides an alternative psychic structure for the articulation of narcissism:

> To this ideal ego is now directed the self-love which the real ego enjoyed in childhood. The narcissism seems to be now displaced on to this new ideal ego, which, like the infantile ego, deems itself the possessor of all perfections.
>
> (Ibid.: 74)

Freud seems to distinguish feminine narcissistic vanity from masculine narcissistic ideal-formation on the basis of the former being a turning of the 'object-libido' back upon the self, while the latter is an extension of the 'ego-libido' to an ideal of the self – so a vain woman loves primarily her own image, but a narcissistic man loves primarily the idea of what he could be. However, in both cases the figure of the homosexual is invoked as an example. In the case of vanity (object-libido returned to the self), homosexuals are equivalent to the vain woman because they 'are plainly seeking themselves as a love-object and their type of object choice may be termed *narcissistic*' (ibid.: 69). And in the case of narcissistic idealism (ego-libido deflected to the ego-ideal): 'Large quantities of libido which is essentially homosexual are in this way drawn into the formation of the narcissistic ego-ideal and find outlet and gratification in maintaining it' (ibid.: 76). (Here once again we see the tendency of the Freudian homosexual to engage in idealistic behaviour – not only as a sublimation of repressed libido, but also as a way of loving the ideal self.)

The Freudian homosexual, then, becomes a figure who can stand in for both the feminized narcissism of vanity and the masculinized narcissism of the ego-ideal. While Freud's pathologizing of homosexual desire may be an anathema to the contemporary gay patrons of Splash, we can usefully draw upon his complex, contradictory analysis of homosexual narcissism to further our understanding of the relationship between display and public space in surveillance-related sexual behaviour.

## Vanity and conscience

Narcissism may be at root phallic, as Irigaray (1985) argues, but within our society it is made to appear as feminine and feminizing. The masculine narcissism of the ego-ideal is desexualized and is recognized not as narcissism, but rather as a form of moral value. Freud (1963b: 75) specifically links this narcissistic ego-ideal with the popular concept of the conscience:

> It would not surprise us if we were to find a special institution in the mind which performs the task of seeing that narcissistic gratification is secured from the ego-ideal and that, with this end in view, it constantly watches the real ego and measures it by that ideal. If such an institution does exist, it cannot possibly be something which we have not yet discovered; we only

need to recognize it, and we may say that what we call our conscience has
the required characteristics.

If we accept Freud's suggestion that homosexual male desire
relates both to vanity of the body and to the ideal self, we will not
be surprised to see both conscience and self-display functioning in
scenes of gay desire. And this conflation is surely precisely what
we do see in the practice of public sex. The public sex described
and promoted by a viewpoint such as that of *Steam* occurs within
structures of desire that relate sexuality both to an erotics of display
and to moral/parental prohibitions intrinsic to the development of
desire. In the world of *Steam* (as opposed to the utopianism of Califia)
the very prohibition of desire can be desired. The eye of conscience
– which as part of its character disapproves of homosexuality – can
become a part of the structure of that sexuality, since it is itself (as
male ideal) a potential object of desire. *Steam*'s public sex negotiates
this sexualization of the conscience, the internalized law, by placing
the same-sex act within the realm of the law's disapproval (the public
space).

Splash's shower scene works more directly with the apparatus
of surveillance and the structures of narcissism. In this scene, the
surveillance camera can be viewed as standing in simultaneously
for the mirror of feminized vanity and for the disapproving eye of
conscience. The self-involvement of the dancer is part of the erotic
charge of the scene. The dancer's body is presented as if for his own
pleasure – touching himself, enjoying himself. Whereas in a recorded
video the camera would be as if absent, in this performance it is
marked as present. The camera acts like a mirror – marking the dancer's self-involvement as display – as vanity. However, the camera is
– through all of its associations with policing, evidence and the law
– also, by extension, the eye of conscience. On the fictional narrative
level, it suggests an intrusion of the public eye into the private, masturbatory space. On an associative level, it suggests that the erotics of
this masturbatory space have always depended upon the frame of an
internalized disapproval, upon the frisson of conscience.

The scene has a frisson because it introduces the viewer into a
structural relationship to display and desire different to that which
he is used to in the safe, idealized gay space of Splash. It allows

him access to the kinds of transgressive feelings associated with the 'seedier' goings-on of *Steam*, and reintroduces the desiring structures of disapproval into a gay scene that might seem to be all about self-satisfaction.

The positioning of the camera-as-eye also complicates the scenario by introducing a double audience identification – as a degraded, non-ideal conscience (the prying camera-eye), and simultaneously as a vain, feminized ideal body (the boy). Watching this scene, with its multiple narcissisms, we no longer know where we are and where the other is – a deliciously homosexual position to be in.

The pleasure of the scene is associated with the perverse alignment of terms here. It is the physicality of the boy that is idealized, not the conscience. Vanity and the super-ego, seemingly so distinct, mix in a confusion of identifications. The public/private binary which parallels this distinction of female vanity (private/domestic) and male conscience (public/legal) is transgressed, perverted, deconstructed.[5]

## Webs of desire

While a bar with a similar name and the same owner still exists at the Splash location, the surveillance shower performance has long gone from the repertoire. In the early twenty-first century, the commercial club- and bar-centred gay world continues to thrive (though perhaps without quite the energy of its mid-1990s heyday), but another gay realm has opened up which is perhaps equally important as a locus of gay sexual activity, and is undoubtedly an arena where the complexities of surveillance imagery and the gay body can be explored in far more detail than the stage of Splash allows. Today, much of the gay male conversation and 'cruising' that would once have taken place in bars and parks takes place on the World Wide Web.

While it is unlikely that the web will replace the need for bars like Splash, where physical location in a 'gay space' is celebrated, it has undoubtedly replaced the need for publications like *Steam*, with many a web site now devoted to guidance on cruising spots. But gay male activity on the web provides much more than information and reference to a 'real' gay world. Through chat rooms, webcams, webrings and personal profiles, gay men on the Internet (we will look at related heterosexual activity below) have eagerly incorporated the kinds of viewing dynamics explored in the Splash shower scene into desiring exchanges via computer.

Among the (largely heterosexual male) commentators on surveillance, the incorporation of computer networks into sexual practice is usually viewed with a dismay reminiscent of a fall from Edenic grace. David Lyon (2001: 15) worries about 'disappearing bodies' and seeks to re-embody us. Paul Virilio (1997) has railed at the prospect of 'prostheticization' in a way which suggests a short journey from computer assistance to disability to castration, and William Bogard (1996: 153) concludes an initially stimulating argument about the interdependence of simulation and surveillance in contemporary 'telematic society' with a thoroughly dystopic vision of sexuality in this society:

> Telematic societies at the end of the twentieth century are distinguished by both an excess of sex – an expenditure of sexual energy beyond any conceivable utility – and the absolute disappearance of sex, its reduction to the zero degree. This isn't a contradiction. Rather both are complementary effects of a general obscenity that characterises the contemporary social order itself, an order where sex (and sexuality) is so thoroughly hyperreal and overcoded that it vanishes without a trace.

As our Freudian examination of gay male sexual practice suggests, however, the idea of a difference in kind between some concept of 'embodied' sexuality and a mediated, computerized, prostheticized practice is not nearly so self-evident when a notion of enclosed, private sexual space has never been available. Instead of contrasting some fantasy of self-present sexual experience with the mediated addictions of computer sex, gay men have, by and large, fairly smoothly transferred the sexual practices that characterized their culture and behaviour already into the interactions facilitated by the Internet.

Core to these interactions are the conventions and choices that relate to the dynamics of display – exhibitionism, voyeurism, narcissism, paranoia – that we have examined above. Every gay man who uses the Internet as part of his social and/or sexual interactions is immediately engaged in a series of decisions of great relevance to our understanding of subjectivity under surveillance.

Not that these decisions are self-evident, rational or consistent with the subject's characteristics in the 'real' world. I consider myself, for example, a pretty thoroughly out gay man, living and working in a society which makes that a relatively easy position to take. I also recognize in myself several of the characteristics that link homo-sexuality to surveillance in our Freudian narrative. Since childhood I have had a narcissistic involvement in my own image (though one characterized more by a worried obsession with my own reflection than any satisfaction with how I look). I have also been told since childhood that I 'stare' at people too much, and I am happy to have discovered the profession of theatre directing, which allows me to practise such voyeurism. To a lesser but significant degree I have exhibitionist tendencies – though not sufficiently strong to make an actor of me. The one Freudian 'homosexual' characteristic I have never much experienced is paranoia. I have been (justifiably) scared as a gay man, particularly when very young, of what people might think or say about me, but this has never translated into any general-ized psychological or sexual experience.

On the web, however, a form of paranoia is probably my defining characteristic. I have never digitized a photo of myself and sent it to anyone. I have my browser set to announce and, by default, decline all cookies that are sent my way, and if I do not encrypt my email it is largely because I don't believe that it does much good anyway. I assume that all my messages are read by the FBI and self-censor accordingly.

My fear of self-exposure on the web is, I think, largely tied in to the thought of there being uncontrolled versions of me out there. Whereas my narcissism causes me to check my bodily self in every mirror I pass, if I set up a web site or personal profile with my image on, that image can be copied by anyone, shown anywhere, without my knowledge or control.

On a rational level, this fear is absurd to me. I really don't care if someone wants to take my image and distort it. Anyone with an ounce of sense these days knows that any image can be doctored and would no more take an out-of-character photograph as evidence than they would any other form of rumour.

Moreover, if I am perfectly happy to be seen going into a gay bar or club by all and sundry, why would the thought of my picture on a gay personal profile site looking for exactly the same things I am looking for in the bar – love, friendship, sex – fill me with horror and dread?

But, of course, the rational has little sway over the psychology of desire – and horror and dread are exactly what I feel.

Other individuals display equally contradictory positions. A recent visit to the primary UK gay profile/chat room site, Gaydar, introduced me to a young man who likes to perform sexually for a live camera according to the sometimes quite extreme instructions of an online sexual partner. While the young man prefers the partner to have a camera rigged up too, so both can see each other, he will also perform for an anonymous, invisible figure. He said that he had never done anything like this in real life, but felt safe and protected in the virtual encounter. The safety aspect is reasonable and sensible, but the young man also said that what he particularly liked about this way of doing things was that he was being watched at a distance and via the camera, that he really enjoyed this sense of 'showing off'. I asked if he minded not knowing who might see or record these things, and whether his friends knew what he did. He replied that in the rest of his life he was usually very discreet, that, although he was out as gay, his friends had no idea that he did this, and that he would be very embarrassed if they found out. However, somehow when he was having sex in this way he felt protected from these dangers.

Another man I spoke to has a very revealing photograph of his ass on the front of his personal profile. Elsewhere he also has pictures of his cock and of his face. He said that people often recognize him in clubs and comment on his site. He has a responsible job in the media, but isn't really concerned about anyone seeing his site because 'it's only an ass and everyone's got one'. However, he said that he was worried about the cock pictures and was thinking of taking them off because they were 'far more personal'.

My own and these other examples of gay male behaviour on the web display a mix of rational and irrational attitudes, largely justified by a sense of how things 'feel'. These feelings don't necessarily concur with our feelings in other non-web situations – someone may be exhibitionist in one environment and paranoid in another, for example. The experience of and behaviour in gay web space is dependent on the viewing structures of that space. A key element here (seen in all three examples above) is the nature of the subject's relationship with the unseen, unknown viewer. In some cases (such as mine) the notion of this unseeable, unfixable presence may initiate the kind of fear of the 'hidden photographer' that in other kinds of space has never figured. In other cases (the young webcam exhibitionist) the distant, uncontrollable figure may feel benevolent and protective. For some people (our man with the much recognized ass) the unknowable viewer may reflect in a very satisfactory way the moral–behavioural perspective of the subject (ass pics OK, cock pics dodgy) and allow for safety or frisson based upon an entirely self-referential moral code. In all of these cases, this absent viewing figure is crucial to the experience and meaning of the desiring space in which the subject finds himself.

## The security guard

In surveillance outside the web, this absent viewing figure is most frequently imagined as a security guard. We will examine this ambivalent figure in more detail in Chapter 5, but for now it is important to note that the security guard participates in a lot of the contradictions and conflations noted in the surveillance sex (as opposed to public sex) scenes examined above. Unlike 'the law' or 'conscience', the security guard is far from ideal (though he may be erotically idealized) – as a presence in our society he (or occasionally she) clearly possesses very limited and specific authority. Moreover, he is often distant, sleeping or not there at all. Most importantly, he is not 'the public'.

Participants in 'surveillance sex' do not enjoy the protection of theatrical space. Nor, however, do they enter into public space. By incorporating the absent security guard into the terms of their sexual act, they create a new space involving this absent other, a performative space brought about by the doing of certain acts in view of a surveillance camera. Clearly, such acts make no claim to privacy, but nor to they engage with the open realm of the public. We have seen in Chapter 1 that performative surveillance spaces involve us in experiences and understandings very different from direct representation – from the equivalence with the public field of evidence and law which the visual ideologies of surveillance lead us to expect. Analysis of the sexual terms on which subjects may begin to create such performative spaces adds an understanding of the ways that these spaces may be pervaded by, or even constructed from, vectors of desire. Moreover, desires in surveillance space are not independent of prior spatial dichotomies of public and private. Rather, they are active perversions of this binary, drawing upon its conditioning force while undercutting its stability and resolutions. An understanding of surveillance sex in terms of such performative perversion implies that the position of the viewer (the security guard) should not be legally equated with that of a member of the public. Sexual acts in surveillance space impact only upon those who are in some way involved in a desire to know about them.

## Brian's triumph

The degree to the public has already come to embrace a shifting sexual morality and politics based upon surveillance technology was demonstrated in particular by the second UK series of reality television show *Big Brother*. This format, which involves twelve 'housemates' locked in under twenty-four-hour total surveillance, with one evicted by popular vote each week until a winner emerges, has been internationally successful, and particularly so in the UK, that most surveyed of countries. Part of the enjoyment of the series has always resulted from the sexual tensions in the house, and the question (which has pushed the boundaries of acceptability in television) of whether any of the participants would in some way be caught on camera in sexual activity. One of the interesting elements of the show is the way in which the boundaries of what defines sexual activity become interrogated. The conventional version of acceptable sex – in the private bedroom with the lights off – is of course unavailable to the housemates (who sleep in dormitories under infra-red cameras at night), and under the eyes of the cameras all sorts of activity becomes reinterpretable as sexual.

We will discuss in more detail in Chapter 6 the ways in which *Big Brother* demonstrates the generalized desire for, and desiring relationship with, surveillance that is, I believe, replacing all ideologies of crime prevention and privacy protection. However, here I want particularly to examine the moment in UK popular culture when two gay men entered the *Big Brother* house, and one of them won.

Twenty-three-year-old Brian Dowling was one of the most popular *Big Brother* housemates from day one of the second UK series. He was funny, pleasant to look at, took part in group activities with enthusiasm and was interested in all the kinds of day-to-day gossip and trivia that fill the kind of papers and magazines that are also packed with *Big Brother* updates. He was also quite openly gay and, while not particularly overtly sexual or experienced, he was happy to discuss the limited experiences he had had. He was very popular with the other housemates, and the heterosexual men adjusted to sharing life and a bedroom with him far more quickly than might have been imagined. The British public also did not behave exactly as might have been predicted. Whereas commentators have often suggested that in the UK entertainers can be as camp as they want but must never come out as gay for fear of complete public rejection, Brian's self-revelation in the surveillance space of the *Big Brother* house was immediately and consistently embraced by the public. It was as though there was a consensus that, if we were to engage in the kind of total intrusion that is the basis of *Big Brother*, we could no longer resent or punish sexual disclosure. The celebration of Brian – who won the show by a wide margin and is now, of all things, a successful children's television presenter – seemed almost to symbolize a public choice of surveillance sexuality over the public/private binary. Moreover, in rewarding Brian for his out, gay behaviour we could perhaps say that the public was recognizing that, as a gay man, Brian was particularly well equipped for life in surveillance space. He was used to having to make revelations about himself that were challenging; he was used to having to win people over rather than assume a natural affinity. His exhibitionism and humorous self-involvement made him engaging and interesting to watch. As a gay man, he seemed already to understand and to have practised how to engage socially in the post-private world. He seemed to be teaching everyone how they could survive and prosper in surveillance space.

Of course, things are rarely that simple and complete, as the case of UK *Big Brother 2*'s second gay contestant, Josh Rafter, demonstrated. Josh (aged thirty-two) was a very different kind of gay man to Brian. With a beautiful, gym-developed and tanned body, a handsome, chiselled face and a soft, well-spoken voice, he was immediately recognizable to many British gay men as the archetypal urban gay male – the 'Soho queen'. However, to much of the rest of society – including initially all of the other *Big Brother* housemates – he at first appeared to be a particularly handsome and desirable heterosexual man. Josh entered the house late and in a slightly odd way. As a means of enlivening the new series, viewers were asked to 'vote in' an extra housemate at the end of the first week, from three candidates whose adverts for themselves were shown each night that week. In his ad, Josh was described as single and keen on the gym and was shown exercising and wearing typical gay fashions. However, he did not explicitly mention that he was gay. Competing with two women candidates, he easily won the vote, supported no doubt by heterosexual female voters just as much as by gay men.

Inside the house, the confusions continued. Several of the women housemates were clearly attracted to him, and several of the men were defensive and jealous. Even Brian did not recognize Josh as gay. On his first evening Josh had to create a very definite coming-out scene, far more revelatory (and reminiscent of the embarrassment of much gay male coming out) than Brian's self-evident status. The response of the other housemates remained interesting. Some of the women continued to flirt, and one of the men continued to state that he thought Josh was pretending to be gay in order to get close to the women! Brian took an ongoing dislike to Josh, and often used his wit to undercut him.

Having voted him in, the public never took to Josh again, and he was voted out in week 7 of the show. While to some degree this was undoubtedly because he had a less tele-friendly personality than the witty Brian and a couple of the other housemates (particularly the heterosexual Helen and Paul, who were forever almost engaging in on-camera sex), there is a sense also that Josh was being punished by everyone for the sexual confusion he had caused. Even gay men criticized him for failing to state his sexuality in his initial advertisement for inclusion in the house, though neither of the other candidates stated their sexual preference.

Whereas Brian appears to have made people in general feel positive about the surveyed future, Josh was clearly a more ambivalent figure. His desirable but confusing presence implied all sorts of ways in which heavily surveyed space creates not transparency but complexities – including desire with no appropriate object. His expulsion from the house and failure to have any media shelf-life beyond the series indicate that, although the public may be ready to embrace the transparencies and openness of sex in surveyed society, the confusions of desire that surveillance space is creating are still threatening. As such, *Big Brother* perhaps acts equally as a way of embracing and understanding certain shifts occurring in our lived experience through surveillance, while also perhaps, temporarily at least, immunizing us from some of our surveillance society's more disturbing personal effects.

## Unmarked space

Freud's example of the hidden photographer has productively introduced us to a relationship between surveillance and homosexuality. However, as noted in first discussing Freud's analysis, the case repeats a conflation, often found in Freud's treatments of homosexuality, between male and female experiences. Such conflation would imply the paradox that in homosexual women the difference between woman and man, elsewhere psychoanalytically emphasized, is suspended. The narcissism that structures the homosexual relationship to the public/private binary, and which potentially perverts that binary when a surveillance context is introduced, has so far been discussed wholly in relation to gay male experience. As noted earlier, public space tends to be gendered as male, and the gay male relation to that space is undoubtedly different to that of the female. By extension, the female sexual experience of surveillance cannot be equated with that of the male.

In our analysis of the relation between visual and audio surveillance in Chapter 1, we noted that the visual field is founded upon the exclusion of the interior associations of audio surveillance. In developing an analysis of the surveyed subject, it is important to bear in mind the exclusions of the visual field and the complicated relations of these exclusions to the concepts of privacy and domesticity.

In her analysis of Yvonne Rainer's movie *The Man Who Envied Women* (Phelan, 1993: 71–92), Peggy Phelan develops the key thesis of her book, *Unmarked*, that a demand for representation does not necessarily satisfy the need for the creative exploration of the position of 'the Other'. Referencing Joan Copjec's critique that feminist film theory tends to apply the Foucauldian concept of panoptic vision overliterally, Phelan resists a concern with the 'male gaze' and proposes a filmic/artistic practice which values the inward gaze. The title of Phelan's chapter on Rainer, 'Spatial envy', reverses the Freudian proposition of penis envy, exploring instead the many ways in which desire for space draws upon a male perception that women hold space within them.[6] Phelan (1993: 88–9) suggests that, ultimately, Rainer's movie (in which the female protagonist never appears but is represented by her voice) is proposing a disruption of the male desire to colonize this (and all) spaces: 'Rainer's *filmic* architecture takes flexibility and flow as defining principles, and film's inevitable failure to meet the desire to fix or possess space itself as its philosophic spine.'

In this filmic architecture (which Phelan also closely relates to the 'disappearance' characteristic of live performance) the object-less 'inward gaze' and the 'failure of the Other to appear representationally' (ibid.: 91) potentially bring about a reconfiguration of the relations of subject, object and visual field.

Phelan's argument emphasizes the degree to which female-as-other is excluded not only from the public representational field but from the public/private binary itself. The unrepresentable space of the interior gaze is not the always-already colonized private sphere, it is what is left unrepresented after the public/private binary has been established.

In analysing the disruption of the public/private binary brought about by the operation of narcissism in the visual surveillance field, we should not fall into the representational trap of equating value with exposure to view. While the bringing of the 'male gaze' of the law/conscience into the viewed/erotic structure subverts a concept of invisible authority in a way which potentially has very real positive social and political consequences, we should be careful not to erase the value of the 'unmarked'. Specifically relating to the question of vanity and the super-ego, Luce Irigaray (1985: 124) would argue that both sides of this split narcissism simply reiterate phallic value and that, in fact, the female never has access to any narcissism at all:

> Now, besides the fact that the definition of 'ego' in woman is far from settled, the feelings of inferiority from which woman suffers and which are

77

essential to the sexual and social role she is allotted do not promote the development of the narcissistic libido.

She is narcissistic, in fact, only by phallic mandate, for, as we have seen, any narcissization of her own sex organ(s) is completely out of the question.

[. . .] the 'physical vanity' of women, the 'fetishization' of her body – a process patterned after that of the model and prototype of all fetishes: the penis – are mandatory if she is to be a desirable 'object' and if he is to want to possess her.

(Ibid.: 113–14)

What then happens to the 'not-all' of woman in surveillance society? Hints of an answer have already been introduced in our analysis of the space of audio surveillance, and the links here with Rainer's filmic solution of a female protagonist who appears only in the form of her voice are clear. Phelan, however, is not content with a theorizing which places this not-all entirely outside the visual sphere. In her reading of filmic space as a disruption of architectural space, and in her discussion of the disappearance characteristic of live performance, we begin to see ways in which the structuring of the visual space of surveillance may suggest experiences other than that of representation.

## Camera positions

The all-seeing surveillance camera actually depends for much of its fascination on the limitations of its gaze. The surveillance image is pored over in crime shows and pirate videos partly for the hints of what is happening off-camera, for the event obscured from view, for the distorting effects of two-dimensionality. Whereas the conventions of film carefully use the sequence of shots to create a sense of a whole place, the surveillance camera displays the limits of its relation to the real place it is recording. While conventions of evidence and representation may be insisted upon in the policing/judicial context of most surveillance reception, the comforting completeness of the Hollywood or television world is never achieved. The inevitable sense of lack in relation to the limitations of the surveillance shot potentially introduces a wider sense of lack in relation to the field of representation in general. While such lack is skilfully compensated for and disguised in the camera work and editing of mainstream movies and television, there are other, rougher genres in which it becomes apparent more easily, and which can therefore be usefully compared with surveillance footage. In particular, a significant comparison can be made with the figuring of female lack in pornographic videos.

In her analysis of porn movies, *Hard Core: Power, Pleasure and the Frenzy of the Visible*, Linda Williams (1989) discusses the ways in which the inability of porn movies to represent female pleasure and its location inside a woman's body leads to the development of a series of compensatory fetishisms as part of the genre of hard-core porn, the most notable of these being the 'money shot' – the scene of male ejaculation outside the woman's body. The irony of the money shot is, of course, that it represents solitary male pleasure at the very moment that the male focus 'ought' to be most thoroughly fixed on the interior space of the woman. The money shot is a disturbingly literal appearance of the Lacanian phallus as signifier of lack:

> The paradox of contemporary feature-length pornography and its fetish of the money shot might therefore be described as follows: it is the obsessive attempt of a phallic visual economy to represent and 'fix' the exact moment of the sexual act's involuntary convulsion of pleasure. The money shot utterly fails to represent the satisfaction of desire as involving a desire for, or of, the other, it can only figure satisfaction as failing to do what masculine sexual ideology frequently claims that the man does to the woman: to occupy, penetrate, possess her.
>
> (Ibid: 113–14)

Williams goes on to suggest, however, that this failure in hard-core porn does not so much reify the erect porn penis into the raping weapon of Andrea Dworkin's critiques (Dworkin, 1979) as it reveals and permits a disruption of the fetishizing completeness of the conventional cinematic model. In porn's obsessive relation to the representation of pleasure, resolution under the phallic sign of the money shot can not satisfy the 'frenzy' of porn in the same way as objectification of the female body can satisfy the conventional film narrative; nor, however, can the fetishized female body properly function as phallic signifier in the porn movie, since it too clearly in this context reminds the male viewer of what he cannot fully know.

Williams follows an optimistic reading of Irigaray, whereby the revelation of the phallus as universal signifier predicts its collapse under the weight of its own lack. Importantly, and here we may link Williams to Phelan, it is in the failure of, and frenzied desire to, represent the interior space of female pleasure that the phallus is both asserted and revealed as lacking.

A more pessimistic account of the economy of pornography (and one to which Williams also gives considerable weight) is that the lack in the phallic money shot (the Lacanian *objet a*) will function perfectly well within a fetishistically organized consumer economy to ensure return by the viewer for other viewings, new videos, more money shots. Williams is not suggesting that this does not happen any more than Phelan is suggesting that Yvonne Rainer now runs Universal Studios. But she does suggest that, within the representational medium of the porn film/video, certain structural possibilities, certain consequences of the medium, make themselves felt, and that some of these possibilities and consequences are in fact counter-hegemonic to the phallic, fetishizing male gaze.

## Money shoot-outs

In the visual economy of surveillance, the equivalent of the money shot is, perhaps, very literally a money shot – the footage in which the gunman enters, shoots and takes the money. This sequence is the model towards which innumerable other pieces of surveillance footage – of bungled robberies, credit card frauds, convenience store mayhem – refer. It is, of course, itself a borrowed reference to innumerable bank heist movies, some of which cast the gunman as sympathetic protagonist. The desired result built into such scenes is that the gun will go off, the money will be stolen and the gunman will get away. (However much the ideology of crime may invite us to engage in capturing the perpetrator, without an escape there is no gunman to catch or identify and no justification for broadcasting the footage.)

Williams' analysis encourages us to look for the lack in this surveillance money shot. One interesting comparison with the porn scenario is immediately apparent: when the 'money shot' surveillance scene is placed into sequence by crime shows or when surveillance footage is used as a device in movies, the stick-up shot is often followed by the image of a screaming face of a woman. This screaming woman's face – silent, since CCTV has no soundtrack – is barely different from the ecstatically screaming woman's face which often follows the money shot in a porn movie, as the actress simulates orgasm. The relation of the silence of the surveillance scream to the dubbed sound of the porn climax will be analysed further below. First, though, it may be worth exploring whether the two screams and the two money shots bear any relations in terms of visual structure.

The shot of the woman's face in a porn movie shores up the climaxing penis against its lack. By focusing the eyes of the woman on the penis fetish, the importance and power of the male organ is reinforced. At the same time, the mouth of the woman stands as a secondary representation of that which is not figured – the interior female organs, the woman's pleasure. The screaming, climaxing woman has her cock (visually) without eating it (and causing it to disappear from sight). The face of the woman, unlike her genitals, allows the possibility (within porn logic) that the woman can be most sexually stimulated by the visual, exterior presence of the penis (Williams, 1989: 101).

What equivalent work could the screaming surveillance woman be doing? Must she too compensate for a dangerous lack in the money shot? What is it in this surveillance money shot that we do not get to see?

Of course, there are many things that we do not get to see. Usually, we do not get to see the face of the perpetrator, nor the full effect of the gunshot, sometimes not even the money. By cinematic viewing standards the surveillance shot is always sadly inadequate. We are used to seeing more than this. The compensatory shot of the screaming woman reinforces the power of the surveillance money shot in that the woman – site of excessive emotion – testifies with her expression to the 'fact' that we have indeed seen a lot, seen something exceptional. The move to this shot of the female/feminized viewer is a cinematic (point of view) compensation for surveillance's cinematic failures.

However, the relation of the lacking shot and the compensatory shot can be read as functioning on another level also. For the victim's scream, the news commentator's stern face, the return to Hollywood colour that follow the surveillance money shot also prevent us from lingering too long on the surveillance image, from beginning to see not just its central event but its edges, its exclusions and obscurities. If we did watch for too long, we might begin to see in a whole range of cases exactly what the jury in the Rodney King case chose to see – that in fact the surveillance image shows nothing at all, that it is so stained with its lacking relation to the lost object of the event itself that any 'real-world' decision based upon this footage is absurd. Usually it is in the interests of crime prevention to ensure that such focus on lack is not encouraged. Hence, the variety of reaction shots reinforcing the power of the surveillance money shot while moving our gaze away from the money shot itself. As with the hard-core movie's ejaculating penis, we are not allowed too much time to watch things wilt.

But again, as with the hard-core movie, the reaction shot also draws attention to the lack by reminding us of what the money shot can never represent. In surveillance as opposed to hard core, this unrepresentable element is not necessarily the literal experience of female pleasure, but, in a gendered economy of representation, we can perhaps say that the unrepresentable of surveillance will be in a structural relationship to female pleasure just as the 'money shot' of the bank heist is in a structural relation to male power.

## Guns and pleasure

Two Hollywood treatments of female crime, both of which use surveillance footage as part of their movie language, demonstrate these issues through the productive confusions that they generate when women participate as subjects in the money shot of the heist. In *Thelma and Louise* (directed by Ridley Scott, 1991) and in *Set it Off* (directed by F. Gary Gray, 1997), women who would not otherwise be the likeliest crime suspects are fixed as criminals and located within the logic of the movie by surveillance recordings of them engaged in gunpoint robberies. In both movies, there are extended scenes of police viewing or responding to these tapes, as though only by repeated viewing can women be fixed into narrative as perpetrators of the phallic act of gunpoint robbery. Meanwhile, in the non-surveillance film footage surrounding these key scenes, the display of female sexual pleasure enters into an excess explicitly disrupting Hollywood conventions of female sexuality. In *Thelma and Louise*, Geena Davis's passionate night with Brad Pitt not only fails to progress into any relationship, it also explicitly fetishizes the boyish male body as instrument of female pleasure (as opposed to dominant cause of female pleasure) and is specifically used to underline the sexual failure of Davis's macho husband in Thelma's comment to Susan Sarandon's Louise the morning after her night with Brad: 'I finally understand what all the fuss is about'. Meanwhile, the sexual 'frisson' between Davis and Sarandon builds and builds.

In *Set it Off*, the representation of female sexual pleasure which is in some way 'set off' by the surveillance footage of women as phallic gunmen is even more explicit. (Here the terms are complicated by race, and the image of the black male body is also interrogated within the movie.) The movie involves a (for Hollywood) very explicit lesbian sexual relationship, shown in scenes between Queen Latifah's Cleo and Samantha Maclachlan's Ursula. Sex scenes between these two female characters are uncompromising in the degree to which they are about sex rather than friendship or bonding (Ursula is not one of the four female friends who undertake the bank robberies). The relationship is also very explicitly butch/femme. In contrast to Geena Davis's blonde feminine presence in the surveillance footage of *Thelma and Louise's* convenience store heist, Queen Latifah displays a shockingly masculine appearance as a gun-loving 'gangsta'. This difference is carried over into the two movies' versions of lesbianism, which in *Thelma and Louise* amounts ultimately to 'crush'-like declarations of love at the moment of mutual suicide and in *Set it Off* adds up to raunchy sex scenes involving role play and lace underwear. We might surmise that the degree to which the female character is 'fixed' by the surveillance camera in the masculine role directly affects the degree to which female sexuality in the non-surveillance-related scenes of the movie exceeds the bounds of cinematic convention.

The importance of the *surveillance* convention in introducing the female to the male role and in consequently disrupting the sexual conventions of the rest of the movie lies in the very limitations noted as aspects of the surveillance 'shot'. The awareness of the frame, and of people wandering out of it, the obscuring of aspects of the scene through obstructions and bad camera angles – limitations which all film cameras are manipulated to disguise – these limitations are highlighted as part of the defining characteristics of surveillance footage. When introduced to a movie, even a big-budget Hollywood movie, such footage generates a reminder of, in Phelan's words, 'film's inevitable failure to meet the desire to fix or possess space itself' (Phelan, 1993: 88). There is, the surveillance footage implies through its very lack, a whole field beyond that which is represented. Lesbian sexuality is part of (or signifies) this unrepresented field. It is ironic that this field then *is* apparently represented through the naturalizing conventions of Hollywood cinema in the movies that we have been discussing, but this is where hard-core porn as analysed by Linda Williams can perhaps help our analysis more than the conscious manipulations of Yvonne Rainer. Because it is in the exchange between failures – between the money shot and the faked female ecstasy, between the pseudosurveillance scene and the Hollywood romance – that the presence of desires, pleasures, experiences beyond the frame begin to make themselves felt.

In *Thelma and Louise* and *Set it Off*, the insertion of the female subject into the 'wrong' side of the binary – into the money shot – sets off a disruptive ricochet in which Hollywood convention no longer knows where it is at in relation to the figure of woman. If no satisfying representation of female sexual agency can fully emerge through such movies (both movies can be criticized for their clichéd versions of lesbianism and of female sexuality in general), nonetheless there is a breakdown in the representational control of female sexuality and an outbreak of possibilities of agency.

Williams also emphasizes the degree to which porn movies break the continuity of Hollywood dramas. She compares the sex scenes in hard-core movies to the numbers in Hollywood musicals, in which there is a fairly sudden switch to a 'different' reality. Williams uses Richard Dyer's analysis (Dyer, 1981) of how differing versions of the musical genre utilize or dissolve this split, and applies it to the history of hard-core porn (Williams, 1989: 160). While both Williams and Dyer emphasize that there are a variety of forms and degrees of separation between 'narrative' and 'numbers', they also make the point that the very existence of the two 'realms' initiates a dialectic quite different to the organic completeness of the world conjured by the purely narrative Hollywood drama. I think that the insertion of 'surveillance-style' footage into a Hollywood movie tends to have the same effect; moving the representational structure of the movie from one of organic whole to one of dialectic contradiction. Williams argues that, once such a dialectic is introduced into the representational structure, issues of sexual difference will tend to arise with disruptive energy. The examples of *Thelma and Louise* and *Set It Off* indicate, in their outbreaks of lesbian sexuality, that the introduction of surveillance footage has precisely the effect upon movie representation that Williams' argument would suggest.

## Acoustic narcissism?

Both Williams and Phelan make specific reference in their analyses to Kaja Silverman's book *The Acoustic Mirror* (Silverman, 1988) in which she explores the possibilities of identification with the acoustic and specifically argues for the feminist possibilities of the movie soundtrack which is separated from the visual narrative. Rainer's *The Man Who Envied Women*, as analysed by Phelan, is an almost textbook exploration of the possibilities of such a separation, of the differing identifications that occur with the acoustic and of the differing relations that occur with the visual narrative when identification occurs primarily at the level of the acoustic. Williams discusses the convention of post-dubbed sound in porn movies, with their emphasis on sound recorded very close and played loud, and on inarticulate female cries. She notes that, as sound functions differently from visual reproduction, so the ways in which it is used to represent sexual pleasure differ. For this doubling of representational possibilities, the porn viewer is happy to surrender the representational unity so important to mainstream cinema:

> As Mary Ann Doane points out in 'The Voice of the Cinema' (1980, 39) sound cannot be 'framed' as the image can, for sound is all over the theater, it '*envelops* the spectator'. It is this nondiscrete, enveloping quality that, when added to the close-miked, non-synchronous sounds of pleasure, seems particularly important in the hard-core auditor-viewer's pleasure in sound.
>
> (Williams, 1989: 125)

She goes on to note that the quality of sound as seeming to come from the interior gives it particular resonance as a signifier of female pleasure.

As analysed in Chapter 1, there is a strong philosophical tradition that implicitly displaces the experience of sound in establishing the 'common sense' of the world of phenomena and which consequently produces a potential for 'interior-to-interior' identification when the external field is disrupted by the 'evidence' of intimate, 'overheard' sound recording. We examined the ways in which the interiority produced by covert, intimate recordings created a space which functioned disruptively in relation to surveillance imagery's presumed representational qualities. Williams' suggestion that the sound of sexual pleasure – reproduced in the enveloping aural environment of the cinema – signifies the invisible intimacy of the female adds an additional dynamic to our consideration of interior sound space. Extending Williams' argument, we can see ways in which the sound of surveillance is, in general, sexual in tone. That is to say, not only does it point towards the gendered exclusions of the representational field – the 'not all' of woman – but it specifically carries associations of female sexuality.

Moreover, it is not only audio surveillance which carries these associations with female sexuality. The exclusions, the silences, of the visual field also refer us to this unrepresentable experience. As we have noted, the field of visual representation under surveillance is separated from sound: most surveillance cameras do not have microphones, sound is considered either secondary or irrelevant to the direct evidence of visual reproduction. In porn, the sound of female pleasure, disruptive though it is in its disjunction from the visible, is nonetheless ultimately represented in the artificial screams and moans of the porn actress; it is reintroduced as a fake. In visual surveillance imagery, however, sound is usually left as an unknown: the silent scream, the smoking gun. In its absence, the sound of surveillance infests our experience of this imagery not only with lack, but also with the suggestion of female agency.

Whereas male visual narcissism under surveillance disrupts the public/private binary by eroticizing the very invisible forms of law and conscience which hold this binary in place, the absent female sound space of surveillance suggests a location of pleasure and

86

agency entirely unimaginable within the field of visual representation. By implication, the more the surveillance camera intrudes into the private space, the more it will discover that this space is not the location of the feminine at all.

Kaja Silverman (1988: 164) notes the importance in mainstream cinema of suturing the female voice to the body, referring to this disciplinary representational system as a 'surveillance':

> Both constituents of the surveillance system – visual and auditory – must be in effect for it to be really successful. To permit a female character to be seen without being heard would be to activate the hermeneutic and cultural codes which define woman as 'enigma', inaccessible to definitive male interpretation. To allow her to be heard without being seen would be even more dangerous, since it would disrupt the specular regime upon which dominant cinema relies.

For Silverman, the productivities of the female voice in cinema are complexly structured by a narcissistic relationship with the mirror of the mother's voice, through which the subject first comes to consciousness (ibid.: 120–4). Silverman's key proposition is that the desiring, discursive relationship with the mother is located not in some pre-Oedipal realm, but within the symbolic order:

> To situate the daughter's passion for the mother within the Oedipus complex, on the other hand, as I think we are obliged to do, is to make it an effect of language and loss, and so to contextualize both it and the sexuality it implies firmly within the symbolic. It also brings it within desire, and hence psychic 'reality'. Finally, and most important, it is not to foreclose upon what might be called a 'libidinal politics', but to make it possible to speak for the first time about a genuinely oppositional desire – to speak about a desire which challenges dominance from within representation and meaning, rather than from the place of a mutely resistant biology or sexual 'essence'.
>
> (Ibid.: 123–4)

The psychoanalytic failure to acknowledge the narcissistic, self-defining relationship with the mother's voice is produced in part by 'the alignment of femininity with an unpleasurable and disempowering interiority' (ibid.: 100).

Silverman's argument potentially helps develop our analysis of surveillance subjectivity in two ways. First, her exploration of a 'feminine' (though not exclusively female[7]) narcissism separated from the visual field challenges readings of surveillance restricted to the display of the body. Secondly, her insistence that female interiority is an effect produced by the masculinized visual sphere suggests that a reading of surveillance space which simply contrasts the referentiality of the visual sphere with the interiority of the aural will continue to replicate a gendered binary.

Silverman's argument suggests that a recognition of the narcissistic structures of the acoustic realm open this realm into relational, discursive possibilities foreclosed by the notion of interiority. An acoustic understanding of surveillance has already revealed to us the importance and productivity of code, of rhythm, of languages, which exceed representation. Silverman encourages us to understand such coded audio spaces as discursive, narcissistically structured fields.

The silent surveillance image, though in many ways opposite to the feminist movies analysed by Silverman (which emphasize the female voice), potentially opens up similar possibilities.[8] The surveillance image implicitly equates the absence of the soundtrack with the various other failures of its representational capabilities – its borders, its obscured viewpoints. Unlike the pornographic camera, which attempts to penetrate the interior and which, failing, returns to the phallus, the surveillance camera only ever glances at the surface; it offers no move towards the interior. This failure of interiority leaves the not-all, the unrepresented, unfixable within the flickering bodies of the image. These poorly resolved images do not seem to be hiding places of mystery. Rather, it is in the borders and limitations of the visible that mystery seems to lie. The silence of the surveillance image, once noticed and engaged in, encourages a reading of the image's absences and edges.

A subjective practice of surveillance that draws attention to such absences and edges reintroduces the excessive productivity of the not-all, the unrepresentable. It suggests that, just as much as for the gay male display analysed in the first part of this chapter, there is a role for partial concealment, for muttered, unrecorded sounds, for bodies covering other bodies, in the development of radical surveillance possibilities.

The surveillance space implied by Silverman's arguments is neither visualized nor interior. Whereas 'gay male' surveillance display perverts the public/private binary by embodying and eroticizing the abstract forces that structure it, 'feminine' surveillance concealment disrupts this binary by pointing towards places and experiences unlocatable on either side of the split. The concealments of surveillance imagery and its absent sounds exist outside the private realm but are unreachable within the public. They imply intimacies, mutterings, secret languages and signals, bodies too close to separate; but these obscurings are neither indoors nor interior – they are the surfaces that cannot be seen.

## The disabling gaze

It is important to emphasize, however, that such radical potentials for behaviour under surveillance, while they may indicate paths towards agency, do not imply a voluntaristic relation to the effects of surveillance. The displays and concealments which potentially disrupt the representational self-evidence of surveillance are rooted in the psychic traumas through which the subject comes to function in the symbolic realm. The use of the term 'narcissism' as a key to exploring the subjective possibilities of surveillance reminds us that such possibilities continually return us to the painful relations of self and object which structure our psyches. Active engagement in surveillance practices by gay men and by women is less a choice than an inevitable result of the shaky relations of these subject positions to the certainties of the symbolic, a shakiness emphasized when a profound shift in representational culture is occurring.

The degree to which the development of agency under surveillance involves a long and painstaking process is underlined by an examination of the experience of members of perhaps the most heavily surveyed of all populations in the Western world – disabled people. In his book *The Creatures Time Forgot*, disabled photographer David Hevey (1992: 30) analyses the phenomenon of advertising by 'disability' charities in Britain, and links it to a Foucauldian reading of the Victorian practice of 'categorization photography' within a eugenically focused medical establishment:

... negative genes would manifest themselves in bodily distinctions. This was the basis for much of the Victorian categorization photography which sought to prove that bodily difference entailed difference in the entire psychic and social behaviour and make up. The body became the signifier of difference for disabled people as it still is very much today in charity advertising.

Hevey (ibid.: 54) makes the point that disabled people are both concealed and surveyed within special institutions – segregated schools, medical establishments, etc. Their appearance as images in the public realm is 'to demonstrate the successes of their administrators'.

The experience of disabled people is particularly important to the current analysis in that they are a population under an unprecedented degree of surveillance while being allowed into the public representational field only under the most controlled and disempowering terms. In particular, in relation to a discussion of the sexuality of surveillance, the experience of disabled people in Western society demonstrates how a totalization of surveillance can produce an erasure of sexuality. The link with eugenics is not casual; the extreme and unnecessary intervention of a variety of surveillances in disabled people's lives is undoubtedly linked to the prevailing Victorian fear that they might reproduce, and the exclusion of all but the most careful (and usually infantilizing) charity images from the field of representation ensures that the possibility of disabled people's sexual activity is kept far from the public mind.

In his book, Hevey discusses a variety of techniques that he uses in workshops with other disabled people to introduce the disabled person as subject into the visual frame of the photograph. He comments that, of course, it is not simply a question of giving disabled people a camera or of asking them to set their own pose in a picture. Disabled subjects have inevitably internalized or naturalized much of what we might call the 'disabling gaze' of the representational economy:

When I have run workshops with disabled people working on self- and social-representation, one thing has consistently struck me. This is the essential passivity of the participants in front of the camera .... It works because at the point when the subjects, those photographed, are having the camera pointed at them and the 125th-of-a-second shutter is about to click, they must focus themselves as a vessel of signs from larger discourses which they may understand but do not control. Their life expectancy is summed up for the camera.

(Ibid.: 112)

Interestingly, Hevey adapts many of his workshop techniques from radical theatre practice. Several aspects of the choices that he encourages workshop participants to engage in also relate very closely to characteristics of surveillance recordings that have been noted above: 'This direction would include focusing, editing the body in or out of the frame, the camera direction in relation to the body and so on' (ibid.: 115).

Working in pairs, Hevey encourages participants to play with photographic composition, or rather, perhaps, with their own composition by photographs, in order to denaturalize the heavily ideological 'normal' photograph of the disabled person as a medicalized object of charity and control. Abstracting from Hevey's description of his workshop process, and also examining his own photographs, it seems that one of the key questions addressed might be that of the boundaries of the body itself – so seemingly clear until the viewer is made to think about an image of a wheelchair user. Hevey analyses the evocation of the absent 'normal' body in mainstream images of disabled people – the disappearance of Franklin D. Roosevelt's wheelchair from all but two of 35,000 photographs of America's disabled president (ibid.: 102), the focus on the place where a leg 'normally' would be in a photograph of a young amputee: 'Its absence is accentuated and impairment here is read as loss' (ibid.: 55). When the disabled body is imaged as the loss of the normal body, one of the elements of normality that inevitably becomes 'lost' is sexuality. Moreover, as the disabled person is traditionally continually under surveillance, watched by a representational regime (medically, institutionally or domestically in the form of relatives or helpers), this imagery of loss, and particularly loss of sexuality, is reinforced constantly.

Whereas the gay man as analysed above is sexually highlighted by surveillance, and women's sexuality tends to remain unsurveyable, the disabled person's sexuality seems to be removed by the process of surveillance.[9]

91

It is in the context of the representational field analysed by Hevey, the 'public' outcry in the UK over David Cronenburg's movie *Crash* (1996) (fervently opposed by Britain's right-wing media) begins to make sense. Cronenburg took J.G. Ballard's story of a cult-like group obsessed with traffic accidents and the prostheticization of the body and turned it into a sumptuous and graphic movie. In sexualizing images of disability, particularly in relation to car crashes, Cronenburg's visual world raised the possibility that the carefully maintained balance between universal surveillance and representational control could collapse. The movie, of course, is not about surveillance; it is 'about' the eroticization of traffic accidents. But in Britain, where the outcry against the movie (usually condemned unseen) was particularly strong, a link is easily made, since there is a comprehensive system of road surveillance. Whereas currently disability is contained by a kind of naturalized Foucauldian panopticon – disabled lives carefully monitored but mainly kept from view – the emergence of an excess of forms of surveillance makes the maintenance of representational codes ever more difficult. Without intentionally addressing a specific politics of disability, Cronenburg's movie implies the dangerous thought that universal surveillance will display how sexual society's most aggressively desexualized members may be. The combination of sex, disability and traffic accidents is a nightmare condensation in contemporary English society. The reality behind this nightmare – sexually active disabled people – potentially demands the thought of technologies and individuals that assist others in the sexual act. For a culture in which the concept of sexuality as inherently private remains a key principle, a questioning of sexual privacy, erupting, via the imagery of surveillance, in the thought of disabled people's sexual practice, is disruptive on a structurally fundamental level.

For the disabled subjects who find their sexuality and agency erased by a history of surveillance, the appearance of a movie, however shocking to Britain's film critics it may be, is not going to undo the psychic consequences. As a narrative, indeed, *Crash* (both in the movie and in the original novel) tends to see the post-traffic-accident body only in relation to a pre-existing natural body. (Hevey's 'loss' is replaced by augmentation.) However, the crack in the representational field which the response to the movie indicates is important. As Hevey's photography workshops indicate, the erasure of sexuality through surveillance experienced by disabled people cannot be repaired by a resort to privacy. 'Private' sexuality inherently reasserts a myth of the whole and heterosexual body. It is a space where disabled people's sexuality can only fail. Rather, it is through rearticulation of the camera, of imagery, that a slow, painful resistance to the paradoxically concealing force of surveillance occurs. As both Hevey's workshops and the reception of *Crash* imply, it is in an excess of surveillance imagery that the possibility of resistance to surveillance control lies.

The transition from surveillance as a tool in erasing sexuality to surveillance as a site where current sexual structures are under pressure is particularly graphically illustrated in relation to disabled people's sexuality, but the thought emerges in each of the areas discussed in this chapter that increase in surveillance is simultaneously both an increase in capacity for control and increase in pressure for collapse of a sexual culture structured on the public/private binary. It would be unwise, of course, at this point to underestimate Foucault's warning that an expansion of the discourse of sexuality is simultaneously a means of increasing sexual/social containment (Foucault, 1978), is in fact a 'panopticization' of sexual behaviour. However, a Foucauldian reading may also help us to think through the ways in which surveillance technologies potentially participate in a radical sexualizing discourse, a discourse that deconstructs the enduring mythology that there is a bodily present and private place where sexual pleasure properly occurs.

The discussion of disabled people's experiences indicates that a proliferation of technologies potentially results in a transformation of surveillance's role from that of erasing 'inappropriate' sexuality to that of excessively revealing the non-idealized sexual body and all its non-bodily supports (from wheelchairs to sex toys to cameras). Surveillance technologies potentially move us from an aestheticization of sex to a 'prostheticization' of sex.[10]

The omnipresence of surveillance technologies implies the involvement of technologies in all sexual scenes. The myth of the self-present sexual experience is deconstructed by the expectation of recording, transmission over space, subsequent experience of the scene by the participant as well as non-participants. Once the technology of the camera, the microphone, etc., enters the very terms of the sexual experience, there is no line left to draw against the further 'prostheticizing' of the sexual scene by technologies and by other individuals. The sexual scene, in fact, becomes uncontainable within any single space. It spills in both excessive presence and perpetual lack through all representational discourses.

## Surveillance sex toys

In October 2002, a few weeks after it had finished a weekly series of supplements on surveillance compiled very much from a privacy protection agenda, the *Guardian* newspaper put a photograph of a camcorder on the front of its G2 section, with the headline, 'How this became the sex toy or our age'. After a series of recent tabloid stories in which famous people's ex-lovers had revealed the presence of videos of them having sex with their partners, the *Guardian* chose to explain how the camcorder is introducing us to a different kind of sexual experience. The article interviewed a range of people who film themselves having sex, concluding with quotes from 'Richard, who is 29':

> In one sense it distances you from the act because there's another presence there, even if it is a piece of machinery. You're used to abandoning yourself to the moment, and then it being over. But with this other eye there, suddenly it's about seeing a different side of yourself because you can enjoy it afterwards too.
>
> If I wanted to have a really emotional sexual experience I certainly wouldn't imagine filming it being a part of that. There's something about watching or recording which is quite dirty and lacking in intimacy, though it can be incredibly arousing.
>
> (*Guardian*, G2, 29 October 2002)

In this male conclusion to a liberal news article, sex incorporating a camera becomes an interesting and tolerated arena of experiment but not quite the 'real thing'. However, the point that sex in front of a camera can be 'incredibly arousing' goes unaddressed in this analysis. Consistent with the *Guardian's* general privacy-orientated approach to surveillance, the article focuses primarily on encouraging us to be careful what we reveal – the subsequent public exposure of camcorder sex is considered a danger attendant on a titillating but ultimately frivolous sex game.

In fact, the source of the 'incredible' arousal *is*, as Richard implies, the geographical and temporal disruption of the sexual scene. It is the fact that Richard finds himself not quite present – already cast into a future where he is watching the tape, and also displaced into the viewing space of a potential other who may watch the scene and who is figured by the presence of the camera – which is the source of his erotic engagement. That is to say, the distancing, the spacing, characteristic of surveillance creates the erotic charge. Whereas the *Guardian* seems to think that this charge can be contained in the private bedroom as long as we are careful and do not leave the tapes lying around, it is the very impossibility of such containment that creates the erotic effect of self-recorded sex.

Interviewing heterosexual couples who video themselves having sex and show the images on the web, Amory Peart, presenter of UK Channel 4's *Future Sex,* met a range of married partners whose personal engagement in the erotics of self-filmed sex has gone on to involve the creation of web sites and even thriving businesses. In the case of Jon and Cherie Messner from Maryland, USA, initial self-filming has grown into a particularly significant online business, The Wetlands web site has 400,000 subscribers; its studio is visited by couples who travel to Maryland from all around the country to have sex on camera while thousands watch and sometimes interact via live chat. Peart has a utopian view of this activity – noting that it is opening up new sexual possibilities and satisfaction to thousands of ordinary people. As web site founder Jon suggests, 'hopefully it will become a movement'. If so, this movement will involve the spacing and distance of surveillance as well as a utopian sharing. As one of the married participants in a webcast sex scene with his partner comments: 'It turns you on knowing other people are getting some excitement out of what you're doing.' However, this is no orgy – in many cases only the married couple are actually present in the bed – the absence, the distance, of the viewers is clearly one of their key characteristics.

It is interesting that most of the examples of web-based sexual display given in these pieces of journalism, and many others,[11] are of heterosexual, often married, couples choosing such activity. To a degree this may simply be a question of newsworthiness: it is more of a story when formerly polite married people start displaying their sexual lives than when sexual outlaws do it. Certainly, there are plenty of sites on the web where the non-married, from gay men to fully fledged porn stars, video themselves for public show. However, there does seem to be a significant proportion of web display from the formerly private heterosexual bedroom. In terms of the analysis undertaken in this chapter, it seems that a sizeable minority of heterosexual couples are embracing the opportunities for post-private sexual behaviours offered by recording and distribution technologies such as camcorders and the Internet. It is notable that this heterosexual deviance, though, does not take place in relation to the public realm, but rather to the 'other' realm of cyberspace. While there may always have been 'readers' wives' who were ready or persuaded to display themselves in magazines, the volume of engagement with self-filmed sex on the Internet is far higher. This seems not least to be due to the fact that the sexual acts filmed in this way need never directly involve a body outside the marriage – the partners can, if they want, engage only with each other in the filming, and only ever encounter their viewers as words or maybe images online.

The fact that heterosexual couples seem to have embraced this form of 'surveillance sex' as fully as the more traditional deviants indicates the degree to which this sexual activity exists outside the public/private binary which has, in modern Western culture, kept the perverts out of the family home.[12] Whereas very few such couples would make the move into the public sexual realm often inhabited by gay men, this other space of self-surveillance seems far more accessible to them. Rather than crossing the borders of a binary, they are perhaps simply slipping into a space where that binary, that boundary, has lost its force.

## Sexual uptake

In Chapter 1, we discussed the idea that an Austinian notion of 'uptake' could be applied to the notion of 'performative spaces' of surveillance, and noted that, whereas in speech act theory uptake involves the understanding that a particular performative utterance has been enacted (e.g. that I have been dared), in relation to surveillance uptake may rather involve the understanding that a new form of space has been initiated (i.e. the uptake is of the possibility of performativity). In discussing the sexual subject of surveillance, we begin to see the degree to which this uptake is not a voluntary matter or a question of opinion. The viewer of sexual surveillance footage – whether one of the original 'performers' or another person – is almost certainly 'uptaking' the concept of performativity in that she or he is probably as much excited/interested by the fact that the scene is 'non-professional' yet for the camera as by the actual revelation of bodies. Whereas uptake of performativity in the *Caught in the Act* videos discussed in Chapter 1 involved the viewer 'criminalizing' the scene of private activity through watching via surveillance, here performativity involves a sexualizing not just of the scene (since it is already sexual) but of the camera's involvement in the scene – as prosthetic extension of the 'performers'' sexual bodies. The key difference is in the relation of the video's subjects to the camera. In the former case (*Caught In The Act*), it is their lack of knowledge of the camera's presence that structures the viewer's relation to them via the camera. In the latter case (video or webcam sex), it is their active knowledge of the camera that structures the relationship. The sexual scene under surveillance becomes all the more interesting if the subjects know that the camera is there – if they have placed it there or placed themselves in relation to it.

In the sexual surveillance scene, then, the subject is far closer to the speaker of a speech act than in the criminal surveillance scene. As such, the perlocutionary effects subsequent to uptake may, as opposed to the examples in Chapter 1, be subject to some form of intent by the subject. The phenomenon of sexuality under surveillance points the way into thinking about agency among the subjects of surveillance society. It underlines, however, that such agency is not likely to be one of limitation or legislation. That is to say, it is not likely to grow out of calls for an enhanced right to privacy, but rather involves a consciousness of and engagement in the prosthetic structures of sur-veillance. In such engagement, the subject of surveillance replaces a right to privacy with a proposition that the body's boundaries are not easily drawn or contained within a binary, and that the performative space of surveillance involves as much an extension of the body into all space as it does an intrusion of the public into the private.

## Suspense and secrecy

Freud's patient, terrorized by the hidden photographer, was, we assume, unable to continue a happy relation with the man she was seeing. Of course, if Freud's intimations of homosexuality are correct, such happiness was never on the cards. In retrospect, and with a far from Freudian gloss, we may even begin to see the hidden photographer so insistently conjured by the woman in Freud's analysis as a fearful yet fascinated premonition of the end of the private sexual act. If the woman was indeed homosexual, or otherwise unable to function happily sexually within a scene recuperable by the marriage bedroom, her enemy was not the hidden photographer, whose photographs would not have revealed her 'real' illicit desire, but rather privacy itself, which bound her sexual imagination and possibilities within a frame in which her desires could not be realized. So, the fantasy of the hidden photographer does not so much represent the danger of revelation, but the frustration that her sexuality cannot come into revelation. In destroying the privacy of the heterosexual bedroom, the hidden photographer begins to enact the possibility of a sexuality, of a selfhood, contained neither by that privacy nor by an alternative public sphere.

The woman was not happy with her hidden photographer, and we may all feel many discomforts under his more literal descendant's eye. Even in full consciousness of surveillance's performativity we are left with the uncertainties of illocutionary suspense discussed in Chapter 1: we cannot be sure how our performative acts in surveillance space will be taken. However, if the hidden photographer does his cultural job, we will at least know that the 'perlocutionary effects' of our acts under surveillance should not involve their misinterpretation as public or private, and the suspense which we will continue to experience may perhaps be closer to that of a performer awaiting an audience's response than of an accused man awaiting the jury's verdict.

# 3

# Accidental death

Besides, death is always the name of a secret, since it signs the irreplaceable
singularity. It puts forth the public name, the common name of a secret, the
common name of the proper name without a name. It is therefore always a
shibboleth, for the manifest name of a secret is from the beginning a private
name, so that language about death is nothing but the long history of a
secret society, neither public nor private, semi-private, semi-public, on the
border between the two . . .

(Derrida, 1993: 74)

We have seen that the experience of surveillance is as dependent
upon an image's representational limits as it is upon any equivalence
with the recorded event. An understanding of surveillance as space,
by subject or viewer of the footage, leads to an engagement in the
edges, the concealments, the silent sounds, the absent personnel, the
deferred participants, which structure and inhabit this space. I have
also suggested that this space is 'performative' in nature, i.e. that it
does not pre-exist but comes about in the moment when we experience it.

'Performativity' implies that the relation of the subject to the
performative is neither voluntaristic nor entirely conditioned. In a
speech act, both the speaker and receiver of the performative utterance function as distinct individuals within the citational frame of
language. A speech act cannot simple be invented, free of citational
authority, but its enunciation is chosen and its results are unpredictable. I have suggested that the predominant, common-sense ideology
of surveillance as crime prevention tends to obscure the performative, spatial qualities of surveillance much as the constative tradition
in language philosophy is described by Austin as obscuring the
qualities of the speech act. I have also indicated that subjects who are
positioned at the crisis point of surveillance – at its boundary with
privacy – are likely to recognize surveillance's spatial qualities and

act in relation to these qualities rather than within a framework of privacy or crime prevention.

However, in speech act theory, and in notions such as gender performativity which apply Austin's linguistic findings on a cultural level, the effects of performativity are not limited to those who recognize them as such. We do not fail to be married, to participate in a bet, to undertake a dare, because we mistakenly think of our words as descriptive. Nor are we any the less conditioned as a boy or girl because we imagine these states to be the pure outcomes of biology. I have suggested that 'uptake' of spatial performativity involves acceptance of the general proposition that our experience of surveillance involves participation in new spaces. However, if this leaves those who do not recognize spatial performativity entirely free of its effects, much, if not all, of the usefulness of the term 'performativity' – the concept of an effect which is both immediate and citational – is lost.

Our discussion of the sexual subject under surveillance to some degree addresses these issues. The individual who acts sexually in relation to surveillance technology is incorporating that technology into complex psychological structures which are far from free of the sexual conditioning predating the surveillance moment. I have suggested, moreover, that by involving the sexual response of the viewer or receiver of the surveillance recording the sexual subject incorporates this viewer in the scene, the space, in a non-voluntaristic way, though not with predictable responses. However, the citational framework of such sexual surveillance acts could be said to be the general psychological/cultural structures of the symbolic/social realm rather than any language of surveillance per se. A question remains as to whether there is a surveillance culture which itself structures our acts in, and responses to, surveillance space. Is there a citational framework of surveillance?

In this chapter, I will examine the extreme case of death under surveillance – the particular ways in which imagery of death circulates and carries meaning in a world of surveillance images. I will suggest that our experience of death has been radically changed in surveillance society. Ultimately, I will argue that it is this experience of death that informs the performativity of surveillance space – which defines the specificity of surveillance culture.

## Death on camera

Narey almost saved himself with his arms. As he fell, his right shoulder glanced off the wall, and his knee was bruising, but the rest of him thudded unscathed to the concrete. Except that he began to vomit, his stomach rebelling at the jarring, and as he lay, surprised and winded and suddenly unconscious, he breathed it in. He began to die.

He was being watched: nearby, high on the side of his tower block, a security camera perched. Bradford City Council had positioned it there to stare protectively down at the estate's tenants and their visitors, and record them. Around 12.15 that night, the camera caught Narey's stagger and fall, and fed it back – a small, flailing blur – to one of four screens in the security office. Each screen was split seven ways, one grainy postcard for each camera on the estate; a single security guard, marooned out of sight in another tower block up the hill, watched them all.

(Beckett, 1997: 26)

The story of Kevin Narey, as recounted by Andy Beckett, is one structured by ironies – of secrecy, of security, of surveillance. Narey was a member of the Militant Tendency, a far left grouping which in the 1980s attempted to infiltrate the British Labour Party, campaigning to have its members elected as Labour councillors and MPs. Narey was, in Beckett's account, a well-meaning, passionate individual, perhaps somewhat too given to the kind of intrigue inherent in extreme political factions, but genuinely concerned to implement local community reforms. One of the improvements in the local environment he had campaigned for was the installation of the surveillance cameras under whose watch he eventually died. Narey collapsed after a binge of celebration following the victory of the Labour Party in the 1997 British parliamentary elections. Ironically, the victory was ascribed in part to the Labour Party's success in the 1990s in expelling supporters of the Militant Tendency and generally moving towards more centrist policies.

At the coroner's inquest into Narey's death, the ironies multiplied:

Why had the security guard called the police so late? Why hadn't the security camera, as it turned out, recorded what it saw? Why hadn't he gone to help?

The answers were as saddening and routine as the beige courtroom walls. Security guards were not permitted to leave their posts: they might be attacked or deliberately distracted. An ambulance had not been called because drunks had abused ambulancemen. The police had not arrived for an hour because they had been dealing with an armed robbery . . .

(Beckett, 1997: 32)

The fact that Narey probably died within three or four minutes of his fall does not seem to have deflated the urgency with which these questions were raised by his brother and other friends at the inquest. At the most, however, if the surveillance systems had functioned fully, the emergency services would have reached a dead body sooner, and a permanent record of his dying would have been available on video.

Narey's death, in all its ironies, system failures and secrecies, is a useful emblem of the ways in which death functions as both as image and absence in surveillance culture. The questions it raises can act as a guide through a discussion of the characteristics of death under surveillance.

## Agency and imagery

Beckett's article is only one example of a steady trickle of journalism which increases the interest in a report of death or murder with the additional information that the death was in some way recorded – usually through security cameras. I have chosen this example to analyse because of its ironic structuring, its detailing of the actual path and fate of the video signals, and also because of its relation, through the connections with Militant Tendency, to issues around secrecy which, we will find, in line with Derrida's argument above, are surprisingly important in analysing the impacts of an apparent 'openness' to imagery of death in surveillance society

However, it is important to emphasize the degree to which the growth in surveillance technologies has led in general to an unprecedented public availability and circulation of imagery of death.

Moreover, the imagery of death made available through surveillance is not only greater in quantity than previous imagery (primarily television war footage) but also different in kind. Whereas previous imagery of death either bears the distance of representation (fictionalized, albeit 'realistic', movie deaths) or the problem of agency (the responsibility of the cameraman in relation to the death recorded), surveillance footage of death is able to circulate as apparently 'real' and yet 'innocent', in that the unmanned camera has 'accidentally' recorded the death with no question of agency within the scene.

Agency is, to some degree, doubly removed in the surveillance death scene. In cases of accident or unexpected bodily failure such as Narey's above, there is no clear agent in the 'doing' of the death. Even in the case of shootings or other deliberate killings, however, while there is agency in relation to the death, there is no clear agent of the recording. That is to say, the murderer or equivalent does not know that the camera is recording his or her actions and is not in a 'performative' relation to the camera in the ways analysed in the previous chapter.[1] In general, the reception of the death scene under surveillance will almost always involve an understanding that this recording exists 'by accident' and, therefore, that the viewer is not implicated in the ethics of its production. This accidental nature of recordings of death under surveillance has allowed a freedom of circulation of imagery of 'real' death perhaps unprecedented in the West outside of war zones and since the disappearance of spectacles of execution.[2]

This last point refers us, of course, to Foucault (1991), who, in tracing the development of the panopticon in *Discipline and Punish*, first documents the disappearance of the spectacles of death. As noted in the previous chapter in relation to the question of 'panoptic' control of disabled people's bodies, there may be instances when the development of surveillance technologies actually results at a certain point (though perhaps a future imaginary point) in the inversion of panoptic control into an imagistic surfeit. We saw that the surveillance of disabled people has historically eliminated the disabled person as subject (particularly sexual subject) from the imagistic realm, but that the omnipresence of recording devices threatens to invert this surveillance control. Likewise, in relation to images of death, whereas the culture of panoptic disciplinarity eliminated the need for death as spectacle, a surfeit of surveillance seems actually to be reintroducing, in a much changed form, such spectacle. Indeed, in relation to Foucault's grand history, the question arises as to whether the newly developing surfeit of images of 'real' death is symptomatic of the epistemological break with enlightenment humanism predicted in much of his work.

## Circulation and agency

The importance of the question of death in surveillance society is underlined by the ways in which imagery of death is treated in a variety of contemporary cultural products. In Mark Ravenhill's self-consciously nihilistic play, *Shopping and Fucking* (1996), Lulu, one of the play's young, bewildered protagonists, is late for a meeting having witnessed a stabbing in a Seven Eleven all-night store. Describing the incident, Lulu agonizes over her own lack of action, her failure to alert anyone to the attack. Her friend Robbie comforts her: 'Look, they'll have a video. There's always like a security camera. They'll have his face.' (Ravenhill, 1996: 27).

The popular ideology of surveillance kicks in. The presence of a camera somehow compensates for Lulu's inaction by suturing the event into a crime-fighting sequence. But this ideology also has its worries for Lulu, who has used the attack as an opportunity to leave the store with a stolen chocolate bar (ibid.: 29).

*Lulu:*     They'll have me on the video. With the chocolate.
*Robbie:*   They'll be after him. Not you.

Later in the play, after a bungled drug deal, Lulu and Robbie turn to phone sex as a way to make some money quickly. Lulu is distraught when one of her clients describes the video he is masturbating to. The video has been passed on to him by a friend and is the recording of the assistant in the Seven Eleven being stabbed.

While the plot by which Ravenhill reaches this revelation may seem forced, the implications of this story within the play are interesting. Ravenhill implies that all remaining social activity – shopping, clubbing, stealing, drug taking – have become flattened into an equivalence with sexuality, 'fucking', which is both addictive and unsatisfying. In particular, for our purposes, the circulation of the recording of the stabbing in the Seven Eleven enters inevitably within the play's logic into a sexualized economy in which the most extreme events, images and stories are the most valued, the most orgasmic. Under this logic, death inevitably has the greatest value as the most extreme event, and yet is also emptied of any value or meaning as just another item for circulation. (Unlike most things in the play, the video of the death is not for sale but passed on by a friend – a mark of both its special value and its ultimate valuelessness.) Lulu's dilemma is that she is upset about nothing. The man masturbating to the video is causing no-one harm, and yet her sexual implication in this scene via the phone sex line is unbearable to her, and is the one point in the play at which she becomes entirely immobilized. Ravenhill marks this dilemma particularly emphatically by having the video in which Lulu becomes sexually implicated be the exact same scene in which she failed to intervene, succumbing instead to her own version of the 'ideology of crime' in surveillance and stealing the chocolate bar. However, the revulsion conjured in the audience by the report of the phone sex scene is not primarily due to its connection with Lulu's previous experience in the Seven Eleven (if anything this plot revelation lightens the impact of the phone sex story, deflecting attention to the link). The revulsion, demonstrated when I saw the play in a mass audience shudder, is more to do with the circulation of any scene of death for sexual stimulation. To some degree the audience recognizes that, in its acceptance of a cultural economy in which surveillance recordings of death are freely circulated for a variety of reasons, we have assented to the inevitability of the use of these recordings for purposes of which, taken in isolation, we would disapprove. No censor in the world has managed to legislate against specific responses as opposed to specific representations.

Lulu's predicament symbolizes a cultural dilemma in relation to surveillance imagery of death. This circulation, while under no obvious need for restraint or censorship according to current norms, raises the feeling, the possibility, that we are in some way failing to stop death happening, and that the reason for this failure is that in some way we profit from or enjoy the circulation.

This anxiety of circulation is very different from the anxiety of agency in relation to, say, journalistic war footage. Public reception, and media processing, of war footage depends largely upon intermediary figures – war reporters who will stand between the representation and the event. The figure of the war reporter acts as a guarantee of the image's veracity – the image replicates or represents the events that he or she has seen. As such, the war photographer/reporter as agent of these images and recordings has achieved a kind of elevated status in our society as one uniquely suffering the dilemmas of witnessing, without being able to prevent, death. The war reporter, we allow ourselves to believe, has suffered a present, bodily relationship to the facts of war. This bold but compromised individual has refrained from intervening in the event of death in order to fulfil the greater purpose of reporting the war to us. The reporter embodies the dilemma of agency – the ethics of witnessing rather than acting, of not acting in order to witness. This centrality of the reporter allows us to organize our relationship to the imagery of death via the figure of this agent, the individual who makes a choice. As a result, the war reporter is delegated an almost priestly role in our society, as one who will be tortured on our behalf by the contradictions of agency, of the choice to watch, not intervene. The genre of war reporters' autobiography is almost always a testimony to this personal anguish. In terms of public response, evidence of this elevated status ranges from the continued popularity of Vietnam reporters' memoirs to the election of BBC war reporter Martin Bell to the British parliament as an anti-corruption candidate.

Surveillance footage of death lacks the buffer of this reporter-agent. As such, it is presented as less problematic and therefore as more readily available for circulation. No choice was made to record these deaths, there was no decision not to intervene. However, as indicated by the intensity of Lulu's reaction to the experience of the circulated recording of death, the absence of the agent as priest/transgressor brings the viewer/audience of the surveillance recording of death into a relation with the circulated representation which seems disturbingly direct.

## Death and the other

To understand more fully the relationship between the viewer and the surveillance image of death, we should first examine in more depth the relation between self, death and other which is so satisfyingly deflected by substitute relations with the agency of a reporter or actor. In his discussion of death, *Aporias*, Jacques Derrida (1993: 72) focuses on an analysis of the complexities and limitations of Heidegger's 'existential' exploration of the relation of Dasein to death: the uniquely human relation to the 'possibility of impossibility' – one's own non-being. Derrida teases out the distinctions in Heidegger between the human/existential experience of death and biological 'perishing'; he also notes the degree to which, in Heidegger's argument, such existential analysis must be 'superordinate' to any other analysis of death (biological, anthropological, cultural). A cultural analysis such as the current one will mean nothing if it has failed to place itself in some relation to the questions of this 'possibility of impossibility'. In fact, there is a good basis in Derrida's own arguments for the discussion of the particular cultural role of circulated representations of death. For, as Derrida emphasizes throughout *Aporias* (while carefully avoiding the implication that this thought contrasts with Heidegger's position), the existential dilemma of the 'possibility of impossibility' can never be separated from the relation to death of the other:

> For, conversely, if death is indeed the possibility of the impossible and therefore the possibility of appearing as such of the impossibility of appearing as such either, then man, or man as Dasein, never has a relation to death as such, but only to perishing, to demising, and to the death of the other, who is not the other. The death of the other thus becomes again 'first', always first.
>
> (Ibid.: 76)

Derrida refers to a trinity in modernity's understanding of death – Heidegger, Levinas and Freud – and while his analysis focuses almost entirely on Heidegger's work it is shadowed throughout by the far more centralized relations to the other in the works of Freud and Levinas. Derrida writes that:

> Levinas . . . is saying 'the death of the other is the first death' and 'it is for the death of the other that I am responsible, to the point of including myself in death. This may be phrased in a more acceptable proposition: "I am responsible for the other insofar as he is mortal"', . . .
>
> (Ibid.: 39)[3]

Levinas's Hegelian position is that it is only in relation to the death of the other that any experience or expectation of the 'possibility of impossibility' – one's own death – is mediated. Derrida finds this position less in conflict with Heidegger's analysis than Levinas believes, and also rightly links it to the Freudian discussions of mourning and of the death drive.

Accepting this understanding of death as an existential experience of the possibility of impossibility necessarily formed in relation to the death of the other, the crisis in Lulu's (and the audience's) reaction to the sexualized report of the Seven Eleven murder tape takes on further levels of significance. In a non-surveillance portrayal of death on camera, a second other stands between the viewer and the dying body – either an actor or a reporter/camera operator. It is with this second other that we usually choose to make our relations, allowing this viewing ultimately to be not about death at all, but about skill in acting perhaps or, as noted above, the angst of the reporter. In a surveillance recording of death, this other other is not available and we are forced into the existential contemplation of the dying body.

However, the example of *Shopping and Fucking* also implies a more extreme consequence of the circulation of surveillance footage of death in contemporary society. The differing intensities of Lulu's reactions, first to the stabbing and, secondly, to the report of the surveillance recording of the stabbing, imply that it is the second experience that is the more shocking. It is the recording and not the live event which creates an aporia, a limit of comprehension.

How could a reported electronic signal impel the crisis of understanding that is the thought of death more strongly than the actual witnessing of the death of the other? One possible reason is the power of narrative to socialize even the most extreme experience. The actual Seven Eleven stabbing takes place within a chain of events that Lulu witnesses and takes part in; it also bears reference to sequences commonly presented through television and movies: 'And I didn't see anything. Like the blade or anything. But I suppose he must have hit her artery. Because there was blood everywhere.' (Ravenhill, 1996: 27).

By contrast, the surveillance recording of the same death appears narratively displaced, in the disturbingly inappropriate 'genre' of phone sex. Such narrative defamiliarizing allows the shock of the incomprehensible event – death itself – to remain in view.

Additionally, the particular shift of genre from that of crime prevention to pornography has implications with regards to the relationship between viewer and image. In the previous chapter we saw how surveillance images experienced sexually tended to involve the recognition by the viewer of a structured sexual relationship to the viewee. Such association with 'relationship' in the transition of the Seven Eleven footage from crime setting to sexual frame might initiate the kinds of existential responses suggested by Levinas and Derrida.

In addition, however, I would suggest that there are elements of the recording as recording which make it, in contemporary culture, a more direct, more affecting, experience, or at least an experience less susceptible to the elimination of affect, than the directly witnessed death.

Unlike the 'live' death, the recording of death circulates. As such, it behaves according to the qualities associated with value in contemporary society – the fetish positions of money, capital, commodity. Bodies, particularly bodies economically stranded in set geographical locations, maintain only a rubric of value. Faced with the death of the other, it is relatively easy to dissociate myself because I am not in that place, it could not 'just as easily have happened to me'; I am, in fact, asserting my relative economic value in moving away. Of the live killing which took place in front of her, Lulu says: 'It's like it's not really happening there – the same time, the same place as you. You're here. And it's there. And you just watch.' (ibid.: 27).

The surveillance recording of death, moving fetishistically through society's most sophisticated distribution networks, always inhabits the place where I am, and does so in the character of commodity value. The surveillance recording of death is more likely than the 'live' death to bring us to the aporia, the limit point of understanding where we encounter the possibility of the impossibility of our own non-being.

Such an aporetic moment necessarily conjures contradictory responses – fascination and revulsion, horror and hilarity. It is the fetishistic emptiness of the image – no-one actually dying, just electronic signals, nothing to intervene in, nothing to worry about – which, as with all fetishes, allows it its power.

The surveillance image of death combines the emptied potency of the fetish, specifically the circulating fetish of contemporary capitalist society, with the aporetic shock of the death of the other, enforcing the existential recognition of the impossible possibility of the death of the self.

## Death as trash

Surveillance imagery of death, then, exhibits a variety of contradictions in relation to more familiar views of the dying other. It is more easily accessible because it is unburdened by the problems of responsibility associated with agency. And yet this very separation from agency makes us feel closer to, more psychically implicated in, this accidental recording than in other imagery of death. At the same time, the status of the surveillance image as a circulating commodity attaches it to value in our society, a value higher than that placed on present production, from which we can geographically and temporally distance ourselves. This commodity value evokes and depends upon a fetishizing of the surveillance image, which we simultaneously avow is entirely detached from real death and its responsibilities, and yet at the same time experience as a more profound psychic encounter with death than a 'live' witnessing.

*Shopping and Fucking* does not take up the challenge, implied in its own subjects and structures, to explore the possibility that it is in the seemingly affectless realm of the circulated image that affect and even meaning begin to re-emerge. (The play ends rather with a sentimental reaffirmation of the power of narrative.) However, there are undoubtedly artists who are addressing the question of this paradoxical relationship to imagery of death.

Greg Araki's movies and Dennis Cooper's novels each take as their subject matter drug use, sexual ambiguity and extremity, and general loss of affect among young Americans. For Araki, the filmic landscape of west coast USA is as naturally populated by video cameras as by cops, cars and senseless death. Despite what can be seen as a nihilistic, youth-obsessed uniformity to Araki's cinematic vision, a series of his movies in the 1990s explores the relations of death and imagery in different ways. In his 1994 film about LA teenagers, *Totally Fucked Up*, the protagonists, a loose group of friends, perpetually video each other as part of the means of their communication. The pointing of a camera at the person talking becomes at once a way of paying attention and of separating the moment from its context. At the end of the film, after one of the boys has committed suicide, his best friend plays and replays footage of him on an edit suite, trying to splice his life back into the present. For the audience, and in a way for the characters, the strangeness of the moment is that the dead boy seems as present as he ever was. In contrast to the ritual of mourning usually enacted by the replay of soft-focus moments at the end of a movie, *Totally Fucked Up* has prepared us to perceive these video images as heightened versions of the recorded person, separated from the mundanity of teenage life. The dead character becomes more fully himself once video is left to speak for him.

Two other movies, made either side of *Totally Fucked Up* – *The Living Edge* (1992) and *Doom Generation* (1995) – explore this question of the relation of death to the value of the visual image in differing ways. A Generation X AIDS road movie, *The Living Edge* gains much of its power through a separation of death from the visible: the split between the raging minds and the engaging bodies of its HIV-positive characters. The cause of death is hidden within. At the point that one of the characters starts to become visibly, physically ill, the movie ends. Araki provocatively suggests that, within the artifice of a movie fiction, it is the non-signification of death by the dying body which reveals the drama and pain of AIDS.

In his later film, *Doom Generation*, Araki makes a similar but more explicit point about the relation of the video signal to the body. The film follows the story of three characters on the run as they become involved in a string of semi-accidental and increasingly gory murders. In this film, Araki uses special effects for the first time: the kind of gruesome, over-the-top special effects associated with splatter movies. Convenience store owners are killed in vast oceans of blood, with strange second heads appearing after the first head has been decapitated. Bar-room brawls lead to limbs flying across the room, taking on a life of their own. However, within the convenience store, surveillance cameras film realistic images of the protagonists, identifying them to police. As in *Totally Fucked Up*, reality within the movie seems to be more reliable, more consequential, when recorded on camera than when enacted in life. By showing death as ridiculously artificial in *Doom Generation*, Araki returns in a very different way to the separation of death and the image explored in *The Living Edge.* The goriness of the special effects call attention to the fact that the whole movie is a trick of camera and film; but in cheap video surveillance technology, images, and specifically death images, recirculate with renewed meaning.

In each of the three movies, Araki locates death as separated from the movie narrative. In *The Living Edge,* it is inaccessible to view, inside the characters' bodies. In *Totally Fucked Up*, death is meaningless within the daily lives of the movie's characters, but through the video recordings taken by those characters, it achieves a meaning – separating, editing the video body from the less fully realized character in the main narrative. Finally, in *Doom Generation*, life is exposed as a B-movie fake, whose budget is never big enough for the required thrills, and it is only the unmanned surveillance video recording that is able to register and circulate the facts of a senseless convenience store killing.

Araki's obsessive relationship to death in his movies is matched by a vast cynicism as to its importance, and yet at the same time death is the only value functioning in these movies – the poignancy of, the anger at, the engagement in death. The problem of filmic representation of death means that the movie camera can never provide a meaningful image of death – the movie camera reaches an aporia. But unlike most movies, Hollywood or otherwise, Araki does not deflect attention from this missed moment – the death itself – with the forward thrust of narrative. Instead, he draws attention to this failure within the movie, marking death's resonant absence. When images captured by video cameras within the movie's narrative reappear to remind us of this absent death, they bring with them an affect missing in the first telling of the death. We are, like Lulu in the phone sex scene, suddenly confronted, via home video or surveillance, with a report of a death that we thought we had placed at a distance. Recirculating as electronic image, the death gains currency.

Another west-coast artist, Dennis Cooper, explores this currency of circulating death with particular complexity. Cooper's novel *Frisk*

(1991) deals with a psyche permanently affected by early adolescent encounter with a 'snuff' photograph:

> I didn't understand what was happening in the pictures at first, but after three or four I realized that the model was dead and not laughing or yelling like I'd originally thought. He was lying face up on a bed. His wrists and ankles were tied with heavy rope, and there was a rope around his neck that I imagined had killed him. His eyes and his mouth were wide open. That's why I'd thought he was laughing. He was pale, cute, and had long, straight black hair. There was nobody else in the photographs with him.
>
> In the last couple of photos somebody had rolled the boy over, so we could see what he looked like on both sides, I guess. That's when I knew for sure he was dead because instead of an asscrack, he had a crater. It looked as if someone had set off a bomb in his rectum.
>
> (Cooper, 1991: 27)

Cooper's complexly structured narrative goes on to describe the life of a character (I/Dennis, though not always told in the first person or from that character's viewpoint), whose psyche, and ultimately whose life, are determined by an obsessive relationship with the sexualized death scene. Dennis believes that the images 'went on to completely direct or destroy my life in a way' (ibid.: 30), even though he finds out at the age of seventeen that they were faked, when he has sex with the boy who modelled for them. The story turns into a balancing act between action and affect. We become increasingly unclear whether Dennis is heading towards the reality of serial killing or an almost schizophrenic confusion between the intensity of his sexual fantasies and the responsibilities of agency. At the end of the novel this tension is finally relieved by the description of the 'snuff' photographs Dennis has taken:

> Close-up. The 'wound' is actually a glop of paint, ink, makeup, tape, cotton, tissue, and papier-mâché sculpted to suggest the inside of a human body. It sits on the ass, crushed and deflated. In the central indentation there's a smaller notch maybe one half-inch deep. It's a bit out of focus. Still, you can see the fingerprints of the person or persons who made it.
>
> (ibid.: 128)

This extraordinary conclusion to the novel inspires a range of reactions in the reader. There is a narrative relief at the discovery that Dennis is not a murderer and yet at the same time a sense of loss in that the mystery of the initial snuff photograph is dissipated. This dilemma of the loss of death is crucial to both Cooper's and Araki's work. Death is absented from any conventional representations of its form: the movie death scene (sentimental or shoot-up), the literary description, cannot present us with death, and so these artists and the characters they depict show an affectless relation to attempts to describe or represent death – to what common-sense culture thinks of as death itself. Paradoxically for Araki and Cooper, as for Ravenhill in Lulu's phone sex/surveillance scene, it is in the trashy circulated images and signals of consumer society that death can momentarily re-emerge as a direct experience: as the experience of death of the other, formative of our comprehension of the possibility of the impossibility of our own death.

Faced with this paradox, Cooper and Araki (as opposed to Ravenhill) do not deflect their gaze towards other comforts (Ravenhill's appeal to the timelessness, the immortality of stories); they maintain focus on the degraded apparition of death, seek even (particularly in Cooper's *Frisk*) to develop its reach, its possibilities. Often faced with criticism for their perceived nihilism, these artists are in fact making the shocking proposition that it is only the devotees of splatter movies, snuff movies and surveillance shoot-outs who are actually engaged in any contemporary existential struggle with the fundamental question of death.

## Circulation and value

I am suggesting that in the contemporary public realm (as opposed to the private experience of, say, death of a loved one) the experience of death of the other is available only in glimpses, in the circulating representations of trashy and/or accidental recordings. I am linking this situation directly to the role of the commodity fetish in contemporary society (although without the assumption that we should necessarily be searching for some alternative production-based value in death). Whereas the carefully prepared representation of death allows a relationship on this existential level only with the agent of the representation, the chance encounter with an unprepared image results, at least momentarily, in an encounter with the possibility of 'raw' death. Even the experience of 'live' death in the social realm (the actual Seven Eleven stabbing) is already mediated by popular representations, and occupies the devalued site of production from which the consumer/spectator can (and usually does) move away. By contrast, the chance image/recording, regardless of its poor quality and low cost, occupies the site of value – circulation – from which, by its ubiquitous, reappearing nature one cannot escape. In its lack of 'production values' and agency, the chance image disallows any relationship to the producer of the representation, and impels the viewer into a confrontation with the death of the other.

Operating in the realm of the commodity fetish, the circulating image of death accrues to itself many of the aspects of the Freudian as well as the Marxian fetish, providing satisfaction all the more fully in its acknowledged emptiness. However, this emptiness of the image does not imply that the subject of the surveillance death scene is rendered irrelevant. If the existential experience of surveillance footage is, ultimately, an experience of the possibility of death through contact with death of the other, the subjectivity of this other will need to be explored.

## Missing the moment

In his film *Silverlake Life: The View From Here*, Tom Joslin creates a work within which lies the possibility of a recording of the film-maker's death. *Silverlake Life* is a 'film' begun by Joslin after both he and his lover, Mark Massi, had been diagnosed with AIDS. Using the ready availability of video technology, Joslin recorded over forty hours of footage: of his attempts to undertake simple domestic tasks as the disease progresses, of intimate moments with Massi, of explanations to the camera about what is happening to his body, of encounters with his family, and of the late stages of the illness, lying semiconscious and skeletal in his bed. The film, edited after both Joslin's and Massi's deaths by Joslin's former student Peter Friedman, is hugely difficult and moving to watch. My own experience of viewing it was of vast, stomach-churning pendulum swings between experiencing the film as a representation, an almost empty signifier of my own fears and losses, and, at the other extreme, feeling numbed by the particularities, the very specific frustrations and sadnesses of Joslin's situation and story. I remember at one point sitting in front of my VCR entirely unable to pause the film for a moment's respite, and yet at the same time frantically checking the video box and my watch to see how many minutes were left to suffer. In all of this I found myself longing for Joslin's death, for the relief, the mourning, that endings allow.

In this longing for death, we are aware of a particular tension arising in *Silverlake Life*. As it becomes clear how intimately Joslin is revealing his life, and how many hours of footage have been shot, the possibility clearly emerges that Joslin's death will be recorded by the video camera. In the end, we do not see the moment of death itself. Instead, we see two moments surrounding the death. One, a few days before (25 June), shows Joslin lying in bed, his gaunt face scarred by Kaposi's sarcoma lesions, his breathing imperceptible. Massi reveals that he has been 'ashamed' to switch on the camera for a few days because he fed Joslin something that disagreed with him and felt responsible for how much worse he was looking. Massi focuses the camera on each of Joslin's eyes in turn. One, the lid covered in lesions, is barely visible; the other is clear: 'that eye he can see in the camera with'. Massi then asks Joslin how he feels and Joslin mutters in a breathy voice, barely intelligible, with Massi attempting to translate: he feels pretty bad, but wants his friends to feel good. The video is showing a frame of Joslin's face, it cuts suddenly to the face again, a slightly different angle. There is a howl then Massi's voice: 'This is the first of July and Tommy's just died.' Joslin's clear eye still stares towards the camera.

This hugely upsetting, terrifyingly memorable sequence gains much of its effect from the decision by Joslin, Massi and Friedman to stick very close in this extreme moment to the video diary format which is the basic frame for the project. While the final film plays with the format at differing times, often ignoring the diary update convention, in this key sequence we return to the basic device of Joslin's face in the camera frame, a voice, though now Massi's not Joslin's, telling us the date, what has recently happened, what is happening now. (The earlier moment in the film when Massi's voice takes over from Joslin's as the primary recorder of dates and sequence is itself a terribly affecting point of both loss and love.) As in the fictional work of Cooper and Araki, this maintaining of the low-grade, low-cost image, in contrast to the death-bed conventions of movies and other mainstream representations, disallows the deflection of our relation to the death onto another agent. The camera pointing only at Joslin's face, measuring only his time, forces us to relate our being in this moment of viewing directly to the process of his dying in some other moment, 1 July, now replayed.

The importance of distinguishing the film viewer's relationship to this dying from the private experience of Massi is underlined by the decision (whether Joslin's as subject, Massi's as partner and in that period camera operator, or Friedman's as editor) not to show us the moment of death itself. We feel, we seem to see, Joslin's death in the cut from one frame of his face to another, in the soundtrack of Massi's howl, but we do not share with Massi the moment (if it is a moment) when life leaves Joslin. The message, the experience of this choice, is that *Silverlake Life* is not ultimately for Joslin, about his death, but for us, about our experience of his death. Separate from this video-for-us there has been another story, a personal story, which, despite the emotional openness of the film, we will never know. This does not mean for a moment that our experience of Joslin's death is distanced or lessened by this separation from the personal event. The opposite is the case: this separating out of Joslin's death-for-Massi from his death-for-us undercuts any tendency to draw away from the death as someone else's private moment, to view not the death but the relationship. This circulated, edited sequence is clearly our public, albeit intensely intimate, experience of a man's death from AIDS. This forcing of a public moment is among the most significant of *Silverlake Life*'s political achievements.[4]

Clearly then, *Silverlake Life* is not a piece of surveillance footage. No matter how exhaustively and intimately the camera seems to observe, the subject is (almost entirely) choosing that observation, and the final product that we see is carefully edited. However, Joslin's video demonstrates a great deal about the difference between the traditional modes of filmic construction – narrative, documentary – and the opportunities opened by the random and uninterrupted availability of cheap recording technologies. Moreover, much of *Silverlake Life*'s power comes from the degree to which it seems to resemble surveillance footage – its incessant watching – and the tension that it therefore sets up around the possibility of revealing the moment of death. The film's structure, its edits and choices, exist in the context of the possibility that anything could be recorded. The missed moment of Joslin's death in *Silverlake Life* is unlike the millions of other deaths from AIDS which are quietly walled behind the private grief of family or friends. By exposing Joslin's dying to an extreme degree of surveillance (in the full sense of the word) and then withdrawing our view momentarily in the instant of passing itself, his film brings his death into the public realm in a way that neutralizes our capacity to subsume it into conventions of sentiment or tragedy.

In this way, Joslin's act in making this video relates very closely to the questions and actions of subjectivity-under-surveillance discussed in the previous chapter. The display of the gay male body, here marked as gay and as sexual by the visibility of AIDS, is clearly an imperative drive in this film. Taking control of, and proliferating, the surveillance under which the ill or disabled person's body is placed is also central to its political and personal agenda. However, it is perhaps most of all in the question of what slips out of view, what is not quite clear, that the film relates to the subjectivities of surveillance discussed earlier. From the missed moment of death in the film, a whole series of other unseen images fan outwards, back and forward through the whole: the virus itself, the moment of infection, the sexual act, the death of Massi, the words that Joslin can no longer pronounce now that he is bedridden, the eye behind the camera, the eye behind the lesion, the feeling of dying, the heat in LA. Like the surveillance image, and in a direct conversation with that image's seeming totality, *Silverlake Life*'s absolute gaze points always towards what is not seen – not because it is private, but because it hovers at an aporia of understanding.

## A space for death?

In her moving analysis of Joslin's film, Peggy Phelan emphasizes images of the gaze, or rather of failure of the gaze: the multitude of cameras, the eye behind the lesion, the lack of shot/counter-shot sequences and hence of the 'reciprocal gaze' that such sequences imply.[5] It is the 'body that can never be confirmed by sight' that Phelan begins to sense emerging in Joslin's sequences. Relating the theme of *Silverlake Life* to her earlier exploration of unmarked subjectivity, Phelan suggests that: 'In *Silverlake Life* Tom Joslin does not try to outlast death . . ., but he does interrogate its borders' (Phelan, 1997a: 167). This interrogation of borders is an exploration of the limits of the visible (the given-to-be-seen):

> It is this vanishing, the dissolution of vision itself, that *Silverlake Life*, uncannily and against all logic, achieves. Dissolving vision, this film composed of seen images, achieves an image against the logic of film itself. It escapes its own terms and sends the spectator into a cinema of his or her own imaginary.
>
> (Ibid.: 168)

Relating Phelan's insight to Derrida's concept of 'the possibility of impossibility', it seems possible that this cinema of the spectator's imaginary contains the scene of the spectator's death – the possibility of the impossibility of one's own death. Or, rather, the imaginary cinema contains a sequence in which this moment has been edited out, and in that editing out becomes present, momentarily shortcircuiting the paradox, the aporia of death.

In the public/cultural sphere, then, the experience of *Silverlake Life* is to make possible the thought of one's own dying in relation to this sphere. For such an effect to be possible, the death of *Silverlake Life* cannot be neatly sutured into its own narrative. In order for us to experience this cultural death as death, it must arise shockingly, unexpectedly. The death sequence in the film, part medical examination, part video diary, part love poem, achieves this shock through the steadiness of the camera's gaze and the juxtaposition of the edit.[6]

## Death and uptake

I have suggested in earlier chapters that the experience of space under surveillance may involve uptake by the viewer and/or 'viewee' of the notion that 'surveillance space' is neither equivalent to the geographical space of the initial event nor a representation of it. In the experience of surveillance, the uptake of this new space carries with it spatially related effects such as the transition from privacy to display, the implication of the absent viewer, the incorporation of future experience into the present moment, the experience of the borders of the surveyed and the divergence of visual and sound spaces.

In the above analysis of the appearances of death in recordings and representations related to surveillance, several similar characteristics emerge. Death is elusive in the recorded realm. The experience of death-of-the-other is easily deflected into a relationship with the agency of the reporter/artist/editor, or subsumed into narrative conventions. While the surveillance recording of death, by its nature, distances the recording from agency and narrative, we have seen in previous chapters how powerfully the representational economy works to reclaim the disruptive effects of surveillance recordings. The common-sense ideology of crime and the libidinal structures of the 'money shot' both operate upon our perceptions of surveillance recordings of death to limit any 'existential' effects.

In *Shopping and Fucking*, the phone sex report of Lulu's client masturbating to the surveillance footage of the Seven Eleven shoot-out implies that, for the client, the death scene has been incorporated into a combined shoot-out/porn climax. Lulu's response, however, demonstrates a much more radical hiatus – a disruption of all activity in the face of death of the other. Lulu, who does not see the recording, is affected by the report of it. The implication of Ravenhill's script, as with Araki's and Cooper's treatment of death recordings, is that at the same time as we pay attention to the image we must simultaneously be deflected, distracted from it.[7] Without such a double movement, the death moment under surveillance can be recouped into the representational mainstream.

In *Silverlake Life*, a deflection of the death moment through the editing process is used to confront the viewer with the political/cultural reality of Joslin's death. As Phelan implies, there is a strange presence of absence within this revealing record which provides a space for a non-mainstream understanding.

Despite the libidinal satisfaction of Ravenhill's fictional phone-caller, such absences pervade the surveillance recording of death. (We could read the need to call a sex line as an attempt to fill the absence of the Seven Eleven recording.) Indeed, as we have seen in examining surveillance's structuring limitations, absences pervade all experiences of surveillance, though representational ideologies often hide them. These present absences, hidden by the common-sense ideologies, are the very basis of surveillance space once that space is 'uptaken'. They are what make the space neither the event nor its representation. I would suggest that the uptake of surveillance space is linked by its present absences to death, whether or not the recording relates to the event of death. Surveillance, in this reading, becomes for our culture structurally 'about' death in the way that theatre was about death for Artaud (see Chapter 4).

## On the border

In surveillance recordings of death, the boundaries, the unseen elements of the recording, are crucial to the effect of the whole. It is the obscured moments, the lack of soundtrack, the bad camera angle, the unsureness of the moment of passing which undercut any narrative suturings and ideological soothings.

As the viewer/auditor of the surveillance death scene allows awareness of these effects to register, he or she is once again engaged in a performative exchange. He or she is accepting effects that are caused not by the recorded event, nor by the recording of the event, but by the inter-relation of event and recording in a space other than that occupied by either event or recording, in a time which is neither past nor present.

Death-of-the-other occurs under surveillance not again, nor in the past, but differently, in a differing space which has been 'uptaken' by the viewer or auditor, and which carries its own unique spatial characteristics. This performative space is not the private space of personal death, nor a public space where death has been sutured into narrative but, to return to Derrida, 'neither public nor private, semi-public, semi-private, on the border between the two' (Derrida, 1993: 74).

## Absence and secrecy

If, as Timothy Gould suggests, performative speech troubles the constative realm with its suspenses and delays, disrupting representational claims for language, the performative space of surveillance can be seen to effect a similar troubling. As recorded images approach more nearly the apparent self-evidence of surveillance, uncut, unmanipulated, unmanned, they simultaneously accrue the characteristics of spatial performativity, with its insertions of the viewer into the scene, its borders, its display of the formerly private, its criminalizations and sexualizations. In Chapter 1, I suggested that 'uptake' in relation to surveillance space had to do with a recognition of this performativity per se, rather than with the acceptance of any particular intent carried with the space. However, in the case that uptake does not occur, that the performativity of the surveillance space is not recognized, but, rather, sutured back into ideologies of evidence and accident, the effects of performativity are not entirely negated. The viewer of surveillance footage of a Seven Eleven murder may understand the viewing only within conventional narratives, but an excess of affect may be seen to occur which continues to trouble the representational realm. This excess is often represented in talk. The Seven Eleven masturbator calls Lulu's sex line; on television there is endless empty discussion of the value of CCTV.

What remains to trouble the reception of surveillance representation when the performativity of surveillance space is not uptaken is a feeling of absence. Whereas uptake of performativity allows acceptance of a space structured around its many borders, disruptions and dualities, refusal or failure of uptake allows no visual means for understanding the experience of watching in precise, apparently unmediated, detail events which are not currently happening. In 'constative' surveillance representation, the absence of the represented event is both denied and felt. That is to say, it is repressed.

Whereas individual psychic repressions produce symptoms that are primarily bodily, and the traditional psychoanalytic approach to them is to engage in the 'talking cure', the social repressions of surveillance may be seen to produce their symptoms in the social body of language. The endless, repetitively uninformed television debates around the value of surveillance outlined in Chapter 1 are examples of this symptom, as are more specific outbreaks of discourse around the suitability of broadcasting particular imagery – and particularly death imagery – for example, Dr Jack Kevorkian's assisted suicide of Thomas Youk on CBS in 1998. As symptom, such speech does not, of course, talk about the actual repressed anxiety, and the uninformative and repetitive nature of such debates is testimony to their status as symptoms. Such debates do, however, allow a space for the energy of anxiety to be expended without impinging on the constatively sutured visual realm.

The Kantian distinction between sound space and visual space comes into play here. Talk (language, particularly as sound) provides an alternative realm to the visual surveillance field, a realm in which the social aspects of interiority and its relation to surveillance may be expressed. In Chapter 1's discussion of the characteristics of surveillance sound space, we found that language under surveillance is popularly conceived of as secret code. The suggestion that surveillance sound needed to be interpreted was, we saw, used as a way to cover up its performative difference from representation, the ways in which it brought about more than it described. In comment-as-symptom there is an almost opposite trajectory, though ultimately with similar effects. The performative difference from reference has emerged spatially in the imagery and has been repressed; its re-emergence is disguised as meaningless language.

In *Aporias* Derrida suggests that the language of death must always be a code: 'death is always the name of a secret . . . it is always a shibboleth . . . so that language about death is nothing but the long history of a secret society' (Derrida, 1993: 74). If language, particularly non-meaningful language, becomes the symptom of the absences felt when surveillance is taken for representation, then perhaps this language is in fact code, a secret name, for death. We have seen that death is figured in surveillance space as and through absences, borders, limitations. When this figuring is disallowed through non-uptake of performative space, there can be no true experience of death in the surveillance image. The images of the surveillance footage may include recordings of people's deaths, but the failure to uptake the relation to the footage in which the death can be existentially experienced disallows any knowledge of death of the other, any approach to the aporia of one's own death. Equally, when the footage contains no representation of death, the repression of the absences inherent to surveillance may equate those absences with the death that they often figure. In this way, a non-performative relation to surveillance footage inevitably represses (and therefore is inherently about) death.

Here we begin to see the full extent to which the spatial qualities of surveillance depend upon structures of performativity. Each occurrence, each uptake of surveillance space, draws upon, occurs in relation to or, we might say, cites the culturally shared knowledge of surveillance's founding absences and edges, a knowledge written in the code of death. Far from being isolated experiences, each uptake of surveillance space occurs in relation to this already circulated knowledge of surveillance's absences and references. Moreover, even the most determinedly representational reading of surveillance relates to this citational frame in its repressions, much as the constative utterance in Austin's reading always carries within it the germ of the performative.

## Secrets, lies and videotape

The example of Kevin Narey's death brings these issues together in an intriguing combination. As noted above, Narey himself had a particular relationship to secrecy as a member of Militant Tendency, one of Britain's most notoriously secretive left-wing political groups. He died in front of surveillance cameras, which he had campaigned to have installed on the council estate where he lived. Yet the surveillance cameras transmitted the image of his death to a security guard who, if he noticed Narey's situation, could do nothing about it. And the images were not recorded.

This last fact, while entirely irrelevant to Narey's fate, seems to have caused consternation among his friends and family. At the coroner's inquest into Narey's death, his brother demanded to know why the security camera had not recorded what it saw (Beckett, 1997: 32). The answer seems to have been an issue of funding, but the brother nonetheless left the inquest promising 'further action'. This sense of conspiracy against someone like Narey reflects the culture of an organization like Militant, used to being plotted against as well as plotting. The fact that it circulates particularly around the lack of a recording which could not have prevented the death nor revealed anything new about it becomes less bewildering once we factor in the above discussion of surveillance, absence and death. In the common-sense ideology of surveillance, the video should have appeared in the courtroom as evidence. Narey's image would be sorted out from the mass of images, having been made exceptional by his collapse. It would then be narrativized as accident, a case not in need of solving. The absence of the tape disrupts the common-sense flow of this process. Surveillance absence makes Narey's death felt in the coroner's court in a way that his dying image could not. The talking, Narey's brother's ultimately pointless questions, which would symptomatically have covered for the repression of the experience of death by the surveillance footage, becomes, in the absence of the footage, the primary space for consideration of, for feeling, the death in the cultural/social sphere. And, helped by Narey's own involvement in secrecy and conspiracy, this talking, already inherently linked with code, with secrets, now becomes associated with a vast, inexplicable sense of conspiratorial falsehood, unrelated to any facts but intimately related to the death of the other.

This case is among the most expressive examples of death-of-the-other in the social/cultural field, reverberating with an existential profundity. In Beckett's article, and, it seems, among Narey's community, the circumstances of this death became a focal point for consideration of many aspects of loss, the passing of time, the effects of historical change, feelings experienced in this moment not through political analysis, nor through personalization, but through a palpable social shudder of recognition.

## Representation and reification

There is a danger in my analysis of a reification of death – a making of this most difficult word into a thing which somehow stands in for all value. Again the example of trash artists such as Araki and Cooper is helpful. Like the fake snuff photo that Cooper's character Dennis eventually and unconvincingly recreates, a theory of surveillance which seeks out death as a grounding value will find instead only empty, artificial surfaces. I do not want to imply that the conflation of 'absence' and 'death' in the above analysis somehow effects a double negative, reintroducing a meaningful experience of death into the surveillance scene. It is not only the relation of absence to death, but also the absence of death, which is keenly felt in surveillance recordings. What I do want to suggest is that in the relatively degraded field of surveillance, as opposed to the 'high arts' of literature and documentary making, the appearances and absences of death, precisely because they are not associated with meaning, because they do not attempt to deal with the subject, impact upon us in ways which higher minded efforts do not. The nature of the aporia of death as revealed under surveillance is that, however close we come to it, however many times we rewind, we do not meet death-as-thing, but find that, in the missing of something, a death has happened.

## Staring at falling

The importance of understanding the relationship between our cultural knowledge of and approach to death and the circulation of accidental video footage has been sharply underlined by the events of September 11, 2001. Of all the electronic images which fill our lives, it is probably safe to estimate that the images of September 11 are the most widely seen, the most widely shared in the world. The planes hitting the towers, the bodies jumping from the buildings, the towers falling; each of these images marked the deaths of thousands of people; each was caught more or less by chance on cameras that were present for other reasons; each was circulated globally.

Responses to the events have, of course, been huge and complex. It is far outside the scope of this study to analyse the geopolitical consequences of an event of this scale. However, when the footage shot is of such surveillance-like, amateur video-cam quality and the governmental response is to increase massively the state's powers of surveillance of its own populations, it seems reasonable to ask whether some of the arguments we have been exploring around the relationship of death to surveillance might be of relevance.

If, as I have suggested, the absences, borders and obscurings intrinsic to surveillance recordings are structurally related to the aporia of death, and specifically to our cultural approach to death in media–commodity society, the sharing on a global public scale of the September 11 footage brings this argument to the centre of contemporary politics and policy. Evidence increasingly suggests that the CIA and FBI had received information that might have led them to anticipate the attacks, but that prevention did not occur primarily because, overwhelmed by the volume of information they had received about a variety of potential threats, the agencies were unable to predict which presented the greatest danger. Nonetheless, one of the primary governmental responses to the attacks has been to rush through legislation that will increase the state's access to information about its own citizens' activities and transactions. It is as though by increasing one of the sources of the problem (an excess of undifferentiated information) the state hopes to prevent the one thing that cannot happen – another attack on the no-longer-existent twin towers. The more likely event – an attack as unlike expectations as the use of a commercial airline to crash into an enormous building was before September 11 – remains unlikely to stand out from the mass of data.

Nonetheless, the increase of surveillance 'seems like' the answer, seems like a way to stop death happening, because we are so troubled by what the surfeit of imagery of September 11 fails to show us. We do not see, recognize or understand the men piloting the planes into the buildings. We hear the voices of the kidnapped passengers on mobile phone recordings, but we do not see their faces. We see the pictures of the towers' inhabitants displayed all over the streets of New York, ostensibly in an attempt to find them if they are alive, but surely rather in an attempt to imagine them in their death – those deaths so revealed and yet obscured in the fall of the towers, and the specks of bodies jumping from the windows.

So – terrified by seeing so much of death and yet feeling that we have not seen it at all, we play the phone messages, tape the photos up all over the city and legislate for more surveillance, more information, more detail. The truth is that the September 11 attacks were not prevented because they were designed not to look like the patterns of terrorism that state surveillance was at that point trained to recognize. The Bali bombings a year later only added to the confusion by looking like the most standard terrorist act imaginable at a point where prevention agencies were focused on the likelihood of something more unusual, more spectacular.

The governmental need to increase its powers of surveillance post-September 11 is in direct structural relation to the anxiety caused by the failure of all the imagery of the attack to reveal useful evidence. In the logic of state control, visual representation should lead to the solution of the crime, the prosecution of the criminal. However, the imagery has had no such effect, and the figure of Osama Bin Laden, despite all of the state machinery employed to capture him, goes uncaught in the camera's eye, other than in the fleeting videos that he releases into the world. The state's response of increased citizen surveillance will do little to solve this problem, but, as long any more complex response to the deaths is repressed, the need for more, better visual imagery will continue to reassert itself.

The deficit produced by the unseeableness, the incomprehension of death in the September 11 events may also be compensated for in the state's response by an increase in secrecy in relation to surveillance evidence. It is unlikely that much of the information on citizen behaviour and transactions gathered under the new 'anti-terrorist' laws will reach the public realm. Consistent with the arguments above, where direct representation continues, inevitably, to fail, the state will return to the logic of code – the need to decipher the evidence and make interpretations. Some of this deciphering may lead to arrest of potential terrorists; some may lead (as there is already evidence to indicate happened in the arrests immediately following September 11) to perfectly innocent individuals being interpreted and punished as conspirators. With the keys to the interpretive code jealously guarded by government, it may be hard for anyone else to tell the difference.

And yet another response to the twin towers attack footage can, and did, exist. Before governments and opinion-makers started to interpret what could not be seen in the obsessively repeated footage of the attacks, started to tell us who did what and why and how it could have been stopped if we had just seen more earlier – before all this there was a direct uninterpreted encounter by millions of people with the shock of the images themselves.[8] In those moments, we all looked at death together or, rather, we looked and death happened and we weren't quite sure what we saw, so we looked again, and again, and again. As the news bulletins joined the bits together, we were presented with a sequence – the planes, the towers, the bodies falling – that did not quite show us the pain and horror we were sure they represented. These images were followed by others of screaming, shocked, sometimes damaged bodies running from the towers, so much more descriptive of the horror, although, of course, these were images of the survivors. Editing the cuts in our minds and memories, we felt a moment between the shots, when faces – similar to those seen running, surviving (so diverse in their age, race, class, gender)

– ran or jumped but did not survive, as the planes crashed, the towers fell. We saw, world-wide, what cannot be seen, what we each have to take inside ourselves and consider, wonder at, take responsibility for – the death of the other. And for a moment, as George W. Bush hid out in his plane, as Osama Bin Laden hid out in his cave, each of us knew that this moment, this death of the other, was our own responsibility, that the blame could not be passed.

Of course, almost immediately the interpretations, the code-breaking began, and we moved from the complex moment of surveillance encounter with death to the assertion of representational control – if only the state had more images, more code-breakers, death would not happen. But it does happen, it will; and it may still be that the shared experience of September 11, if we are not afraid to continue addressing it, may help us to understand how, in the world we have made, we deal with this fact.

## From public to shared

The governmental and ideological recuperations of September 11 ironically but predictably appeal to the public realm – the mantra of public safety – while increasing state secrecy. The possibility for a social response which increases understanding, by contrast, occurs not in the public realm of ceremonies and statements, but in the knowledge that we have shared an approach and a response to death and that we have recognized our own part in this moment. This shared social experience stands outside the public/private binary that surveillance in general disrupts. Likewise, in suggesting that such social responses to death are separate from personal experiences of the loss of a loved one, I am indicating a limit to the scope of the surveillance-based argument, but I am not intending to re-establish a privileged, private realm of understanding.

Ultimately, the separation is a discursive one; this is not a question of drawing a line between 'public' and 'private' death; rather it is a question of insisting that death has meaning, has its structuring, aporetic effect not only in the personal but also in the wider cultural sphere. In particular, an understanding that the necessary citation of death is inherent to our experience of surveillance, even when that citation is repressed, helps to explain the potentially extraordinary effects upon our consciousnesses and culture that surveillance's performativity may enact. The circulating surveillance image – always almost, never quite, showing us death itself – necessitates our compensatory codes, our documentary repressions and our artistic manipulations. In accepting, in living with the consequences of the spatial effects of surveillance, we begin to reimagine our relation to death, our relation to being.

# 4

## Dimensions, doubles and data

## Producing surveillance space

In October 2001, an exhibition, *CTRL [SPACE]: Rhetorics of Surveillance from Bentham to Big Brother*, opened at the ZKM Centre for Arts and Media, Karlsruhe, Germany. Planned over a period of a year, the exhibition was the most comprehensive survey ever of art work produced in response to and using the tools of surveillance technology. Opening in the month that it did, however, the exhibition found itself repositioned in the aftermath of September 11. Suddenly, issues surrounding both security and the visibility of criminal activity on a massive scale were very differently contextualized.

In November of the same year in Manchester, England, the second annual *Futuresonic – A Festival of Sonic Pleasure and Audiovisual Arts* opened. Futuresonic had likewise decided one year previously to theme its 2001 commissions and programme around surveillance, and had specifically moved towards a more activist, even anarchist, stance in its engagement with sound experiment and electronic music by embracing such a socially specific theme. With commissions from such cutting-edge artists and collectives as Coldcut, Ultra Red and D.J. Spooky, the festival also suddenly found itself suspended between the overinsistent presence of September 11 and the more familiar critiques of surveillance that it had perhaps assumed were its ideological starting point.

Ultimately, both events incorporated the inevitable presence of September 11 – *CTRL [SPACE]* in a massive satellite print of Manhattan the day after the attacks, created from commercially purchased satellite imagery by Laura Kurgan; Futuresonic in a sonic and visual sampling of the events by D.J. Spooky (Paul D. Miller). Both artists are New York residents – which was perhaps the inevitable and appropriate artist location for September 11 commentary within these international events, but perhaps also a way of 'containing' the disruption of critique which September 11 potentially unleashed on the events as a whole.

131

This is not for a moment to throw doubt upon the significance and achievement of both of these artistic programmes. *CTRL [SPACE]* and the publication of the same name that accompanied it form the most significant overview of surveillance based art and art-critique ever brought together. *Futuresonic 01*, while much smaller in scale, demonstrated its aliveness to the pulse of the contemporary crossover between activism, art and music in a choice of topic and artists that brought standing room only audiences for debates, performances and viewings. However, the irony of these two events opening, respectively, in October and November 2001 does affect their meaning. In both cases, the critical framework – one which largely, and understandably, distrusts both the 'totalitarianism' of state and corporate surveillance and the consumerism of 'reality' surveillance television – was faced, too immediately to fully theorize answers, with September 11's massive failure of security, the world-wide engagement in repetitive 'reality television' disaster viewing and the governmental response of such legislation as the US Patriot Act, with its vastly increased powers of citizen surveillance. All that the exhibition, publication and festival could really do was register the strange, heavy fact of September 11 in the midst of the sophisticated, complex, probing artwork on display.

In this chapter and the next, I want to look at some of the art and performance work that has been created in the context of surveillance technology, as a means of exploring ways in which such work can help us to think about, respond to, and live in, surveillance space. I have chosen a range of pieces of work to look at, some of it by artists also featured in the *CTRL [SPACE]* exhibition, although usually looking at other examples of their work. I have also chosen some work by artists who are not overtly dealing with surveillance as a theme, but who use surveillance-related tools and techniques to create their works. I am interested here in surveillance less as a subject matter than as a kind of space. As we have already, in previous chapters, developed a particular theoretical perspective on surveillance by examining its uses and appearances in a variety of cultural situations, I am asking of the art work examined here not that it explains to us what we should think of surveillance, but rather that it help us explore ways of living in surveillance society. Again, the art work I am examining is pre-September 11; some – including

Bruce Nauman's seminal work – is over thirty years old. However, with some distance now between us and the events of 2001, we can perhaps start to see how, by examining the ways in which surveillance produces new spatial experiences, these works have in fact introduced us to a mode of experience that does have very direct relevance to the post-September 11 issues of state, security, secrecy and surveillance.

In the first three chapters of this study, I have argued that the experience of surveillance technologies in contemporary society is fundamentally spatial, and that a productive relationship to these technologies is available when the subject 'uptakes' the spatial nature of the surveillance experience. However, a question hangs over this argument – a question of the status of this proposed surveillance space. Is surveillance space a metaphor, a borrowing of the term 'space' to describe certain shared experiences, or does surveillance space have its own status, its own structure? If the latter is the case, can the subject exist within surveillance space, or only outside it, looking in or towards? And if we can be inside surveillance space, what is the ontology of that being? How does it affect, relate to or corrupt our naturalized experience of 'dimensional' space?

In the next two chapters, I will be examining the work of artists who have specifically intervened in these questions, and relating their work to that of thinkers who question common-sense notions of space. In Chapter 5, I will examine works which in some way 'survey' their audience: incorporating the image of the viewer into the work. First, though, I want to examine works of art and performance that use surveillance and related technologies in a more self-contained way. In contrast to most of the videos and images discussed in previous chapters, I will here be using examples of work that is three-dimensional – performance, installation and interactive art – to examine the relationship of surveillance to dimensions, volume and presence.

## Abstract space

So what is surveillance space like? Does it have dimensions? Can we get 'inside' it? Is it real? In *The Production of Space*, Henri Lefebvre (1991) argues that the space in which we live is always produced.

That is to say, it is the result of social relations, ideological concepts and our imaginings. Lefebvre suggests that the production of space is central to historical development and that rather than being a neutral background to, say, economic history, space is the site of power and transformation which underlies and links other progressions. Specifically, Lefebvre argues that the concept of what he calls 'abstract space' – the modern conception of space as a theoretical void to be filled – is a particular historical construct. Abstract space, he suggests, develops under capitalism out of an earlier concept of absolute space – the holy or damned space marked off from general daily space. With the Cartesian world-view as a crucial point of philosophical transition, abstract space – a geometrical emptiness to be filled by the creations of God or man – shifts the conceptualizing of divine or philosophical space from absolute space's geographical separation towards the notion of a pre-existing, structuring framework for all spatial possibilities. Lefebvre (ibid.: 298) notes that abstract space, even (or particularly) in its appearance as the justification of modernist architectural theory, is a 'false consciousness', an ideologically naturalized screen hiding the dynamics of power.

Lefebvre's political contextualization of abstract space helps us to understand the relation of spaces of surveillance to the thought of 'real', dimensional space. Following Lefebvre, it is this latter space, organized through a concept of geometry, that is ideological, whereas our experience of surveillance, lived and felt in spatial terms, may be a real aspect of the space produced in contemporary society. Lefebvre also suggests that contradictions are embedded in the capitalist development of abstract space and that there is reason to hope and aim for a new experience of space, 'differential space', in which 'The truth of space reveals what mental space and social space have in common – and consequently also the differences between them' (ibid.: 399), i.e. where an ideology of space is not allowed to obscure the social experience.

Surveillance space may be analysed as a field where differential space potentially emerges, carrying within itself simultaneous, linked and yet also irreconcilable aspects of the mental and the social. It will be entirely in line with Lefebvre's thinking if we find the differential potentials of surveillance space most fully explored in works of art and performance:

Theoretical thought, carrying reflection on the subject and the object beyond the old concepts, has re-embraced the body along with space, in space, and as the generator (or producer) of space. To say that such theoretical thinking goes 'beyond discourse' means that it takes account, for the purposes of a pedagogy of the body, of the vast store of non-formal knowledge embedded in poetry, music, dance and theater. This store of non-formal knowledge (non-savoir) constitutes a potential true knowledge (connaissance).

(Ibid.: 407)

## Interiors

One of the elements of 'real' space that is immediately problematized by surveillance technology is the very notion of 'dimensions'. Jonas Dahlberg has played amusingly with this feature of surveillance. In 1999, at the Hannover Kunstverein and again during the *CTRL [SPACE]* exhibition at ZKM, Dahlberg placed monitors outside the institution's public toilets, which seemed to present a very revealing view of the toilet spaces themselves. If viewers were uninhibited or desperate enough to go through the doors and into the toilets, however, they found that, although the images shown outside were indeed live images from inside the toilets, what they actually showed were in fact minutely detailed models of the toilet space, which were attached to the toilet walls and were being recorded live by surveillance cameras pointing only at the tiny models.

Dahlberg's piece ultimately rewards us, if we are bold, with an explanation of the dimensional trick. A less immediate, but ultimately more worrying piece by Gary Perkins refuses such reassurance. *–15° at 60 mph* uses a tiny closed-circuit surveillance camera to reveal the surprising interior of a closed space. Michael Archer and Greg Hilty, the curators of the Hayward Gallery's *Material Culture* exhibition, in which the work was shown, describe it as follows:

The work itself is made in two parts. The first part, sitting to the right on a shelf wall, is a 1:24 scale plastic hobby kit model of a refrigerated trailer. Immaculately assembled and minutely detailed with licence plate and statutory stickers, it has also been carefully 'weathered' to give it the appearance of having travelled many hundreds of miles. On another shelf a

135

few feet to the left, a small monitor shows the interior of what appears to be a studio or workshop, not cluttered, but full of materials. It is clear only from the physical relationship of the two parts that the video is relaying in real time the interior of the trailer, like an image of the abstracted mind space within the closed container sitting next to it.

(Archer and Hilty, 1997)

It is interesting that the curators, whose exhibition focused on the object in British Art of the previous twenty years, 'questioning what an object is and how far it can be defined in different directions', jump so quickly from materiality to the 'image of the abstracted mind space' in explaining a work which makes no specific reference to mental processes. It is as though the overlaying of two spaces in one space necessarily brings about an appeal to a pre-existing conceptual space. In Lefebvre's terms, this reading of Perkins' work reasserts a higher Cartesian space in which the contradictions of the juxtaposition can be resolved.

However, such an appeal to abstract space does not respond to the crisis of dimensions pointed to by Perkins and Dahlberg; rather it provides a refuge from the crisis, in a metaphorical elsewhere. Moreover, such a refuge is not really needed if we can accept that dimensions may, in certain cases, not be absolute. My own experience of –15° at 60 mph was the opposite of the curators' – at first (not knowing much about the inside of transport containers) I assumed that the inside of the model truck was what was on show on the monitor, but after a while I began to think that maybe this was a trick, and I started to stare at the on-video workspace for the sign of a body entering, a live body which would fix the dimensions and reveal the joke.

My crisis of dimensions in viewing –15° at 60 mph had little to do with the squeezing of abstracted mental space within a 1:24 scale model. Rather, I was confronted with the simultaneous possibility of two differing real spaces: the inside of the small container and the interior of a full-scale workshop. The nature of surveillance technology made it impossible to judge between the two. The technology, seemingly absolute in its representational clarity, was revealed as unable to indicate a most basic spatial value – size. In relation to this dilemma, Perkins' use of the transport container – an object whose only characteristics are its standardizations – of size, temperature, etc. – is productively ironic, and the piece's title, mentioning two of the standardized elements, speed and temperature (neither of which of course are relevant to the stationary, unrefrigerated model), and ignoring the crucial issue of dimensions, doubles the irony.

The curators' appeal to 'abstracted mind space' in analysing *–15° at 60 mph* humanizes the work, implying that the artist's creativity has in some way rescued the bleak standardization of container space. A reading that emphasizes the role of the surveillance technology in the piece, however, allows us to see how this humanizing instinct plays into the ideologies implicated by Lefebvre in the concept of abstract space.

Replacing the appeal to abstract space, we experience *–15° at 60 mph* as a work which confronts the phenomenon of standardization with a crisis of dimensions, which raises the possibility that in a world of increasing standardization, driven by commercial systems, the very guarantee of relative dimensional value begins to collapse. A centimetre may as well be a metre inside the monitor's image. The more we keep a watchful eye, the less we can distinguish what we see. Following Lefebvre, it is only in the reassertion of differentiality, or spaces irreducible to the abstract, that any value can re-emerge.

## Child-like dimensions

The resonances of the question around dimensionality raised by surveillance video technology are underlined by a brief return to the Bulger case examined in Chapter 1. The surveillance video imagery remembered by thousands of people shows two ten-year-old boys leading away a two-year-old in a shopping mall. Much of the public horror around the crime related to the ages of Thompson and Venables, and watching the video it is hard not to collage the surveillance shots with subsequent photos of two fresh-faced little boys. However, when the police originally viewed the surveillance footage, they assumed that the images were of two teenagers, aged fifteen or sixteen. It was a subsequently discovered security video of the boys outside, away from the shopping mall, walking past a low wall, which revealed their true dimensions. When police visited the site shown on this second footage, they realized just how low the wall was, and therefore how small the boys must be. It was at this point that they put out an appeal for witnesses who had seen two boys of about ten years walking with a boy of two. This detail points us again to the question of dimensions – of what fits in what – and the framework of abstract space. The debate as to whether or not ten-year-old boys can 'be evil' might be rephrased as a question of whether evil can fit inside such small bodies. Interviews with police, lawyers and psychologists all emphasize the shock at meeting Thompson and Venables in real life and realizing how small they were.[1] Even after adjusting their understanding of the surveillance footage to see ten-year-old rather than teenage boys, they were not prepared for the shock of relating the size of the boys to their own bodies. For the public, of course, traumatized by the visual imagery of the abduction, there was no such moment of relativity. It may be that the outpouring of hatred for the perpetrators of this crime was partly permitted by the collapse of dimensional relations under surveillance technology: on video, the boys can seem big enough to fit evil inside. If this is so, then there is surely an added relevance to work which questions and explores the relations of surveillance imagery to dimensional understanding.

## Lurking within

Bruce Nauman's installation, *Learned Helplessness in Rats (Rock and Roll Drummer)* (1988), also explores the irreducibility of surveyed space and imagery to a unified, abstracted notion. The installation is usually shown in a partially walled-off gallery area where a rotating surveillance camera watches an empty Plexiglas maze about nine inches high. The live image of the maze is transmitted on a monitor, but it is alternated with recorded footage of the same maze with rats running inside. Meanwhile, a video projector shows a rock drummer, while the sound of the drums plays loudly over speakers. The piece is based upon an article in *Scientific American* describing how rats behaved helplessly when subjected to strong auditory stress. It is a disorienting piece to view – the doubling of the empty maze with the rat-filled maze plus the movements of the camera and the high-volume drumming lead to an initial confusion. There seems to be a lot happening in the maze, although in fact nothing is happening. The space is restructured by the surveillance doubling; empty Plexiglas easily viewed from above becomes an anxiety-ridden labyrinth in which terrifying animals may be lurking.

In *Learned Helplessness in Rats (Rock and Roll Drummer)*, Nauman is concerned with, among other things, the question of behavioural modification. As Robert Storr (1997: 94) points out, 'the signs of frustrated habit in the movements of the boy [the drummer] and the rat are painfully similar', and Nauman is consciously referring to the possibility that behavioural modification techniques may teach us helplessness rather than sociability. There is a fairly direct comment about surveillance here. The ideology of surveillance proliferation suggests, as we have seen, that surveillance will both reveal crime and make it disappear. Nauman's installation suggests that the stress of existence under a bombardment of technology is as likely to cause a helpless madness as it is to bring about containment.

However, Nauman's placement of his socio-scientific commentary within a surveillance environment has effects beyond ideological critique. Nauman doubles the interior of the maze with itself, the two versions separated by time. The presence of the rat in the monitor's maze, with these shots identical in placement to the live shots of the maze, leads us to assume that a rat was previously in the maze. (Rat droppings in the real empty maze reinforce this supposition.) Perhaps the rat has escaped, perhaps it is dead. The likelihood of these possibilities is, however, lessened by the recorded rat footage, which implies an intention to the difference between live and recorded imagery, and therefore ultimately leads us to assume that the rat has been deliberately removed. To reassure ourselves of the intentional distinction between live and recorded we perhaps bend over the maze or poke our feet towards the boundaries of the camera's trajectory, hoping to catch our own bodies in the rat-free images, and thus separate the two versions of the space with something other than the missing rat.

*Learned Helplessness in Rats (Rock and Roll Drummer)* suggests that, rather than guarding us against crime and unpleasantness, surveillance imagery may introduce demons into the spaces we inhabit. The rat in this piece does not disappear once we realize the emptiness of the maze. Under the auditory stress of the high-volume drumming, we worry about the rat, about why it has been introduced, about the way in which it separates the maze from its images, the images from each other. The present meaning of the work becomes dependent upon the surveillance insertion of what has been removed. Surveillance imagery defines the experience of the space we are inhabiting. Unlike our usual experience of inhabiting surveyed space, however, the camera is carefully positioned so that it will not see us. We are, in this work, caught between the two normal positions of surveyor and surveyed. We inhabit a surveyed space yet are separated out of the surveying. We inhabit a surveyor's view, yet we are removed from the image that fascinates and repels.

Nauman's installation consciously plays with many of the characteristics we have noted in relation to surveillance space: the importance of the boundaries of the surveyed field, the collapse of time (the recorded rat may actually be a live rat elsewhere, the recording of the rat defines our present experience), sound as disorienting and nonsensical (like the codes of audio surveillance), the silent surveillance image, the incorporation of the absent viewer (we are absent from the images, but we are drawn into the space and meaning of the work). Nauman disrupts and explores these characteristics through the simple but extremely effective technique of editing past footage into present surveillance. This doubling of the surveillance space, coupled with the choice of a rat as the signifier of the difference, makes us startlingly aware of how deeply the characteristics of surveillance space trouble us. When the rat, an animal and signifier to which most of us display some degree of phobic response, is the marker of the boundaries of surveillance, its temporal and sonic disruptions, we discover that we do not trust the characteristics of Euclidean geometry or Cartesian philosophy to hold this surveillance rat at bay. In surveillance space, the absent rat becomes perhaps more terrifying than a present rat captured by the camera's gaze. The rat's absence threatens to bite us.

(Of course, the rats also provide a direct link to Orwell's *Nineteen Eighty-Four*, in which it is exposure to rats that ultimately breaks Winston Smith's resistance to Big Brother. In 2001, Newcastle's Northern Stage created a powerful stage version of *Nineteen Eighty-Four*. The introduction of the rats to Smith in room 101 was shown by having the actor playing Smith strapped into an empty 'face-cage', while on vast projection screens rats were seen in a similar cage. The doubling of the empty and rat-filled cages, plus the dimensional distortion of the rats, seen in images much larger that the live actor, created a shocking effect.)

## Representational spaces

We could say that Naumann and Perkins are consciously producing new kinds of space, irreducible to three-dimensional understandings. In Lefebvre's terms, the production of space involves three strands:

1 Spatial practice: the structures, behaviours and relationships that constitute a society's spatial organization.
2 Representations of space: the idea of space that we conceptualize.[2]
3 Representational spaces: 'space as directly lived through its associated images and symbols' (Lefebvre, 1991: 39).[3]

Lefebvre also describes these three strands as 'the triad of the perceived, the conceived and the lived' (ibid.: 39). Of course, the operations of this triad are not independent. Nor, despite Lefebvre's description of conceptualized space as 'the dominant space in any society', are their relative values immutable. Ultimately, Lefebvre tends towards a post-Marxist position which implies that action in the 'lived' field can impact upon the conceived and the perceived.

Works such as *Learned Helplessness in Rats* and *–15° at 60 mph* relate to Lefebvre's distinction between 'lived space' and 'conceptualized space', between 'representational spaces' and 'representations of space'. Both artists insist on placing us within 'representational spaces' – feeling our own bodily and psychic relation to the distortions of normative space enacted by surveillance technologies. They disallow a closure to the experience – a descriptive gesture or summation that would allow us to 'see' this space in our minds. The dilemmas of dimensions and doubling, the temporal disruptions of the spatial field, enacted in these pieces make a mental view of the spaces we are inhabiting impossible. These works describe our spatial surveillance experience by inviting us to live for a moment in a state removed from ideological orientation. Disallowing the conceptualizing position, they encourage us to feel, to live surveillance.

Lefebvre warns us, however, not to reduce this triad of perceived, conceptualized and lived space to a dualism. While there is undoubtedly a progressive narrative in his book which hopes to replace the conceptual dominance of abstract space with the openness of differential space, the question of spatial practice – the day-to-day experience of moving and acting in space – remains equally important. For surveillance art, the link to daily spatial practice is particularly apparent. We still do not see a surveillance camera in a gallery without thinking of surveillance cameras in the streets. Nor does this relation fall easily into one of representational reference: the gallery camera does not seem to stand in for the street camera; rather it is the same technology and does the same things. Disallowing a conceptualization of our spatial experience, a reduction of our relationship with surveillance to an opinion, surveillance art may impact directly (even viscerally) on our spatial practice, on our behaviour in our spatial environment and on our assent or dissent in relation to that environment's developments.

## Performativity and representational space

This particular tendency of surveillance art to link directly with social/spatial practice is at least in part a consequence of the performative nature of surveillance space. Whereas non-performative representations allow the viewer an external relationship to the represented via representation, performative space brings the viewer into the space constructed. As in performative language, in which one of the key factors in 'happiness' of the performative utterance is the status of the auditor (Austin, 1976: 34–5), so in performative space, the space does not exist without the viewer/auditor's implication. Finding it impossible to establish a subject–object relation to the surveillance art work, as he or she is implicated within it, the viewer is equally unable to identify a referent for this non-object, be that referent an object per se, an emotion, a concept or a critique. Instead, the surveillance art viewer lives within the space of the work in the same sense that the auditor of a performative utterance lives within the new reality created by the speaking and uptake of that utterance. And such implication in the performative – as the Austinian examples of the marriage vow, the wager and the promise remind us – is no light matter.

142

This performative involvement of the viewer/auditor in the spaces of surveillance art sits nicely with Lefebvre's definition of a space 'directly lived through its associated images and symbols', although there is, of course, also a tension between Lefebvre's reliance on representation and Austin's distrust of the 'constative' tradition of language as reference. In both theories, however, and in surveillance space as we have analysed it, it is the move away from an absolute referent – real or abstract – which is key.

## Inside spaces

To help us more fully understand the experience of lived space, Lefebvre takes us inside the body. 'The heart as *lived* is strangely different from the heart as *thought* and *perceived*' (Lefebvre, 1991: 48). That is to say, the representational space of the heart is lived as a mixture of emotions, traditions and associations which do not equate with the conceptual realm of medical knowledge or the social perception of the heart as engine of the body's movements and spatial relations. ('This holds a fortiori', adds Lefebvre, 'for the sexual organs.')

In Mona Hatoum's works *Corps Étranger* (1994) and *Deep Throat* (1996), the artist uses a camera inserted inside the orifices and passages of her body to explore such complications in a way which relates very directly to questions of surveillance. In his introduction to the New Museum of Contemporary Art's New York showing of Hatoum's work, Don Cameron (1998) describes *Corps Étranger*:

> Using techniques of microscopic photography most closely associated with exploratory surgery, the artist began the work by passing a camera throughout her body cavity, inserting it in each orifice and extending it as far as possible. Splicing the footage together into a consistent loop, Hatoum added a soundtrack consisting of magnified sounds of the body's internal organs. The video is projected onto the floor of a half-open oval container into which the viewer must enter to see the work clearly. The viewer's required position – standing over the projected image of the body's interior – creates a sense of vertigo, heightened by the degree of magnification and the relatively claustrophobic space.

In relation to the social space of the body, Hatoum's work refers to each of the strands identified by Lefebvre. In terms of spatial practice, it points to the processes of eating, swallowing, digesting, defecating that define much of our social activity and spatial organization. In terms of the conceptual, it draws upon the medical knowledge and techniques whereby we know the anatomy and behaviour of the body's interior and act upon it. As representational space, the work refers to and conjures up our fears and fascinations in relation to the body's interior.

As the video footage alone, *Corps Étranger* might sit uneasily between these strands, pointing to each without particularly exploring our relation to any. However, as Cameron's description indicates, the piece is as much about how the footage is projected and framed as it is about the visual field it represents. By her structuring of a space which the viewer inhabits from the stuff of her own interior, Hatoum disrupts entirely the relations of inner and outer that prevail in both spatial practice and conceptual systems of the body. In *Corps Étranger*, an interior becomes our exterior, what is inside is larger than what is outside, our own interiors are doubled, projected on and around us, what should be invisible (interior organs) is on view in an endlessly looped world.[4]

Placing us in a dimensional work comprising not just imagery, but our positioning in relation to this imagery, Hatoum creates not a representation of a space elsewhere, nor a practice, a behaviour within space, but a new space, a space previously unimagined, and in an impossible relationship to hegemonic space.

Hatoum's piece carries echoes of characteristics we have seen in Perkins' and Nauman's surveillance-based art works. The question of dimensions and the experience of doubling are important aspects of the feelings we have standing in the cylinder of *Corps Étranger*. That the magnified footage refers to a part of ourselves inaccessible to our own eyes, our own direct knowledge, places the work on a border which we could label either as the point beyond which we have moved on from surveillance or as the point at which surveillance is further heightened. In either case, Hatoum's work refers us back to Chapter 2's exploration of the differing 'masculinized' and 'feminized' surveillance spaces, reminding us that much of surveillance, associated with the latter part of this binary, is about what cannot be seen. Hatoum's piece penetrates the boundary of this not-to-be-seen and explores what happens when it becomes seen. Hatoum suggests that this process is more complex than an increasing colonialism of the gaze, that as the spaces of the body are projected over and around our exterior, they refer us back to the still unknown space inside us, never seen by our own eye.

## Deep throat

In her later work *Deep Throat*, Hatoum makes a more specific reference to issues of the gendered gaze. In this piece, similar footage is used to create a rather different representational space. The piece consists of a table set for one, with white table cloth, cutlery and plate. Footage of Hatoum's digestive tract is projected onto the base of the plate, so that the viewer/diner can see it where food should be. Hatoum's title for this piece refers us, of course, to the infamous porn movie, in which Linda Lovelace's character discovers that she needs to fellate oversized penises to achieve orgasm, since her clitoris is located in her throat. Here, Hatoum indicates, is the shot sought after by the pornographic gaze, the interior of the woman, finally revealed. Yet this interior displays not the elusive sign of female pleasure, but digestion, bits of food clinging to the lining of the oesophagus. As in *Corps Étranger,* our own interior is referenced by the footage of Hatoum's. The plate reflects the processes that we will normally go through as the diner, once food is swallowed. Yet this reflection is not a mirroring exactly, since in swallowing the camera's gaze the work interrupts our own swallowing, denies us our food. As in *Learned Helplessness in Rats*, *Deep Throat* enacts a doubling of a temporally displaced process – the rats' presence, our own swallowing – making us aware of our present response to this conjured absence. It is not the representation of the rats or of the swallowing per se that repels or fascinates, it is the effect that this represented absence has upon the present space. In the case of *Deep Throat*, we are also made aware, with the title's help, of a contextual desire (not necessarily of the viewer, but of the visual symbolic realm in which the viewer functions) to penetrate the female unseen. As the camera fails to satisfy this desire, the doubling with our own interior creates, perhaps, a strange mixed awareness of inner emptiness and secrecy.

## Bodies and organs

In his discussion of the body as exemplifying the distinctions of perceived, conceived and lived space, Lefebvre refers, almost in passing, to the work of Antonin Artaud:

> Localizations can absolutely not be taken for granted where the lived experience of the body is concerned: under the pressure of morality, it is even possible to achieve the strange result of a body without organs – a body chastised, as it were, to the point of being castrated.
>
> (Lefebvre, 1991: 40)

Lefebvre's comment relates strangely to Artaud's notorious desire for the body without organs, analysed at length in Deleuze and Guattari's *Anti-Oedipus* (1983). Whereas, for Artaud, the body without organs is an unrealizable desire, for Lefebvre it seems to be an unpleasant possibility. Perhaps it is partly to keep his systematic inquiry at arm's length from the celebration of such extreme notions in Deleuze and Guattari's work that Lefebvre brackets the body without organs as an entirely negative product of morality. However, this body without organs is introduced in relation to the discussion of the perceived–conceived–lived spatial triad, and, in fact, Lefebvre implies that the body without organs can exist only in the realm of the 'lived', of representational spaces.

Works such as Hatoum's *Deep Throat* and *Corps Étranger* relate intriguingly to the Artaudian concept of body without organs: 'The body is the body/it is all by itself/and has no need of organs/the body is never an organism/organisms are the enemy of the body.' (Artaud quoted in Deleuze and Guattari, 1983: 9). In Hatoum's pieces the interior organs themselves become apparently organless: smooth, seamless trajectories of swallowing, ingestion, inseparable into organic parts. Our own bodies are reflected in these moist surroundings, interior become exterior – food, habitat. The largest organ of all, the skin, which separates us from the outside, is sidestepped.

The Artaudian fantasy, celebrated by Deleuze and Guattari as an aspect of the schizophrenic state which they suggest potentially disrupts the stabilities and repressions of social organization, would seem to arise far more centrally than Lefebvre implies in any analysis

Dimensions, doubles and data

of 'lived' spatial representations dealing with the body. Indeed the contradictions of the body without organs are to an extent inherent in an understanding of the body which is simultaneously lived and representational: as Hatoum's work suggests, a constructed spatial experience of the body disrupts the stability of bodily organs – a stability which is always at least in part dependent upon conceptualization – and delivers us into a fluid, unboundaried realm where the body no longer obeys the rule of organic order and proportion.

Inherent to this experience in Hatoum's work is the doubling of the body – the placing of the artist's unboundaried interior in relation to our own body with its interior hidden from sight by its exterior. The notion of doubling is, of course, another key Artaudian term, and is one which can, I think, be used to examine in more detail the ways in which the representational spaces of surveillance draw upon the possibilities of both performativity and performance.

## Inside out

Artaud's notion of the theatrical double is both evocative and elusive. In his theatre manifestos Artaud (1958) implies that, if theatre is liberated from the script, from the requirement to represent a realistic world as imagined by an author, it has the potential instead to refer to, or even embody, another spiritual/mystic realm of intensified states, beyond the material/organic. This other world, the world of the double, the self beyond the mortal body, is conjured particularly by physical, representational and (to a degree) linguistic excess, or heightenedness: hence Artaud's taste for extreme physical action, spectacles of death, and Romantic poetry. If such demands seem clichéd now, this only emphasizes Artaud's influence on the performance world in the second half of the twentieth century, from Grotowski to Fura Del Baus to Pina Bausch.

The doubled body is closely related to the body without organs, though Artaud tends to use the former term (sparingly) to express his theatrical intentions and the latter primarily in relation to his own psychic dilemmas. The doubled body carries a spiritual, symbolic and social impact, separate from (though not independent of) the organic body. The doubled body is revealed, achieved and possibly lived in as a result of the exertions and cruelty placed upon the organic body.

147

In the works of body surveillance described above, Hatoum seems to double not only her own body with the invasive video footage, but also ours. The eternally looped intestines projected over and around us, or into the place of our food, take our minds in the opposite direction to our eyes, travelling about our own insides. However, we cannot, in these installations, think of our interiors simply as functional (perceived) or scientifically known (conceived) spaces. As our eyes focus on Hatoum's apparently unending intestines, we begin to live our insides, and to see the silent, invisible ways in which these insides function in our lives. Hatoum's work reveals our interiors as lived spaces – as representational spaces. That is to say, our actual inner digestive organs are doubled by an experience of the significance of our insides.

As with the Artaudian theatrical double, this experience of our insides in Hatoum's work cannot be put simply into words (reconceptualized). At least as long as we stand in the space of these pieces, our own insides become part of a spatial structure that is irreducible to a concept. (Indeed, the very title of the work *Corps Étranger* enacts its own doubling, pointing us both to the correct translation, 'foreign body', and to the mistranslation we hear in the sound of the words – 'strange corpse'. This sound play in the title reminds us, of course, that the doubled body also inevitably introduces death.)

## Surveillance and its double

*Corps Étranger* brings the viewer physically inside the artwork. Nauman's *Learned Helplessness in Rats,* by contrast, uses surveillance technology itself, rather than physical structures, to place the audience in relation to the work. The positioning of the surveillance camera in this piece means that it scans the Plexiglas maze to its very border, to the point where the audience stands, but it does not cross that border. The audience is excluded from the frame, held tantalizingly at its margins. As noted above, the desire to separate definitively the recorded rat footage from the live imagery intensifies our wish to bend or poke our way into the frame of the surveillance shot, but this cannot be achieved without potentially damaging the maze (an infringement which would not only incur the watching museum guard's wrath, but might also be recorded by the camera). We wander around the work, included but not seen, our visual absence adding to worries already generated by the absent rat. It is as though the rat has displaced us, taken our rightful place on screen. In this way the rat, already doubled by the live/recorded versions of the maze, also doubles as us, becomes our body in the transparent, surveyed labyrinth. Nauman neatly evokes a simultaneous desire to be allowed into the surveillance picture and a horror at our metaphorical presentation within it. His work allows a simultaneous but dissatisfying experience of the two desiring positions examined in Chapter 2 – for narcissistic display and for unrepresentable subjectivity.

In Nauman's work, then, we see that the doubling of the audience body can be achieved in surveillance space without any appearance of a human body. (The drummer in the work is outside the surveillance space, though producing its raucous soundtrack.) In fact, we sense in all of the work described above, that the pushing of the audience body to the edge of the space's frame, far from excluding us, or giving us an external perspective on the work, includes us viscerally through the experience of surveillance doubling.

## Brace up

A good test of this hypothesis is provided by the work of The Wooster Group. Although descended from the quintessentially Grotowskian Performance Group, The Wooster Group has been notable for its re-distancing of the theatrical production from its audience – to the degree that the group's work (alongside that of contemporaries Richard Foreman and Robert Wilson) can seem hermetically sealed, a self-contained world of auto-referenced complexity. Within its work, The Wooster Group has long made extensive and sophisticated use of video and sound technology. Video may be used to introduce sequences previously recorded (such as the 'porn movie' in *Frank Dell's The Temptation of St Anthony*, 1987), to represent those performers who cannot be present owing to other commitments, to give a second view of what is happening within the stage area and most recently, to create a score, seen only by the performers, for them to respond to (*To You, The Birdie!*, 2002). In the company's version of Chekhov's *Three Sisters, Brace Up* (1991), video cameras were particularly used to show action happening in a partially obscured area at the back of the stage.

Unlike conventional theatre's use of video technology, which is usually restricted to televisual effects such as the close-up, The Wooster Group uses video to heighten and complexify the stage space in which the actors are performing. So, in the *Three Sisters* dinner scene, the cast were deliberately placed upstage, off the raised hydraulic platform that is always the company's main playing area, obscured by bars and rails. The video monitors took centre stage, and microphones relayed the conversation, although the video did not necessarily show the face of the speaking performer. As opposed to simply giving us 'more detail' with close-up, or making metaphoric references to the manipulation of television, The Wooster Group used video to displace the body within the performance space, pushing it to the edges, while redoubling it at the centre.

As such, the performers in *Brace Up* were periodically close to inhabiting the position we inhabit in *Learned Helplessness in Rats*: held beyond the perimeter of surveillance inclusion. As the audience watching this spectacle from the other side of the stage area, firmly beyond this line, we became aware of the fragile, incomplete nature of the performance space, the difficulty of physically inhabiting it. The performers' bodies, particularly in the weary world of *Three Sisters*, seemed unable to push themselves for too long to the stage centre, depending upon technology to transport them (unreliably) as they muttered and fiddled at the edges. Just beyond these edges ourselves, we felt our own displacement doubled in that of the actors, and the exclusion, the ironic distance characteristic of the audience's experience of many 'postmodern' performances, transformed into a powerful sense of loss, inertia and frustration. Unlike traditional productions of *Three Sisters*, which engage the audience through character empathy combined with a historically distant overview of the play's world, *Brace Up* used its technology and structuring to create an emotional architecture for the audience. As such, while never undergoing an identification with the characters, the audience experienced a structure which equated with the world of the play. Within this structure, the wholeness of identification was replaced by the disruption of inclusion. Rather than viewing a representation of space on the stage, we were incorporated into a new representational space. As with the other art works discussed in this chapter, this incorporation into surveillance space was achieved via a doubling of the audience's bodies, in this case by the bodies of the actors, held, like us, at the edges of the representational frame.

## The borders of death

Another way in which *Brace Up* related to the Artaudian notion of the double was through the experience of death in the performance. It was suggested in Chapter 3 that, in so far as the surveillance camera's gaze is always about its limits, it is also about death. *Brace Up* was a performance of surveillance that emphasized the limits of the stage, and it had a particularly direct relationship to death and dying.

The second oldest character in *Three Sisters* (a play in which the healthily middle-aged bemoan their advanced years) is the doctor, Chebutykin. Played in *Brace Up* by Paul Schmidt, writer, academic and translator of the Chekhov text for this production, Chebutykin rarely appeared on-stage; instead Schmidt sat in the upstage border area, relayed into the action by camera and microphone. The oldest character, the serving woman/nurse, Anfisa, was actually beyond the limit of the stage. As Kate Valk explained when introducing the character, the actress playing Anfisa was too old to leave her nursing home and was therefore shown on prerecorded video. (In case we might take all this too literally, septuagenarian performance artist Beatrice Roth played the ingénue Irina with gusto, centre stage.)

The progressive ageing out of characters from the live performance space implied that beyond this space lies death. When the camera succeeded in folding the ageing bodies back into the performance, it did so imperfectly. Anfisa's lines were caught in loops or fast forwarded. Eventually, we felt, the technology would not be able to hold on to the bodies. Beyond the limit of the stage and the camera, the audience perhaps felt a shudder of death.

My own experience of death in *Brace Up*, and that of many others, was undoubtedly heightened by the fact that this is the last Wooster Group work in which I saw Ron Vawter perform. Vawter was a key collaborator in a series of Wooster Group works, much admired for his ability to create an extremely complex performance without seeming to 'act', without, that is, attempting to create a coherent character or present a history other than his own. In pieces such as *Frank Dell's Temptation of St Anthony*, Vawter would often stand downstage centre, muttering into the microphone, redefining the audience's understanding of charisma. Vawter's seemingly direct presence was, however, always mediated. The microphone was rarely absent; the performance took place within a complexly ordered structure of mechanical effects, video and sound recording. The apparent bareness of Vawter's performance, in fact, had its effect only in relation to this mediated world of which he was co-creator.

In *Brace Up,* Vawter 'played' Versinin, the melancholy Lieutenant Colonel, who pronounces that 'the day will come when everything which seems essential to us now will be forgotten, or seem futile' (Chekhov, 1979: 12). Like most Wooster Group pieces, *Brace Up* showed for several years in various stages of development. But by the time of Vawter's last run in the show, it was public knowledge that he was dying of AIDS. For many of the audience at these shows, the performances were as much about the dying of Vawter as anything. There he stood, this strangely charismatic man, bald and middle-aged but notoriously sexually attractive, seemingly at the height of his powers, yet publicly dying. With the resonances of Chekhov's text and the memory of other Wooster Group works echoing through the performance, the audience strained to see in this parade of loss – these many texts of loss – the agency of death, disease, terror, that is taking things away from us even as we feel, like Versinin, that we have already lost them.[5]

The visual and aural structure of *Brace Up* – the technological centring of that which is disappearing or barely overheard; the emphasis on the limitations, the edges, of the performance space; the disregard of the audience beyond the line of the stage, the surveyable – this structure becomes retrospectively a place where we can experience the aporia of Vawter's social death, the loss of an extraordinary artist. This effect is enhanced by the fact that *Brace Up* (like much of The Wooster Group's work) spills out beyond itself, reminding us subsequently that part of what was seen was the limit of seeing. At Vawter's memorial service – packed with thousands who had seen his performance – video footage was played of Vawter-as-Versinin in the final act of *Three Sisters,* an act which was never performed as part of *Brace Up.* Takes were shown of Versinin's 'farewell' speech, with Vawter periodically asking for more glycerine to make him cry. (Those familiar with The Wooster Group's work know that these 'out-of-character' moments are at least as likely to make it into the eventual performance as the speech itself.) This final act of *Three Sisters* had, it seems, already been planned as an element of a production separate from *Brace Up*, with Vawter performing Versinin's role on video, and indeed The Wooster Group went on to make this piece, *Fish Story* (1994).[6] Now it is no longer age or the process of dying which separates us from the centre-stage image, it is death itself. At the memorial, this video footage was perhaps the moment in which Vawter least seemed lost, as his mediated absence was so in tune with the performance structures by which we as audience had come to know him. Our attendance at Wooster Group performances, and at *Brace Up* in particular, had prepared us instinctively to accept that the disappearance into death would be balanced by a central appearance on video. This does not mean, however, that the video memorialized or elegized Vawter. Rather, its throwaway qualities made us feel like we were catching a glimpse of Vawter, overhearing him again. And in this circulation of seemingly accidental footage, we were both confronted with, and able to start accepting, his death.

## Stage effects

It was part of Artaud's vision to bring the experience of death to the audience via theatre. Artaud did not necessarily expect real spectacles of sacrifice in the theatre, but he believed that performance could achieve sufficient intensity that the audience would undergo the experience of watching death through the double created by the stage spectacle. By contrast, J.L. Austin used the stage as a prime example of a space in which the performative utterance was unachievable – a marriage vow, an oath, a threat, issued on stage has no real effect: 'a performative utterance will, for example, be *in a peculiar way* hollow or void if said by an actor on the stage, or if introduced in a poem, or spoken in soliloquy' (Austin, 1976: 22, his italics). In my analysis of surveillance space, I have suggested that we can 'uptake' a performative space under surveillance, a space which differs from conventional space in its relation to time, to borders and to our own bodies. In this chapter, I have gone on to argue that this performative space is akin to Lefebvre's representational/lived space – a space made of representations. To say that performative space is representational is not per se to contradict the Austinian roots of our viewpoint, since the performative utterance in Austin is, of course, 'made of' language – language that is judged primarily by its action, not by its reference (though the two can never be distinct, in Austin or in questions of surveillance). However, at the point that we are discussing consciously constructed art works, we have to ask the Austinian question of whether performativity can continue to function in this 'artificial' environment.

Here, the difference between Tom Joslin's *Silverlake Life* and The Wooster Group's *Brace Up* seems significant. Joslin set out to make a film about his own dying. Via the medium of cheap, ever-present video, we live, as audience, a version of the real death. We inhabit a social space of Joslin's dying, marked by the characteristics of performative surveillance space – the consciousness of edges, the disruption of time. By contrast, in making *Brace Up*, The Wooster Group was undoubtedly dealing with the illness of Vawter as part of the personal and shared material it brought to the piece. However, the work itself does not use imagery of the 'real' dying of Vawter. Vawter is present as a performer; video footage is footage of performances. It would at first seem reasonable to suggest that *Silverlake Life* – dealing directly with representations of reality and yet bringing about new spaces, new experiences, through the ways in which these representations are manipulated – follows a pattern equivalent to that of performative speech, which uses the (representational) structures of language to 'do things'; in contrast, The Wooster Group's performance is artificial, ultimately non-serious. In Artaudian terms, however, a stage performance can evoke its double – a 'spiritual' level of experience, the world of the body without organs. If the body without organs is unthinkable, so, as we have explored at length in Chapter 3, is death. A work such as *Brace Up*, which carefully places the human body in a relation to technology that continually points towards death, allows us to approach the thought of death, even as it remains beyond thought. It is in this artificially constructed environment that we are most able to clear away the paraphernalia of associations (blood, sentiment, the death scene itself) which obscure our approach to this aporia. We have seen that surveillance imagery functions within a framework which refers – through its borders, its silences, its obscurities – to the impossible possibility of death. As a stage work which cites this same framework, *Brace Up* brings about a new space, a new experience in its performance, an experience which, far from being a 'non-serious' version of real death, in fact reintroduces death, newly confronted, in a unique combination of surveillance and the theatrical double.

## Citation and absence

The question of citation, and its relation to representation, is clearly important to an understanding of surveillance space. In his essay 'Signature/Event/Context', Derrida extends Austin's analysis of performativity to reveal the 'iterability' (and hence the writing) underlying all language acts. Derrida (1977: 5) particularly emphasizes the importance of absence in the structure of language:

> The absence of the sender, of the receiver [destinateur] from the mark that he abandons, and which cuts itself off from him and continues to produce effects independently of his presence and of the present actuality of his intentions [vouloir-dire] indeed even after his death, his absence, which moreover belongs to the structure of all writing – and, I shall add further on, of all language in general . . .

Much twentieth-century theatre, particularly in the 'Artaudian' tradition, has laboured under a claim of presence – of the actor, of the event, of the spoken word. In his essay 'La parole soufflée', Derrida (1982: 169–95) deconstructs the concept of present voice in Artaud's writing. However, reading Artaud primarily as a theorist not of presence, but of the double, i.e. of an always emphasized absence, an artificiality of the perceived event which nonetheless conjures another possibility, we have seen how the representational spaces of surveillance may equate in a contemporary culture to Artaud's theatre. It is here that the extension of Lefebvre's notion of representational spaces, in the case of surveillance, into the concept of performative spaces comes into focus. Because the force (to use Derrida's term) of the surveillance space comes not simply from its representational nature, but from its relation to iterability. Moreover, as we saw in Chapter 3, the iterability, the citational frame of surveillance culture consists not primarily of what surveillance shows, but of the ways in which it fails to show. That is to say, surveillance space is not constructed simply, or even primarily, from the scenes and bodies that it seems to reproduce, but from the context of unreproducible moments, obscured events and significant exclusions in relation to which it is structured. Surveillance space does not so much rely upon its referents for effect as it relies upon the absence of its referents. Ultimately, following Derrida (1977: 8), this absence becomes also an absence of producer and audience:

> To be what it is, all writing must, therefore, be capable of functioning in the radical absence of every empirically determined receiver in general. And this absence is not a continuous modification of presence, it is a rupture in presence, the 'death' or the possibility of the 'death' of the receiver inscribed in the structure of the mark . . .

The same death of sender and receiver is inscribed in the experience of surveillance space.

In this deconstruction of Austin, the ghost of intentionality in relation to performativity is put to rest. It is not, in Derrida, the intention of the author which produces writing – and ultimately, therefore, it is not the intention of the speaker which produces the speech act. Rather, performativity is made possible by the machine of writing which produces the language effects within which the speaker/writer moves – just as the machine of surveillance produces the spatial possibilities within which various subjects, with varying degrees of intention, produce performative space:

> For a writing to be a writing it must continue to 'act' and to be readable even when what is called the author of the writing no longer answers for what he has written, for what he seems to have signed, be it because of a temporary absence, because he is dead or, more generally, because he has not employed his absolutely actual and present intention or attention, the plenitude of his desire to say what he means, in order to sustain what seems to be written 'in his name'.
>
> (Ibid.: 8)

It is in the performativity of surveillance space that the profound absence, the death, which frames surveillance is realized. The

Artaudian double brought about in surveillance art works is, then, intimately linked to this performativity.


## Force and weakness

As we saw in Chapter 1, Timothy Gould problematizes Derrida's reading of Austin, emphasizing the degree to which Derrida relies on a concept of force to characterize the performative. Gould suggests that such Nietzschean force has tyrannical associations (the edict of the ruler) equal to those of the constative language tradition. By contrast, Gould emphasizes the delay/suspense inherent to the effects of performativity as a useful counter-balance to this force. He suggests that the 'illocutionary suspense' which comes between uptake of performativity and our response to that uptake introduces an uncertainty that undercuts the tyranny of constative sense and, by extension, of language as force. Similarly, Parker and Sedgwick (1995: 1–16) have suggested that the 'etiolation', the effete, decadent weakness that Austin locates in the stage performance, may, in fact, prove perversely productive, queering the normative stabilities of language. In a performance such as *Brace Up*, we see a performative citation of the framework of surveillance; we also see a stage doubling – a conjuring of what is absent. These two processes come together in this work to produce a resonant experience of death. We might say, following Gould and Parker and Sedgwick that *Brace Up* combines the force of the speech act with the productive weakness of the stage act.[7]


## Data and doubles

These art works which hold us over the border, which deny us the incorporation of our image into their surveillance spaces each in their way double us, incorporating us through our absence. While this experience of exclusion is very different from the daily reproduction we participate in as we pass the massed security cameras of street, store and workplace, it actually relates very closely to an even more common surveillance phenomenon – the electronic database.

In *The Electronic Eye*, David Lyon (1994: 8) centralizes the database in his definition of contemporary surveillance: 'Electronic surveillance has to do with the ways that computer databases are used to store and process information on different kinds of populations.'

Lyon exhaustively charts the extraordinary rise in the past three decades of technology's capability to store, sort and retrieve information on individuals. He also describes the ways in which these information stores transform individuals into statistical/demographic groups. Lyon rightly emphasizes the degree to which the citizen–consumer becomes a member of a majority grouping whose worst fear is to fall out of the data net – to lose credit, insurability, citizen rights – and he neatly identifies a surveillance/surveillance dichotomy, whereby to fall-out of this majority data surveillance net is to become subject to the disciplinary surveillance of the underclass.

> Things have changed since Orwell's time, and consumption for the masses has emerged as the new inclusionary reality. Only the minority, the so-called underclass, whose position prevents them from participating freely in consumption, now experience the hard edge of exclusionary and punitive surveillance.
>
> (Ibid.: 61)

Lyon emphasizes the dual nature of surveillance data – potentially protective (for example in epidemology[8]) as well as invasive. Bearing in mind the arguments of Chapter 2, I would extend this sociological duality to a subjective contradiction – desire for, as well as fear of, surveillance. In an advanced consumer society, in which much of consumer privilege is dependent upon inclusion in data banks – where credit rating is the mark of the successful citizen – protection in relation to data (such as the UK Data Protection Act) has concentrated on an individual's right of access to details stored about him or her. Secondarily, the issue of access to data by others is an issue. (The infamous case of Lotus Household Marketplace, a commercially available database detailing names, addresses and incomes of eighty million American householders, which was eventually withdrawn in response to public, but not legal, pressure, is only the best-known instance of the massive recirculation of information given willingly in credit applications etc.) However, as we attest with every bank form we fill in, in general, worries about how we are represented in data banks are outweighed by our desire to be included as creditworthy data citizens. A greater fear operates in relation to government databases. Here, the Orwellian shadow is longer and an association with negative status – having a police record – operates. (In the USA, most data protection relates to government records.) However, we willingly engage in the rush to be recognized as passport holders, legitimate users of health and social benefits, voters.

If the ideology of surveillance exhibits a marginalized body (the young black male, but also the disabled person and the homosexual) as its legitimate visual object, it should not be surprising if we feel relatively comfortable with the non-visual images of ourselves circulating in data banks, particularly in areas, such as credit listings, to which the marginalized person is unlikely to be permitted full entry. However, the analysis we have undertaken in counterpoint to this ideological frame has suggested that far more complex relations to imagery and reproduction underlie these ideological reassurances. Mark Poster (1990: 98) has suggested that the data files collected on us circulate like extra bodies, with their own lives and histories. In this chapter we have seen how a subject on the invisible side of a representational border discovers his or her self in a very direct relationship to a double created by conscious use of surveillance technologies. What, then, do we feel when we come close to the data selves that circulate on the other side of visibility's horizon?

Our 'data bodies' carry stains that are perhaps harder to clean than mud or sin – the marks of past late payments or motoring offences. They pursue us, confronting us as we apply for mortgages or visas, but they are also manipulated by us, ignorant as they are of our cash transactions or new tattoo. Sociologist Liz Stanley has suggested that such data selves can be, and indeed as a matter of course are, constructed consciously as we respond to the constant pressure of audit.[9] These 'audit selves' are habitually invented to fit the expectations of the particular auditing body – immigration authorities, prospective employers, insurance companies. Gay men in the UK, for example, tend to have two separate medical record selves. One, held by their GP (primary doctor), lists visits for flu and backache and cholesterol tests; the other, held anonymously in a hospital or clinic, carries the result of an HIV test which, whether positive or negative, might destroy the chances of a mortgage or insurance if held in the (unprotected in British law) main medical record. As such, two selves

159

circulate, one with no sexual identity, the other unusually free of all health and medical problems other than those related to sexual activity. Likewise, CVs are constructed to disguise periods of unemployment and credit records hide a long-evaded debt. As Stanley warned in her talk, such 'audit selves' may later be met unexpectedly, an inconsistency between a past and current self creating a crisis of identity – who is this person who pretends he never banked at Citibank, worked for K-Mart or visited Cuba? Perhaps, also, such audit selves may enter the system like viruses, infecting it with their half-truths.

## Identity snatchers

The unsettling implications of the 'data double' are underlined by the practice of 'identity theft'. While theft of passports, credit cards and any other useful data carried by an individual has existed pretty much as long as the information itself, in the late 1990s, a concept began to emerge of 'identity theft' – a misuse of individual details which was complete enough for the 'thief' to in some way take over the identity of the victim. Journalist Tony Thomson introduced this concept to readers of London's *Time Out* magazine in June 1998 in a gruesome, thriller-movie manner:

On the afternoon of July 22 1990, Beverly Ann McGowan arrived at Heathrow on British Airways Flight 292 from Miami. She picked up the rental car she had booked a few days earlier and drove off towards central London.

Meanwhile, back in Miami, homicide detectives were trying to put a name to a mutilated female body which had washed up on a canal bank. The killer had done their best to frustrate identification: the head and hands had been severed with blows from a machete and a flap of skin from the stomach – the site of a distinctive tattoo – had been sliced away. It was only when a tiny second tattoo of a yellow butterfly, missed by the murderer, was found on the woman's ankle, that the police were able to work out who the victim was. The body belonged to Beverly Ann McGowan.

It would be six years before detectives could establish that McGowan had been murdered purely so that the killer could steal her identity. It was

one of the earliest cases of what the FBI describes as the fastest growing
consumer crime in America – identity theft.

(Thomson, 1998)

As the article goes on to point out, in most cases of identity theft
the victim is not murdered, but rather can remain unaware of the
crime for several years – mysteriously unable to get credit, or even
a passport. However, Thomson's choice to frame the article with this
murder story points to the fear, the horror, that underlies the idea
that this other self, this other identity, may be stolen. Interestingly, a
related racial fear also runs through the piece:

It was a similar story in April 1993 when Customs officers discovered eight
air-mail letters, each stuffed with cocaine, which were being sent to a
house in Wembley. When the house was raided, the police found Susan
Cole trying to climb out of a back window, but when detectives went to see
Cole's parents, they realized that they were dealing with a clever impostor.
The real Susan Cole lived in Kent and was platinum blonde. The woman they
had arrested was black.

In Thomson's alarmist article, the invisible world of data bodies
is prowled by body snatchers from those very populations who, in
the world of video surveillance, are hyper-visible – criminals, black
people. The desirability of data representation is undermined by
the nightmare of the good citizen that he or she will suddenly and
unknowingly be made other. 'Our' placing in relation to this realm
of data bodies is not dissimilar to that inhabited by the viewer in the
art works described above. As in Nauman's or Hatoum's constructs,
we are placed across the border of a representational realm in which
we cannot see ourselves, but in which we are nonetheless implicated,
conjured. This representational realm-across-the-data-border evokes
something in us – our double – which is intimately related to our
fears and aporias, perhaps continuing beyond our lives, perhaps
bringing about our deaths. This is a realm where, although we cannot become visualized, a rich visual imagery nonetheless operates
– of killers and criminals, body snatchers and ghosts. Like the rats in
Nauman's art work, these images pursue our invisible selves through
the data maze.

Post-September 11, the image of the terrorist has perhaps become the archetype of the 'other' across the data border. In the wake of the attacks, a previously innocent history of enrolment in flight school or religious attendance was, combined with a particular type of surname or country of origin, enough to produce a detainment of a real body which had no actual engagement in terrorist activity. Data produced terrorists, and the living bodies associated with those data terrorists were arrested.

Lyon (and to a degree other sociologists of surveillance mirror this attitude through a disciplinary emphasis on systems and statistics) suggests that the Foucauldian model misrepresents contemporary surveillance by applying a visual metaphor to what is overwhelmingly a data phenomenon. While far from following a straightforward Foucauldian reading in this study, I have suggested that a spatial understanding is key to an effective analysis of the contemporary culture of surveillance. In understanding the ways in which our experience of artworks such as Nauman's and Hatoum's, and of performances such as The Wooster Group's, relate to our experience of data surveillance, we begin to see how important such spatial analysis is to the theorizing of a range of surveillance phenomena.

As Lefebvre argues in relation to economic activity, the common-sense argument that spatial relations are produced by prior social relations severely underestimates the importance of space in ordering our lives. A spatial analysis of data surveillance is not the post-hoc application of visual imagery to a non-dimensional field; rather it functions as a way of stripping away a normalizing, fearfully clung-to ideology which suggests, against all lived evidence, that data surveillance is either a simple organizational tool facilitating our transactions or a bureaucratic invasion of (the fantasy of) privacy. A spatial analysis of data surveillance discovers the ways in which doubles of self and images of others function in a realm whose borders we cannot cross. Data surveillance is, in many ways, Lefebvre's representational space par excellence – resistant both to perception and conceptualization, but definitely lived.

When we accept or uptake this spatialization of data surveillance, that is to say when we knowingly situate our experience of data surveillance in relation to the uncrossable border and its production of doubles, the impasse of terrified good citizenship (maintaining perfect credit, horrified by thoughts of data thieves or computer errors, troubled by the possible data impact of job loss or ill health) potentially transforms into a very different spatial relationship. In this performative space of data surveillance – this particular space in which we cannot appear, in which we are (mis)represented by our own doubles, we may enact performances. Sending the consciously constructed bodies of credit, medical, immigration selves into the data zone, we may act parts on the stage of data surveillance – parts which, far from being etiolated in their effects, have real and dangerous consequences.

## Surveillance selves

The spatialization of data surveillance allows us to rethink these records of ourselves as doubled bodies, allowing for the possibility of agency, and replacing a fearful relationship to embodiment – its criminal associations in surveillance ideology – with the idea that these other data bodies are our products, our performances. While the ways in which a spatial reading of dataveillance might help a wrongfully arrested non-terrorist are not straightforward; as the debate about record creation and access intensifies and develops, an understanding of the gap and the exchange between physical identities and data bodies will be crucial in formulating an understanding of how the law may function in a world populated by data selves.

In the post-September 11 period, when the governmental accumulation, use and abuse of data on all of us has entered a new phase of comprehensiveness, the ways in which we engage in imagining our doubled selves, in finding ways to act with and upon our data bodies, will be crucial to the very nature of the world in which we are starting to live.

# 5

## Staging the spectator

The opening scene of Copolla's *The Conversation* (1974) inevitably runs through my mind as I tap on the darkened window of a white van parked on a north London street. In the movie we would cut to a space of inner technology, the muscles of Gene Hackman's face tightening with the tension of the operation, the whispered messages from the cameramen and the microphone operators inside and circulating the vehicle. Gene Hackman goes to the back of the van and cautiously opens the door.

In fact, nothing happens. It turns out I'm knocking on the window of a dry cleaning delivery van. With little concern for my Hollywood plotline, Blast Theory have long ago taken their own white surveillance vehicle off in pursuit of an unpredictable audience member.

Audience member? Or maybe participant? Or raw material? In Blast Theory's 1998 piece *Kidnap*, the distinction achieved a rare degree of blurring. The performance began early in the year with a film made by the company, shown at cinemas as a short before the main feature, asking the audience, 'Have you ever felt the need to get away for a few days, have some time for yourself?' The film offered you the chance to enrol as a potential victim in a kidnap. For a £10 fee you could join a list of people who were willing to be abducted by the company later that year, with the two-day kidnap broadcast live on the Internet. From the individuals who enrolled (200 people did so), a computer would choose ten who would be placed under surveillance during a two-week period. From these ten, two would subsequently be selected for the kidnap. On a given day these two would be surprised, snatched from work, home or social pursuits and taken to a safe house where they would be kept for forty-eight hours. While in the safe house, their captivity would be witnessed on the Internet. At registration, participants could (for an extra fee) determine input into their kidnap experience with optional extras ranging from doughnuts (25p) to a bedtime story (£10) to being kept naked (£1) to being treated as the child of a millionaire or a left-wing politician kidnapped by the secret service (£30).

When I met up with Blast Theory (they eventually returned to the designated spot) they were in the second stage of the process – keeping ten individuals under surveillance. In each case they would stake the 'victim' until they had a sense of his or her daily activities, then attempt to take a photo without the subject's knowledge in the context of day-to-day social life. The photo would be mailed to the subject with the message: 'You have been placed under surveillance by Blast Theory.' The individuals would each then know they had a one in five chance of being kidnapped in a week's time.

Inside Blast Theory's van, things were disappointingly low-tech. A single telephoto lens camera peeked from a window obscured by black trash bags. There were no microphones. Owing to budget restrictions, the cellular phone wouldn't be available until the next week. Founder member of the company, Matt Adams, explained the genesis of the piece – a desire to explore issues of control and power; the relation of these issues to sexual fantasy and practice;[1] the logical extension of the company's tendency to involve the audience directly in their work; interest in the idea of a 'contract' between audience and performers; a desire to problematize the notion that the creator of an artwork is the 'most interesting' person involved. I asked Matt and his collaborator, Ju Row Farr, about the experience of the surveillance stake-out. I had noticed how seriously the team was taking the pursuit of its victims. They reminded me of political activists, whose precision and timing are essential to the public and media effect of their action. The urgency was also similar to that of a regular theatre tech week – an intense seriousness applied to choices and priorities in the service of something fictional. Matt talked about the alternation of long hours of boredom with moments of urgent activity, the feeling of criminality associated with the covert activity, the thrill of getting a good shot and staying concealed. Ju talked about the stories she developed for herself about the victims, the fascination of seeing the different roles they played during the day.

Two weeks later, I sit in the ICA's (London's Institute for Contemporary Arts) New Media Centre. Four or five people are trying to negotiate their way through the *Kidnap* web site. Most of these people have little Internet experience; they keep closing down the connection by mistake. The press releases have promised that the camera in the safe house can be manipulated live from the ICA, but this ambitious piece of technology isn't working. There is no sound.

I email Matt and Ju: 'There are five people here and the sound is a mess – I guess this *is* theatre after all.' Next to the computer is a folder filled with printouts of emails sent to the company during the project. At the front is my own first email to the group, explaining who I am, my history and the nature of my research. Suddenly I feel horribly exposed. Though no-one else in the room is looking at the documents, or could know that my body is associated with the email, I feel a strong desire to rip my message from the folder and run off with it. Restraining myself, I go for coffee.

## The right to reproduction

In this chapter, I will examine in particular works of art and perform-ance in which the audience is in some way the object of surveillance. Key to this examination will be an exploration of our desire as audi-ence for surveillance, and also of our relationship to the surveyors. The works analysed each take as their subject the various desires and identifications that structure our experiences under surveillance, and a reading of these art works (with the support of a variety of theo-retical perspectives examining the political and libidinal structure of our relations to image and performance) can open up a far fuller understanding of the complex range of impulses we each bring into, and are brought to by, surveillance space.

In 'The work of art in the age of mechanical reproduction', Walter Benjamin makes the surprising assertion that individuals have a right to self-reproduction: 'modern man's legitimate claim to being repro-duced' (Benjamin, 1969: 232). The idea that such self-reproduction and reproduction of selves would in some way be a right, that it would be an important part of the life and values of the modern subject, has been underdeveloped in a subsequent history of media studies which emphasizes issues of objectification, simulation or representation in the demographic sense. In a world in which the scramble to appear on television in anything from talk shows to 'reality' television is exceeded in its frenzy only by the bewildered disapproval of the upmarket media, the idea that a twentieth-century thinker would locate self-reproduction in mass media as a necessary aspect of modern subjectivity puts an unfamiliar light on an overdiscussed phenomenon. Why would Benjamin consider this reproduction of self a necessary subjective tool, rather than subsuming it in a wider view of consumption (as in Adorno's critique of cinema, or in Baudrillard's recent weary rant against reality television)? (Baudrillard in Levin et al., 2002: 480).

Benjamin's essay famously discusses the loss of 'aura' in the world of mechanical reproduction, the loss, that is, of the sense of unique wholeness surrounding the traditional art work – held at a distance from us, self-contained and mysterious. He contrasts this traditional viewing of the art work with the experience of the architecture of a public building, which we enter, feel around us, learn in passing through it. The great buildings of the modern era, emphasizing space, not facade, are the template for understanding the ways in which twentieth-century art – mass art – can be experienced. Rather than being viewed, such work will be inhabited.

The danger which Benjamin identified was that modern subjects, rather than finding themselves in a self-aware, spatial relation to contemporary culture, would instead be manipulated into overwhelmed, self-annihilating fascination with the unapproachable excess of the mass-produced cultural artefact. The respectful relation to aura would be replaced not with an inhabiting but with a self-prostration before the might of reproductive technology. In relation to such danger (to such actuality), the right to self-reproduction – and the need to become talk show fare – makes more than a degree of sense. If technologically reproduced cultural artefacts can be understood only by inhabiting them, the rush for five minutes of fame on *The Jerry Springer Show* is perhaps a dash for survival, for a moment of placing one's own body within the space of televisual reproduction.

The 'legitimate claim' for self-representation is, then, a spatial claim. The desire to feature in talk shows or fly-on-the-wall documentaries is not, as critics usually assume, an unquestioning acceptance of the ideology of television, an assumption that any appearance in the medium associates the subject with the *Lifestyles of the Rich and Famous*. Rather, with a Benjaminian spatial understanding, we see that the impulse is a survival tactic, an attempt to comprehend televisual space from within – to replace prostration before the post-auratic object with a bodily relation to its complexities.

Such a desire for self-reproduction would not necessarily have been expected from our analysis of surveillance space up to this

point. In relation to the ways in which an 'ideology of crime' functions in *Crimewatch* and similar television programmes, a desire for
television representation is in some ways a contradictory instinct.
We have seen that the ideological structuring of *Crimewatch* is such
that the viewer is encouraged to identify with the non-visualized
position; the visualized is the black, the criminal, the other. The
viewer is reassured that his or her image has been sorted through and
passed as law-abiding and therefore does not need to be circulated. In
examining the phenomenon of data representation we also saw that
it is in this non-visual realm that the citizen–consumer feels most at
ease, separated from the visualized underclass. As noted in Chapter
2, certain minority positions – particularly the gay male – tend to
inhabit a psychosexual relation to the ideological (super-ego) bar
on surveillance auto-representation, which encourages entry into
surveillance space. In the same chapter we also saw heterosexual,
even married, bodies slipping into willing sexual visibility in web
space in a way that they would probably not do in public space. For
the mass audience, however, the desire for television representation
would seem to contradict the ideologically defined instinct towards
surveillance invisibility.

We have seen in the previous chapter how art and performance
works have interrogated the invisibility of the audience under surveillance, and particularly how a concept of the double helps us to
understand the ways in which an audience across the boundary of
visibility is incorporated into surveillance space. Works of art and
performance which actively incorporate the image of the audience
may help us to understand how the desire for reproduction, and
its fulfilment, play out in relation to surveillance's ideologies and
performativities.

## Going around corners

Bruce Nauman's *Going Around the Corner Piece* (1970) examines
the desire for self-reproduction in a remarkably simple way. The
piece consists of four video cameras and four monitors placed at the
corners of a large square of wooden walls. The cameras and monitors
are arranged in such a way that, as viewers turn the corner around
the outer edge of the wooden square, they see a rear view of their

own body in the monitor ahead. As they complete the movement around the corner, the image of the body turns around the corner on the monitor ahead, and disappears from sight.[2] The piece creates the effect of pursuing one's own image around the corners of the square. Inevitably, the viewer speeds up, hoping to catch up. Equally inevitably, the image speeds up too. Despite understanding the logic of the piece quite quickly, viewers often stay with it for a while, circulating at different speeds, tantalized by the impossible possibility of catching their own images. As this impossibility of encountering one's own image, mirror-like, is established, the desirability of such an encounter grows. Seeing one's self perpetually disappearing around the corner, glanced from behind, the longing for a meeting with this particular self-image intensifies.

One of the important features of *Going Around the Corner Piece* for the purposes of this chapter is that without the viewer it does not exist. As a physical construct, *Going Around the Corner Piece* is simply a square of plywood walls and some equipment. (The monitor screens are not visible as we stand back to look at the work as a whole.) Viewing the piece other than in the action of going around its corners there is nothing much to see. In Benjamin's terms, the piece has no aura whatsoever, there is nothing to stand back from, no unique presence. Nor is there the sleek, consumable surface of the commodity fetish. There is nothing but a possibility, hinted at by a title. Moreover, the presence of other viewers at the piece makes little or no difference to its function or meaning. It is only in going around the corner one's self that one brings the work and its meanings into being.

The fascination with the elusive self-image in *Going Around the Corner Piece* points us towards an incompletion, a dissatisfaction, inherent in self-reproduction. As with the Lacanian love object, we seek to see that which the image as other cannot know it has, yet which will, in being revealed, complete us. Our self-images almost inevitably disappoint us, and so we seek another vision, take another holiday snap in another location. The images of ourselves going around Bruce Nauman's corners entice because they leave us; they do not linger for our scrutiny. As such, they never allow the revelation of their incompleteness. But this is not their only fascination. These images also have a spatial relationship to us. Unlike our Kodaks, or even our holiday video, they relate to us in ways involving our bodies and movements. In Lefebvre's terms, they create representational spaces; in Benjamin's imagery, they introduce us to architectures of experience.

One of the key ways in which Benjamin linked the viewing of reproduced imagery (movies etc.) to the experience of buildings was in the notion of 'distracted' viewing – the idea that, rather than focusing on the whole object, we experience it as we wander through it, our minds mainly on other things. The experience of *Going Around the Corner Piece* is necessarily distracted: we never quite arrive at the experience of it, but in retrospect we inhabited it. As an art work, *Going Around the Corner Piece* seems less tangible than *Learned Helplessness in Rats* or *Corps Étranger*. There is little to hold onto, other than the vague feeling of needing to pursue oneself around the corner one more time. It is a distracted piece, one which never quite appears.

I would suggest that the insertion of the viewer/audience into the (surveillance) art work tends to engender such distraction, emphasizing an element of time, of missed moments, in the spatial construct. Whereas we have established that works such as *Learned Helplessness in Rats* and *Corps Étranger* depend upon the uptake, on the part of the viewer, of the spatial performativity of the work and the implication of the body's doubles in that work, surveillance-related art which actively incorporates the image of the viewer into its space contrarily seems to expel us from its space, to make us aware of our non-connection with the work, its non-presence to us, its non-identity with us. While this is no less a spatial, no less a performative, experience than that of surveillance art work in which we are not visually reproduced, it suggests that self-reproduction within the work complicates, rather than resolves, the relation of the performative space of surveillance to the dimensional space inhabited by the viewer's body.

## Spectators at an event

Susan Marshall's 1994 dance piece *Spectators at an Event* was inspired by Weegee's photographs of crowds of spectators at the site of accidents in 1940s New York. Performed at the Brooklyn Academy of Music, the piece incorporated a large projection screen on which Weegee's images were shown as the dancers' groupings and movements explored the dynamics of a crowd whose attention is focused on a single (unrepresented) event. During the piece, several of the performers wandered through the audience, one of them with the video camera that would inevitably appear in such a crowd scene today. Later in the performance, images of the audience suddenly replaced Weegee's photographs on the on-stage screen.

The chain of identification and viewing for the audience in this piece was quite complex. Clearly, we were spectators at an event – the dance. We sat in our seats and watched the dancers execute movements designed to provoke thoughts about the body and spectatorship. The dancers, too, were playing spectators of an event – their movements were based upon the configurations of spectatorship. In this stage construct, the event (a fictional accident) was off-stage, gazed at but never seen. The performers also pointed towards another event, removed in time – the event of Weegee's original spectators, the inspiration, the impetus behind this dance, who we were reminded of in their projected images. And, in these images, these referents also stared off at their own objects of spectatorship – the long-ago accidents, the details of which we will never know.

When a performer points a video camera at the audience, these chains of spectatorship are interrupted. The reference to the past is broken by the presence of the video camera. Our own spectatorship is briefly reflected back upon us – we watch the performers viewing us. When images of the audience appear, hugely magnified, on the on-stage screen, the disruptions are multiplied. Our own images take the place of the dance's historical referents. We watch ourselves, and we watch the dancers in a performance now based on our own watching. The movements of the dancers become commentaries intervening within our spectatorship of ourselves. Their rhythms and groupings draw attention to and function within the gap between our viewing selves and our viewed selves, implying that it is neither in the spectatorship nor in the accident that the event truly occurs, but in the space of the watching, the space created in the act of watching.

Our reaction to the imagery of ourselves is not (at least in my experience of appearing on the screen) one of embarrassment or of satisfaction. Rather, we are distracted for a moment by the trickery, the joke, of the video. Then we become newly aware of the dancers, framed on both sides now by our spectatorship, and tiny in comparison with the huge projected faces. We also become aware of our neighbours in the audience, and of the huge auditorium within which the dance is happening. We do not feel that we have been brought 'on-stage' with the performers, but rather that the dancers are performing within the space of our watching. This shared space becomes the subject of *Spectators at an Event*.

The piece, then, takes the traditional stage proscenium and gradually, through its multiplication of spectatorships, creates, in Lefebvre's term, a representational space – a space made of representations, those seen and those (the event, the original accident itself) perpetually eluding sight. As with Nauman's *Going around the Corner Piece*, the images that the audience sees of itself are partial and momentary. Again, however, they configure the field, the architecture within which the work takes place. But in the case of *Spectators at an Event*, our experience is only partially one of pursuit. The images of ourselves disappear into the realm of the unseen event, and our focus is always partly upon this missing event in the work. However, we are not left gazing into the wings; our focus is also brought back onto the dancers' bodies and movements – a site where the dilemma of spectatorship is being played with, questioned, enjoyed. The reconfiguration of the traditional theatre space into a representational space of spectatorship changes our relationship to these bodies. As they move in the space of spectatorship, the dancers are less objects of desire and fascination and more vectors, analysing and playing with this space.

In Marshall's piece, then, onstage surveillance of the audience body helps not only to develop the theme of the work, but to reinvent the space within which the performance is happening. In Benjamin's terms, our relation to the space becomes more architectural – a shifting, a wandering around – less fetishistic. It is also more distracted – our attention is taken away from the dance at the same time as we notice it in different ways.

## Surveillance and gestus

In *Spectators at an Event*, we see how performers' bodies and movements can interact with images of the audience to question and complicate the meaning and effects of surveillance. In order to examine this interaction further, it will be helpful to refer to theories of the body in performance which highlight its capacities for ideological critique.

In her essay 'Brechtian theory/feminist theory: toward a gestic feminist criticism', Elin Diamond (1997: 43–55)[3] suggests that a feminist reading of Brecht's theatre theory points towards a practice and criticism in which the body on stage can reveal the social structures acting upon it while also engaging the audience as desiring subject, and refusing to abstract the body:

> This feminist rereading of the gestus makes room, at least theoretically, for a viewing position for the female spectator. Because the semiosis of the gestus involves the gendered bodies of spectator, subject/actor and character, all working together, but never harmoniously, there can be no fetishization and no end to signification. In this Brechtian-feminist paradigm, the spectator's look is freed into 'dialectics, passionate detachment'...
>
> (Ibid.: 54)

Diamond is working with Brecht's concept of the gestus, a central element of his theory, the essence of which is that a particular moment in a stage performance crystallizes the social and historical forces acting upon a character, revealing them as constructed and hence susceptible to change: 'scenes where people adopt attitudes of such a sort that the social laws under which they are acting spring into sight' (Brecht, 1957: 86). Crucial to the structures of stage gestus are the attitudes of the actor to both character/story and audience. This is the infamous alienation effect: 'The first condition for the achievement of the A-effect is that the actor must invest what he has to show with a definite gestus of showing' (ibid.: 136). That is to say, the actor neither identifies with the character nor ignores the audience. Rather, the performance is constructed as a process of showing the character and story to the audience. In contrast to innumerable bad 'Brechtian' productions, the effect is not to denigrate or to lecture the audience, but rather to allow moments of revelation during which the social/historical forces normally naturalized in narrative are startlingly and complexly revealed.

However, Diamond rightly suggests that Brecht tends to imagine a universal (male) subject position as the ideal place from which to view the revelations of gestus. Diamond wants to put the audience's desire for and identification with the actor/character – the audience's specificity – back into the gestic picture, while not allowing us to slip back into an uncritical engagement with stage fiction.

One of the examples of gestus that Diamond gives is taken from the 1994 Mabou Mines production 'Mother',[4] a contemporary American 'rethinking' of the famous 1906 novel by Gorky in which a Russian mother, in the process of reluctantly protecting her revolutionary son, herself becomes an agent and symbol of revolution (Brecht created an agit-prop version of the story in the 1930s):

> . . . spectators sit in fully functioning kitchen areas surrounded by television sets, enabling them to watch live action or watch TV, or both. In her closing soliloquy, an educated embittered Mother (Ruth Maleczech) grabs a video camera and films herself, face pressed up and distorted against the lens, while speaking of her yearning for 'transcendence' – a revolutionary leap beyond the suffering she witnesses. In this agonized moment, spectators' eyes dart uneasily between video screen and performer creating with the latter a gestus that powerfully displays the contradictory relation between political agency and media manipulation, between humanist traditions of protest and postmodern environments.
>
> (Diamond, 1997: 53)

As director of that production, perhaps it will be considered not inappropriately solipsistic in a chapter focusing on self-reproduction if I analyse it a little further, as part of an enquiry as to ways in which a Brechtian/feminist analysis might help our understanding of the effects of audience surveillance in performance and art works.

The scene which Diamond describes took place at the end of 'Mother' and was undoubtedly, as she indicates, an attempt both to reveal and move through the contradictions between the use of the mother figure as an abstracted revolutionary symbol in Gorky's original version of the story (and Brecht's stage adaptation), and the contemporary struggles of a defiantly un-abstractable woman in a political present in which grand narratives of liberation are no longer available. This contradiction was, however, always framed within a context of heightened, and problematized, spectatorship. In the lobby, before the show, the audience were interviewed about their own mothers by a character in early-twentieth-century clothing using a video camera. As they entered the theatre space, converted into multiple fully functioning kitchens in which the audience sat, they were instructed over speakers: 'Because you are under surveillance, it is very important that you behave as realistically as possible.' The voice went on to provide instructions on realistic in-kitchen behaviour, and the audience inevitably obliged by making use of fridges, microwaves, televisions, etc. By the time of Ruth Maleczech's final use of the camera, the audience had appeared on screen on several occasions, in a staging that continuously insisted upon the interplay of mediation and meaning.

In creating the final image of the play, we were determined, as Diamond notes, that the audience should experience a pull between the live performer and the television image. Maleczech stood on a raised platform, away from the audience kitchens, with her back to the audience. This platform, with a few cleaning and cooking instruments and a small monitor on the floor, was the Mother's kitchen – far less realistic than those inhabited by the audience. Inevitably, as Maleczech started the speech, the audience looked towards her, despite her face and actions being largely concealed from them. Her body microphone, however, carried her growling voice to the other end of the auditorium, where it boomed through speakers, pulling the audience's attention away from the performer's body. In this movement they noticed (most of them) the image on the televisions in their own kitchen areas – extreme close-ups of Maleczech's face abstracted by her use of a 'Pixelvision' camera, in a live visual sequence composed as a lyrical accompaniment to writer Patricia Spears Jones's textual evocation of the impossible desire for transcendence.

It was very important to us that it was only on the televisions that a final beautiful image was revealed. This television space had been continuously interrogated during the piece. The audience had been asked to 'act realistically' in order to be seen on the televisions, and their images had periodically reappeared. In insisting on this space we did not have a direct 'Brechtian' lesson that we were looking to teach. Rather, our production was built out of the contradiction between and convergence of our longing for a politics, a future, and an equal engagement in the artifice of mediation. The televisions, the cameras, the surveillance, were as much a part of the desire of the piece as the politics, the transcendence. If the final scene succeeded, it did so because the production built a space that was neither the bodily presence of Maleczech/Mother nor the mediated television-kitchen world, but a space experienced in the move of spectatorship back and forth between the two.

The surveillance of the audience was crucial to the possibility of this other space. In ways that we probably could not have explained in making the piece, the incorporation of the audience's images into the televisions seemed to grow inevitably from the decision to place the audience in the kitchen world that 'should' have been the mother's. Given Diamond's arguments, I would say in retrospect that we were pulled along by a question of identification. In pitting ourselves against and in relation to the abstracting tendencies of a Brechtian model, we were bound to pursue identification, to ask whether, as the place of personalized passion, the emotions it allows us to voice could lead to something other than the bourgeois immobilization so derided by Brecht. Through the use of surveillance images of the audience (imagery at one point gathered by the actor playing the character of the Spy) we were able to suggest an identification of the audience image with the Mother image, while reminding the audience of their own bodies and of their bodily difference from the Mother. Importantly, since the mother's final impetus was double – for political transcendence but also for the obsessive joys of auto-representation – audience identification at the end of the piece was doubled and split: disappearing into the mother's idealizing emotion, but also longing to reappear as she created complex, textured imagery from her own body.

Such double identifications, Diamond suggests, are keys to understanding the possibility of a progressive, feminist performance practice. Writing of Adrianne Kennedy's work she suggests:

> Adrianne Kennedy's texts provide access to identifications that are decidedly double, even multiple, wherein traces of hysterical mimicry (of playing all the parts), of narcissistic rage, ambivalence, and rivalry, of the punishing constraints of parental ego-ideals are all in evidence.
>
> (Diamond, 1997: 112)

A feminist Brechtian theatre allows the audience the possibility of such multiple, contradictory identifications. (Diamond's list of identifications also reminds us of the surveillance shower scene discussed in Chapter 2, in which the identifications of the audience were split across the narcissistic go-go boy and the camera in the position of ego-ideal. Diamond's argument suggests that such multiple identifications need not be restricted to the matrix of same-sex desire and that, although in the case of the shower scene the vectors of identification are doubled with desire, desire and identification do not thereby become equivalent (ibid.: 111).)

The introduction of audience surveillance imagery within the space and sequence of a work is a basic means of highlighting the representational structures of contemporary society and the necessary 'claim to being reproduced' within it. By ensuring that, in a piece like 'Mother', one of the identifications is with the desire for self-reproduction, a multiple, contradictory state of identification is necessarily invoked, since this identification is one that seeks to replace its object with the visible representation of the viewer at the very point where, in traditional viewing structures, the audience's sense of self would be lost in the emotion of identification with the character.

The pieces discussed above each use audience/viewer imagery to create a space of the work other than that of the auratic object or the conventional stage. In each case the space created by this 'staging' of the spectator is not centred on the image of the audience/viewer per se, but is some sort of 'between space' – between the audience and its image, or between the reproductive technologies and the live performer. Once again, we find that a 'surveillance space' is in many ways defined by its margins, that what is pushed to its edges is crucial to our experience of it. The disappearance of our image, or its memory carried in a later moment, may be more important than the moment of our seeing ourselves. Our distractedness, our failure to engage properly with this space, may be key, ultimately, to our experience of it.

## Security by Julia

What, then, happens in the 'between space' of the surveillance art work when the subject matter explored in that space is the technology and paraphernalia of surveillance itself? Do we remain 'distracted' and, if so, how does this affect our capacity to respond to the real-life dilemmas of surveillance?

Julia Scher's work is perhaps unique in the degree and complexity with which it explores the technologies of surveillance in an artistic context. In a body of work going back more than fifteen years, Scher has built a series of gallery and site-specific installations out of the materials of the surveillance industry – cameras, monitors, microphones, speakers, image printers, data questionnaires and the high-powered computers and complex programs that link and run them. As with Nauman's *Going Around the Corner Piece,* Scher's work is defiantly non-auratic. Stepping back from these installations, the audience sees a mass of hardware, a mess of wiring (Scher emphasizes excessive coils and loops of wiring – bringing to view the aspects of security systems normally hidden behind plaster or under floors). But as the viewer enters the space and begins to explore it, the work begins to emerge. As Scher (1995: 188) writes:

> This arrangement of gear only creates a shell for experimental moments – the real gems of the project are created as individuals interact with the system, making, performing and reclaiming images for themselves, or finding a peaceful moment within a string of images.

Unlike Nauman's piece, however, the systems created by Scher are immensely complex, and do not reveal their logic to us. As our images appear on monitors, unexpected lists may appear over the images: 'holding . . . holding . . . surprise, the social sabotage car is outside', 'Danger: "We" vs. "Them" identity stud implants are being activated now' (ibid.: 187–8). The distractedness noted above in relation to surveillance-based art is intensified in Scher's work into an anxious movement of focus between the process of self-reproduction and the unpredictable, unmanageable behaviour of the security machine. Scher's point is that an engagement with surveillance technology reveals both our desires and its intrusions – in an interplay very different from the passivity which characterizes any 'normal' relation to surveillance. Writing of an exhibition of her work, she states:

> The site of surveillance of the body is thus inserted into the structure of the institution and becomes in itself the site of perusal, as individuals render

themselves subjects and monitors of their own behaviour. In other words, the slo-scan video configuration puts the visitor in the position of being simultaneously the watcher and the watched, but not in real time, thereby reifying the tacit agreement that occurs in one's daily existence in which we consent to our own control. Watchers are placed in singular experiential moments in which they are both willing subjects of intrusive security control and the helmspeople of their own surveillance.

(Ibid.: 188)

However, while Scher's theoretical position may be that we need to be awoken from our own passivity in the face of surveillance, her art work also engages in a joyful, and very funny, iconoclastic engagement with security technology. Her involvement in the language of surveillance is playful, even poetic:

We provide nationwide free-for-all directories
For information cultivation and extraction we use the
brightest, newest and fastest

MASTER AND SLAVE VOICE READERS
CONSPIRATORIAL ELECTRICIANS AND ROOM DEBUGGERS
INTRA-GENDER NON-TRACEABLE BANK CARDS
COUNTERSPY TRANSMISSION INTERRUPTERS
FAKE FAMILY SERVICE PROVIDERS
BODY BAG, MORGUE AND HOSPITAL INFORMATION GATEKEEPERS
PIRATES AND LEAKERS
WARRIOR COMPANIES AND GUIDANCE COUNSELLORS
EXHAUSTED MILITARY MARKET SALES ENVOYS
INJECTABLES
AIRPORT HARASSMENT VEHICLES
URINE VAPOR DETECTOR WHIPS
CLEAVAGE TONGS AND BUTTOCK ANALYSIS TONGS
SEARCHERS AND SIFTERS
SYMBOLIC AND REAL LAW ENFORCEMENT
FABRICATED EVIDENCE
SEX BEDS
LIVE INTIMACY – REAL AND FEIGNED
DAYTIME SEDUCTION AND FINGER ANALYSIS
SURVEILLANCE

MACHINES OF DOMINANCE AND DELIGHT BIOMETRICS
MILITARY GENETIC RECORDS
GOVERNMENT DATA SELLERS
TAX FILES
BEIGE COMPUTER INPUT TERMINALS
WELFARE FILES
BLOOD FOOD AND ORAL SWABS
FINGERPRINTS
DENTAL RECORDS
CHILDREN ESCORT SERVICES FOR MALES AND FEMALES

MISSION STATEMENT: We utilize freshly gathered judgments identifications and verifications to make our bright shiny and vitamin-rich data
base, state-of-the-art. We heighten the symbolic and communicative
aspects of filling INFORMATION AMERICA, by using gentle, pleasing and
inviting computer commands on new subjects. Our goal is not to manage
individuals, only space.

> (Sound Piece, Information America, accompanying
> the exhibition *I'll be Gentle* at the Pat Hearn Gallery,
> New York, 1991, quoted in Druckrey, 1996: 53)

The two most resonant claims here are that surveillance, the
category, is merely part of the list (shades of Foucault on Borges in
the introduction to *The Order of Things*, Foucault, 1973: xv), a claim
which challenges our attempt to understand surveillance by theorizing and overview, while also implying that to abandon the attempt
is exactly what the surveillance system wants of us; and the claim
'Our goal is not to manage individuals, only space', to which we will
return later.

Scher also accompanies the technology of her installations with
a productive use of the security trade's peripherals. One exhibition
was staffed by old ladies dressed as security guards in pink uniforms.
In another, *American Fibroids* (1996), young male security guards,
again in pink, supervised tables of the 'bits and pieces' of the security trade: badges, hats, old hard-drives, pass cards, ropes, cameras,
T-shirts, arranged as though for sale – 'a cross between a security
fleamarket and a sex shop', in Timothy Druckrey's (1996) description.
Scher's giddy, camp engagement in the stuff of surveillance (other
highlights include the *Children's Guard Station* (1998) – a full, child-

size guard's security desk in Fisher Price colours) demonstrates an art whose creator desires not only auto-reproduction, but the systems of security themselves – and who imagines the surveillance machine desiring back: 'I offer distinguished and ambient space. I am full and waiting for you', announces the soundtrack to *American Fibroids*. 'It's who you play, not who you are. Come into my area now. Please loosen my access control.' As this voice indicates, we are being invited into a specific space here, a space created by the two-way desire of and for surveillance.

Scher's work destroys the humanist notion that a desire for self-reproduction is ultimately a desire for the completion of a self-encounter. Rather, it is the self processed through the terrifying delights of surveillance systems, made other by them, that Scher fears and desires.

## Security bed

The sado-masochistic imagery that pervades much of Scher's work seems to refer not only to libidinal aspects of the domination and control inherent to security systems but also to a Foucauldian technology of the body, whereby instruments acting upon the body recreate it for desire. It is one of the delights of Scher's work that (unlike many artists dealing with sado-masochism) she manages to combine engagement, critique and humour in a complex, productive whole.

Perhaps the single strongest example of this complexity is Scher's *Security Bed* (1994), in which cameras point onto a bed from four corner posts and the audience is invited to perform on the bed; sometimes Scher herself, in a security uniform, will initiate bondage 'scenes'. The security bed could almost be an emblem of the post-private sexuality explored in this study: a bed which is already in a 'public' space is multiply surveyed in a way which makes it no longer simply 'in a public space' but, rather, demanding of special activity, demanding of performance. This performance, though, will not necessarily, as in Austin, become an 'etiolated' version of a real act, rather it may be an act impossible other than in this overdetermined space. When Julia Scher climbs on the Security Bed in her guard's uniform, her action is not 'simply' a performance. Rather it is, in the terms developed in this analysis, a self-conscious uptake of spatial performativity.

What Scher particularly adds to our discussion of sexuality in the performative space of surveillance is her emphasis on surveillance paraphernalia. Scher resists any tendencies to metaphoricize surveillance – to see it only in terms of super-egos or eyes. She insists that in engaging in surveillance, its materials and systems will enter our libidinal structures as fully as any eyes, orifices or penises. The humour with which Scher nonetheless invests her work – most particularly in this engagement with and sexualization of the systems – indicates that she believes that our desiring of the systems may be an anarchic force, and that one way to unleash this anarchy may be to imagine the system desiring back.

Scher's work, then, suggests that the self reproduced under surveillance is different from the 'original' self not just in an incompletion, but also in an accretion, in its desirable processing and additions under surveillance. Scher contrasts the manipulated bodies of her art works with selves created daily by institutional security systems:

> In our everyday lives – when controllers and machines intentionally archive, file away and ultimately define our experience, where surveillance registers all and selects accordingly, thereby reconstructing a body in private, out of view, furthering a strategy of domination – we live in a reality where resignation is the greatest weapon for any control system, any mechanism of suppression.
>
> (Scher, 1995: 188).

Here, recontextualized by Scher, is the invisible, law-abiding body of the 'ideology of crime'; here also is the creditworthy 'data body'. Scher believes that these 'out of view' bodies – these doubles of ourselves not known to ourselves, in somebody else's 'private' – are the true dangers of security systems; and that the only response is to make one's body visible. Importantly, however, the body that we will make visible will also be processed by surveillance – will be prostheticized.

## The right to be reproduced

From Scher's viewpoint, Benjamin's championing of modern man's 'legitimate claim to being reproduced' would need to be more carefully phrased. Scher's nightmare is that we passively assent to multiple invisible reproductions of ourselves, over which we have no control and yet which come to live on our behalf. In Scher's world-view, the racist fantasy of data theft analysed in Chapter 4 – in which the law-abiding data body is appropriated by a black, criminal body – is turned on its head. For Scher, embodiment, making visible within the security matrix, is exactly what needs to happen – and the perversions, inversions and prostheticizations that will occur in such making visible are anarchic potentials for resistance. The 'claim to being reproduced' must be qualified by agency, by the involvement of the subject in the reproduction. As Scher's installations make clear, however, agency does not equate with control. We cannot define in advance what the security matrix will do with our images, our data. But we can insist on having an effect. Moreover, Scher implies that, in having such effect, we will tend to make our surveillance selves visible. This reading coheres easily enough with our analysis of the ideology of surveillance, though it inverts its value, placing danger on the side of invisibility. In this way, Scher's work resolves the contradiction between the television audience's desire for self-reproduction and the desire for surveillance invisibility. She indicates that an engaged experience of surveillance space develops our desire to create hybrid bodies – not ourselves, but ourselves processed by technology.

In contrast to a theory of performativity which separates itself from performance, we might say that in Scher's work her and our (technological and bodily) performances bring a performative space of surveillance into being. This performative space of surveillance is inhabited in Benjamin's architectural sense, in that one needs to explore it. But it is not architectural in that it is not simply dimensional space – we do not experience Scher's work simply by wandering through it, but by doing so from a position of uptake of the performative space created by her/our performances. Only in accepting that this surveillance space is other or more than the visible gallery installation do we experience it. The surveillance space of Scher's work is experienced in terms of its political, visual and existential characteristics.

So, the statement made by the surveillance machine in *I'll Be Gentle*, quoted above – 'Our goal is not to manage individuals, only space' – is revealed in all its irony. For, in the surveillance matrix, it is precisely space which is at stake. Control of our individual bodies and behaviours will not liberate us from the matrix's abusive potential. Only by taking on the security network as space will we attain any agency within it.

## Big sister?

In her statements on her work, Scher seems more or less to buy into the 'Big Brother' critique of surveillance, suggesting that the omni-present surveillance web is a danger per se – that in making its invis-ible versions of the body, security and data systems have somehow endangered our humanity. However, the work itself seems to exceed this critique. The embodiment of the security system within the work – the desiring announcements, the pink-uniformed guards – is far from the faceless authoritarian Big Brother of Orwellian nightmare. This is, of course, a tactic on Scher's part: as in a satirist's cartoons of political figures, making authority ridiculous works to undercut its power. But Scher's embodiment of security authority is not simply ridiculous; her authority 'figures' are also both desiring and, in a va-riety of ways, desirable. The pretty boys dressed in pink uniforms as part of *American Fibroids* are perhaps the simplest dominant/passive inversion of the security sex/power structure. Her security bed is clearly proposed as more desirable, more sexualized, than a regular bed. Old ladies in uniforms are a more complex proposition. But see-ing them in this almost fetishistic guise, we start to imagine them as desiring subjects.

Scher's security net then becomes a web of desire, in which the prostheticizations, inversions, deconstructions of body, role, machine are the stuff of desiring. The viewer entering into her installations is invited to participate in this web of desire, making new hybrid bodies in the matrix.

Whereas in Mabou Mines' '*Mother*' we saw a relation to self-re-production organized, *pace* Diamond, primarily on axes of identifi-cation, in Scher's installations identification is more or less absent; the desire which organizes our energies in her work allows for an objectification and prostheticization of self and others, but there is no person or point in the work where we can locate ourselves other than in our own images. This is not least to do with the roles in which other bodies figure in these different works. In '*Mother*', the performer's body was structurally organized to equate with the audience on many axes – the kitchen settings, the emotions of the text, the placing as object in front of the camera. In Scher's work, the other bodies are usually those of security guards, whether live (*American Fibroids*) or in photographs (the children dressed as guards in Scher's installation *Wonderland*). As seen through reference to Diamond's arguments, in '*Mother*' surveillance encouraged multiple, complex and contradictory identifications: in identifying with a character's desire for auto-reproduction, we both disappear into that identification and simultaneously reappear in our desire to see our own selves reproduced. The desires evoked in Julia Scher's security web are also complex. We (probably) do not desire the old ladies in pink security guard outfits as objects of our gratification, but their appearance in the security matrix evokes a sexualization – a flow of desire – which entices the viewer. Even the more conventionally desirable bodies (the pretty young men in pink uniforms) do not stay in place as objects of desire. As with the dancers in *Spectators at an Event*, the security guards' eyes are always focused elsewhere, moving on from us, this scene, keeping an eye on the point of interest – about to emerge, out of sight. We are watched by them, and watch their watching, but neither of these events is the focus, the true object is about to emerge elsewhere. Scher's quintessential installation, the *Security Bed*, emphasizes this characteristic, typical of surveillance space: the bed is desirable because of its appearance and viewing elsewhere, maybe in another time, which is both crucial to and absent from anything that happens in the bed itself.

In both '*Mother*' and Scher's work, the feminine and feminization play a key role in this complexifying, this deconstructing of the structure of desire and identification. It is through feminization of the authority position, of the manipulator/viewer of the surveillance apparatus, that this complexifying is initiated. When the Mother turns the camera on herself she is both appropriating and subjugating herself to the media eye, the ideological eye which, from Gorky to Brecht to contemporary television drama, fixes her in role of 'Mother'. Feminization of this eye disrupts this structure while continuing to engage in it; our feminized identifications are equivalently complex. When Scher engages our desire in a system in which the points of authority have been feminized, the forms of this desire are no longer held in place, no longer rigidly structured.

Of course, the disruptive potential of such work is in the implication that these structures never are rigid, but only seem to be. This seeming becomes apparent when, encouraged by Scher, we begin to examine the figure of the security guard.

## Subaltern security

The security guard is in a position of peculiarly abject authority. Within the corporate structure of the buildings and complexes they monitor, security guards are among the lowest on the ladders of pay and prestige. Chief security personnel may be retired police officers supplementing their pensions, but the uniformed body staring at the bank of video monitors is likely to be underqualified, low paid and, not unusually, an ex-offender. Whereas programmes such as *Crimewatch* encourage us to focus on the police's use of surveillance footage, the systems installed by corporations, shopping mall owners or local authorities are not usually connected to police authority until the point that a crime is detected. The watching, the filtering, is undertaken by the uniformed but minimally trained private security forces.

It was these personnel, understandably anxious to make a bit of extra income from their unrewarding work, who provided the CCTV footage edited together by the producers of *Caught in the Act* – demonstrating visibly that the mass of security footage, rather than being sorted from the criminal and erased, lingers within the system, liable to many uses and interpretations. Public and media response to evidence of this supplementary use of surveillance footage focuses on fear of criminalizations or outrage at invasion of privacy – quintessentially the use of security equipment to see through people's clothes.

In both these responses, however, there is an underlying anxiety very different from the implied Big Brother intrusions. The disreputable use of surveillance recording raises less the possibility that Big Brother is watching than that persons lacking any Big Brotherly qualifications have access to the security machine. As with Scher's security installations, the operatives in most commercial security systems are quite likely to misuse and distort the images and records gathered along the vectors of their own desire. So, the two demographic types most likely to be followed on video security systems without having done anything suspicious are the black male and the young attractive female, two classes occupying contradictory positions in relation to the ideologies of surveillance, but both associated with the object position in relation to the security guard as (desiring) subject. This thought of the security guard as desiring subject of the security system is potentially as disruptive as the imaginary (artist created) subject in Scher's systems (the messages appearing on screen and soundtrack, the distortions of imagery) because his (or her, sometimes) position does not equate with the imagined position of control. Indeed, as an occupation which is one of few paths into employment for individuals with criminal records, the security guard may inhabit a highly ambivalent relationship to the authority he or she represents. However, this is not to imply that the security guard in any way inhabits a position of agency. Scher carefully avoids giving her feminized security guards a direct or controlling relation to the anarchic/authoritarian desires of the systems they seem to guard. In 'real-life' security systems, most guards are far from occupying an intentionally counter-hegemonic relation to the systems or their employers. Their position might rather be described as subaltern – disempowered participants in a complex cultural structure. Scher's work, in particular, invites us to rethink our position as inhabitants of the security matrix, of surveillance space, in relation to this subaltern security guard, asking us what happens to our mode of being in this space when the fantasy of the controlling, patriarchal eye is displaced.

In her influential essay, 'Can the subaltern speak?', Gayatri Spivak (1988) traces the applications of Gramsci's term 'subaltern' via the Indian 'Subaltern Studies' group to an analysis of the post-colonial subaltern subject. The relation of the 'Western' security matrix to the post-colonial subjects who, in many cases, labour as the producers of its hardware is itself very worthy of analysis. For now, though, I would like to refer to some of Spivak's insights while focusing on a subaltern position more in the Gramscian sense – within the hegemonic structure of a given society.

Spivak's analysis starts with a deconstruction of the positions put forward by Foucault and Deleuze in the conversation translated in the English-language collection *Language/Counter-Memory/Practice* as 'Intellectuals and power' (Foucault, 1977). Spivak takes issue with a seeming agreement between the philosophers that, in Foucault's phrase, 'the masses know perfectly well, clearly; they know far better than [the intellectual] and they certainly say it very well' (Foucault, 1977: 207, quoted in Spivak, 1988: 274[5]). The Foucault–Deleuze conversation often seems rife with a timely political naiveté not necessarily endemic to their work in general, but Spivak argues convincingly that this fantasy of a self-knowing speaking subject continues to be produced in Foucault's and Deleuze's work, not least in their most radical moments. Particularly relevant for the current discussion, she addresses the concept of the desiring machine in Deleuze and Guattari's *Anti-Oedipus* (1983), and the promise that it makes to eradicate the subject:

> Desire does not lack anything; it does not lack its object. It is, rather, the subject that is lacking in desire, or desire that lacks a fixed subject; there is no fixed subject except by repression. Desire and its object are a unity; it is the machine, as a machine of a machine. Desire is a machine, the object of desire is also a connected machine, so that the product is lifted from the process of producing and something detaches itself from producing to product and gives a leftover of the vagabond, nomad subject.
>
> (Deleuze and Guattari, 1983: 26, quoted in Spivak, 1988: 273; Spivak's translation)

This would be a tempting reading of the surveillance machine, particularly as analysed in relation to Scher's work and desire: the vagabond, nomad subject of the desiring being the subaltern security guard. But Spivak warns:

> This definition does not alter the specificity of the desiring subject (or leftover subject-effect) that attaches to specific instances of desire or to production of the desiring machine. Moreover, when the connection between desire and the subject is taken as irrelevant or merely reversed, the subject-effect that surreptitiously emerges is much like the generalized ideological subject of the theorist. [. . .] It is certainly not the desiring subject as other.
>
> (Ibid.: 273)

Spivak suggests that readings of the desiring machine which de-emphasize the subject in fact simply de-problematize it – reinstating a transcendental subject. We have seen throughout our analysis of surveillance space that the self uptaking the performativity of this space finds itself ambiguously placed in relation to subject/object position. As in speech acts, when the object of an enunciation may need to be subjectively involved in the speech act for it to be 'happy', so in our relation to surveillance space we subjectively uptake our object position in the space. As noted particularly in Chapter 2, part of this uptake of our object position may involve the fantasy of a transcendental subject outside ourselves, perhaps linked to the role of the super-ego in our psyches. Scher's installations remind us that this transcendental subject is indeed a fantasy. In fact, there is no Big Brother to watch us. Which is not to say (and Scher certainly would not say) that the effect of surveillance systems cannot be real and ominous.

Certainly, there are agents in the creation of surveillance systems whose intents of control are real; but they are not comprehensive and they are exceeded by the network of systems. Police chiefs may fantasize about total visual overview of city centres; banks may long to link our credit and medical records; politicians may wish to pre-dict and marginalize trouble makers, but the growth of surveillance systems exceeds all of these desires. It is understandable, then, if, as in Spivak's reading of Deleuze and Guattari, the desiring machine of surveillance seems to create a fantasy of a transcendental surveil-lance subject (Big Brother), but, following Spivak, it is dangerous if we confuse this subject with the subaltern operators of surveillance systems.

Spivak's essay asks, in a different context, 'Can the subaltern speak?' It is useful to extend this question to the surveillance sys-tem's security guards. The immediate answer, as in Spivak's essay, is 'no'. The system under consideration does not provide a language for subject statements by its subaltern operators. They may file reports, press camera controls, record data details, but these are programmed, passive responses to the machine. In fact, it is rather in the object position of the watched that we can, as we have seen, enact 'subjec-tive' performances. The security guard can become active only by breaking the rules of the surveillance machine – by misusing the cameras for voyeuristic purposes, by misentering data at random, by selling off footage to *Caught in the Act*, by falling asleep. It is in these misuses of the surveillance machine – these acts of un-surveillance – that the security guard can perhaps assert agency. Of course, it is such 'abuses' of security systems which, as noted above, are most often cited by civil libertarians as indicative of the dangers of surveillance. This confusion of misuse for abuse is symptomatic of the Big Brother critique.

Through Spivak's analysis, we can see the importance of separating a projection of the super-ego in surveillance systems from the production of a naturalized transcendental subject. While the former (the super-ego projection) can function productively within the psychic structures of a performative space, the latter (a naturalized transcendental subject) leads to an elision of the real, disempowered position of security operatives. In her essay, Spivak suggests that, if we avoid this elision, the mute movements of the subaltern subject may, with difficulty, be read. Certain art and performance works may also approach the boundary of this mute subject, assisting in this reading.

## Kidnap

The performance works discussed in this chapter have each placed the performer to some degree in the position of the system operator, whether that is literally (in the case of the performers in *Spectators at an Event* or '*Mother*') holding a camera, or figuratively, as in Scher's pink-uniformed security guards. We have seen that, whereas the Big Brother critique of surveillance tends to assign a transcendental power to the subject of the security matrix, these works reveal the gap between the productiveness of the surveillance system and any agency on the part of the operator. Blast Theory's *Kidnap* – described in the opening to this chapter – demonstrated a particularly intensive relationship to this position of surveillance/security operator on the part of a performance group. In this work, the performers were not simply representing operators of surveillance systems; by inviting members of the public to volunteer to be victims of surveillance and kidnap, the performers/artists themselves took on roles which deliberately blurred the line between agency and performance.

Though most of the media coverage of the project centred on the phenomenon of the volunteer victims – the question of who would choose to do this and why[6] – the work itself seemed to me to have many connections with the tradition of endurance-based performance art, in which the artists test the limits of their own psyches and bodies. Visiting the group during the surveillance stage of the project, it was notable that they were placing themselves under intense pressure to fulfil the operation on the terms that they had set for themselves. Their 'victims' happily went about their business; the goal, at this point, was to disrupt nothing in their lives. The legal dilemma that partly framed the performance – the notorious 'Spanner' case in which British and European courts judged that an individual could be prosecuted for acts of cruelty upon another consenting individual – placed the 'victims' of *Kidnap* in the clear while the performers put themselves into a legal minefield.

At the point of the kidnap itself, the focus, and the weight of inconvenience in the work, shifted. Having secured their victims in the safe house, the kidnappers could, we assume, sit back and relax, occasionally stirring themselves to provide the pre-ordered doughnut or interrogation fantasy. The audience watching on the Internet stared at the victims on camera; the 'performers' were elsewhere, off-camera, off-mike. But, in fact, watching on the Internet, there was nothing really very interesting about these 'victims'. Their personal details could be accessed – age, occupation, kidnap fantasy if any. They sat around in a chip-board-clad room doing not much. Unsurprisingly, given what we have discovered about the importance of the boundaries, the obscurities and limitations of surveillance, what could not be seen soon became more interesting than what was on view. When I saw the images initially, only the male victim could be seen on camera and the microphone was off. The female victim immediately became interesting, the unheard conversations a point of fascination. People in the New Media room at the ICA were urgently emailing the kidnappers about the problems with the camera and microphone. (The company did not reply.) When the female victim came on camera, interest in her subsided. When the sound link started functioning, the main interest was in bits of conversation obscured by poor sound quality.

All of this underlines and refers back to the characteristics of surveillance space noted throughout this study – the importance of borders, of the not quite seen, the separation of the mystic code of audio surveillance from the representations of the image. However, whereas in, say, *Spectators at an Event*, the off-stage gaze of the performers, the deflection away, led to a distracted but productive viewing of the performance, in *Kidnap* it was the performers themselves who were off-camera, over the border, and our gaze, our attention, our focus, turned hopefully/hopelessly always towards them.

*Kidnap* cannily explored the position of the security system operator by appearing to explore the situation of the *Kidnap* victim. Of course, the 'victims' of the piece have not been kidnapped – just as in Austin's example a marriage has not taken place on stage. But something else has happened in this not happening – the creation of a relation between audience/viewers and performers/'kidnappers' – a relation created in a space of surveillance systems through the medium of the victims. There is no 'suspension of disbelief' here; we do not pretend to believe that these victims have 'really' been kidnapped – we are invited to peruse the files which demonstrate in application forms and agreements exactly how contractual, how consensual, this arrangement is. Replacing such suspension, however, is uptake of the proposal that something has been made – some space which we inhabit with the unseeable performers. Rather than an etiolated kidnap, a complex network of borders, codes and watching emerges.

Here, then, in *Kidnap*, in which audience members and their images are most central to the structure of the work, the same audience members and images finally lose any cathectic relationship to our watching. Within this matrix, it is the absent position – the position of the security guard – which becomes our focus. Here, though, the 'weakness' of performance is crucial to our experience. As noted in Chapter 4, surveillance space can be said to combine the 'force' of the speech act with the 'weakness' of the stage act – that is to say, at the moment of uptake, of accepting that we are taking part in the experience, via surveillance, of a new, differing space, we may also experience a delay, a moment of suspense in relation to the effects of this acceptance, which is highlighted and complicated in cases in which the surveillance space involved is in some way the product of an art work or performance. In Blast Theory's *Kidnap*, this combination of performative force and performance weakness particularly structures our relation to the figures and roles of the performers/'kidnappers' within the space of the work.

In choosing kidnapping as the imaginative context for their exploration of control and surveillance, Blast Theory's performers initially associated themselves with a frame of reference far more glamorous than the day-to-day drudgery of the security guard. The idea of kidnap, as the company noted in interviews, is associated with the excitement of movies, the tension and drama of news reports. The processes of surveillance accompanying the piece were also of the investigative kind – linking the performers with Coppola movies, private detectives, danger-defying criminals. These accompanying fantasies engage the audience in the piece. Yet the fact that this is a performance undercuts and weakens the associations – Blast Theory's kidnappers struggle by on skimpy Arts Council budgets, worry about parking tickets, are not really dangerous. In this weakness of performance, our engagement with the fantasy of the kidnappers is not negated, but it is altered. Like security guards in their uniforms, police-like but powerless – the performers in *Kidnap* wear the trappings of agency but in fact can not bring about the events that their power trappings would seem to imply. Complexly, and without direct representational reference, the *Kidnap* performers inhabit and question the position of the security subaltern.

## Love beyond Big Brother

The fantasy of Big Brother (or the super-ego) inevitably inhabits many of our experiences, even the framing conditions, of surveillance space. Yet we find that performance work which introduces the audience image into its representational frame tends to question our construction of this controlling fantasy, reminding us of the weak presence often inhabiting the position of control. As Spivak indicates, our seemingly radical readings of desire will undercut little if they reinscribe the transcendental subject in the place where the subaltern is struggling to achieve expression. The works discussed, however, describe paths of desire and identification which, following Diamond's Brechtian-feminist model, we can read as potentially counter-hegemonic to the dominant structures of surveillance.

In Blast Theory's *Kidnap*, the structures of desire and identification are particularly complex. The audience, logging in on the Internet, or visiting the ICA's New Media Lab, identify with the other 'audience' members – those who have become willing victims of the 'kidnap'. We are fascinated by their choice, their rashness, their whiff of perversion. But we are also bored with them; once they are chosen, once they come into shot, they are insufficient for our identifications, they lack the extra, the mystery, the work that a performer brings to a role. Unsatisfied by the audience victims, who seem to (auto) represent us but lack something, our focus goes off-camera, off-net, to the operators of the system, the performers, the 'kidnappers'. Do we desire the kidnappers? Not quite. Their failing nature undercuts their status as object or as super-ego. There is little to desire. Do we identify with them? Our own position seems too distant, too unknowing to feel ourselves in their place. Distractedly, we wander through the virtual space of the performance's web links.

While we are never 'at' this performance in the way we are at most theatre or movie shows, emerging, it seems that we were, nonetheless, 'in' it, and that our desires and identifications have been complexly evoked by this representational space. To a degree, these desires and identifications have cathected on the space itself, on the kidnap space as body, responding unreliably to our probings, occasionally opening up for us, but failing to reveal its inner secrets. We want to be in this story, this movie, this space. We want to see ourselves within it, we know it better than it knows itself, we want to fulfil it. I found myself emailing the company, amidst the technological breakdowns and confusions at the ICA, in the face of my desire to run away: 'I love this piece.'

Of course, at the point of love, the distinction between desire and identification breaks down. Perhaps we can even say that this breakdown characterizes love. (The loved one is that which we both desire as object and identify with as self.) Winston Smith's epiphany in *Nineteen Eighty-Four* – 'He loved Big Brother' – is a doom-laden warning of the potential of every citizen to become the loving 'subject' of absolute authority. Absenting Big Brother from the space of surveillance, bearing in mind Diamond's proposal that identification with any one figure may be multiple and contradictory, what do we do with our love, our emotional turmoil, in and for a space of reproduced selves unreliably distorted by an always abusive, always failing system?

The love that I felt momentarily for *Kidnap*, the use of the word 'love' to describe my reactions, was partly a citation of theatre parlance (in theatre, 'love' for a show is an easy emotion), but it also came to express something more. My own confusions of identification and desire in relation to the piece, my inability to find Big Brothers or Crime Stoppers, to find secure objects or points of identification, meant that I was moving on always within the work's matrix, tantalized by the power relations, the sexual moments, that I was always almost entering. I wanted to interact with this system, send messages, display emotions. My frustrations, my confusions of desire and identification produced the word 'love'.

In contemporary society our 'legitimate claim to being reproduced' is no longer sternly denied by an industrial capital insisting upon our passive consumption of mass images. Instead, an unreliable, although exploitative, image machine multiplies our bodies in digital data streams – across the border from our consciousness or even our knowledge, but reappearing shockingly, reassuringly, suggestively, disruptively in our lives. Our love, our desires and identifications – hand in hand as always with the longing to destroy, reform, improve, dominate – are simultaneously for these multiple bodies and for the system that produces them. As we start to understand this relation in spatial terms, we see that this love also always involves the glance off, away, to the unfigured, not as a transcendental power, but as ambivalent site and source of the accident, the aporia, the unknown – as much a failing subaltern resistance as a controlling force. We realize that the prostheticized self of surveillance and the subaltern operative are equivalent; that, in the impossible process of visualizing, of relating to these self-others, we undertake the important work of refusing the transcendental rigidities of the unseeable. As we follow our love for surveillance self-others, we find ourselves in a new kind of space. And as we learn to move within and also love this surveillance space, our responses to its problems, its challenges, are no longer yes/no, good/bad, crime prevention/Big Brother, but a subtle and unending array of detours, disruptions, exaggerations and alliances: counter-surveillances.

# 6

# Encountering surveillance

The term 'counter-surveillance' has a range of associations. Perhaps the one that most quickly leaps to mind today is the variety of ways in which surveillance is directly challenged by activists, artists and civil libertarians in forms ranging from web sites and articles to protests and performances. Among the better known of these counter-surveillance practitioners are New York's Surveillance Camera Players, an anarchist group who present anti-surveillance performances in front of CCTV cameras. The group's most famous performance is, perhaps inevitably, George Orwell's *Nineteen Eighty-Four*, but it now largely presents original material commenting on privacy rights and related issues. 'We turn the cameras against their original purpose and use them for ours', comments group member Bill Brown (Levin et al., 2002: 618). The target audience is largely passers-by, but the performances are humorously constructed for the supposed eye of the security guard watching on a monitor – with the lines, for example, written on large placards held up for the cameras. The force and commentary of the work is partly created by an aesthetic which engages with the camera and security guard as part of the work's structure.

The *CTRL [SPACE]* exhibition brought together documentation of a number of similar projects, with differing degrees of political and artistic focus; a range of interventions in the systems of surveillance demonstrating the increasingly naturalized ways in which these systems operate. Examples ranged from projects as simple as the Institute for Applied Autonomy's *iSee* web site, which produces maps of surveillance cameras in Manhattan, allowing individuals to find a (perhaps increasingly futile) 'path of least surveillance' between any two points in the city (Levin et al., 2002: 606) (this tactic is widely repeated now – for example Manchester's *Futuresonic* festival printed city-centre surveillance maps on its publicity brochure), to the hilarious and technologically very advanced attempts by scientist Steve Mann to reflect back day-to-day consumer surveillance in stores by use of wearable computer and camera equipment. Mann's work involves a startling combination of technical know-how and wit. He is a leading figure in research on wearable computers and has developed a range of technologies in which an individual can transmit images from a concealed camera to an off-site receiver or web site. However, his suggestions for use of the technology are as conceptual as they are technical. His proposal for the *Maybe Camera* involves wearing a bulky sweatshirt with a large dark acrylic patch on the front and the words printed: 'For YOUR protection, a video record of you and your establishment *may* be transmitted and recorded at remote locations. ALL CRIMINAL ACTS PROSECUTED!' Only in a few cases would these sweatshirts actually contain a camera. Mann's techniques reflect the logic of surveillance back on itself: another performance, *My Manager*, involves wearing a visible camera in a store where photography is not permitted by customers, yet where surveillance is practised. When approached by security staff, Mann tells them that 'my manager' insists he wears the camera to ensure that he is not wasting his time during his errands – and also to ensure that the store doesn't falsely accuse him of shoplifting. This is not photography, he explains, since the signals are being beamed off-site, where they will be turned into images. Mann blames everything on 'my manager', 'just as representatives in an organization absolve themselves of responsibility for their surveillance systems by blaming surveillance on managers' (ibid.: 540).

On a the less conceptual front, there have been a variety of activist protests against surveillance cameras. For example, Simon Davies reports on anti-CCTV protests in Brighton that involved tactics as simple as using black and yellow stickers to identify and warn of the presence of cameras, and the even more straightforward approach of putting black bin bags over cameras. (Norris et al., 1998: 243) Davies himself, as former director of Privacy International, has led a more campaign-based approach to anti-surveillance activity – ranging from web sites and publications, such as the book *Big Brother: Britain's Web of Surveillance and the New Technological Order* (Davies, 1996), to the annual Big Brother Awards – given by Privacy International to those who have done most to endanger privacy. Other organizations active against surveillance in related ways include the Omega Foundation and civil liberties stalwarts such as the ACLU and Liberty.

While appreciating the wit and passion of much of this work, and entirely concurring in the basic thesis that to ignore the proliferation of surveillance in our daily lives could be very dangerous, it has been the thrust of this analysis to avoid a value judgement about the morality or desirability of surveillance technology per se, and to examine ways in which new understandings of surveillance, and particularly spatial understandings, can help us to live creatively and productively in post-private society. However, it has also been clear throughout this study that the predominant ideologies of surveillance need to be actively and complexly challenged and deconstructed if this is to be achieved. As such, I would not want to ignore the importance of counter-surveillance practice in developing thoughts on surveillance space.

But the relationship of counter-surveillance to surveillance technology is itself ambivalent. While anti-surveillance activists are possibly the first groups that we think of today when we imagine counter-surveillance, there are a variety of other forms of counter-surveillant activity.

Counter-surveillance involves using surveillance equipment in a way that reverses the usual vectors of power. As such, its most basic manifestation may be the video cameras carried at most political demonstrations, on the look-out to record any police brutality. Use of cameras on marches is a tradition going back many decades, but the practice perhaps came into its own in the 1980s when commercial video cameras were available to the public at a reasonable price for the first time. In her essay 'On the make: activist video collectives', Catherine Saalfield (1993) outlines the workings of DIVA TV (Damned Interfering Video Activist Television), one of the video collectives associated with ACT UP (The AIDS Coalition to Unleash Power) New York, and describes the origins of video activism in the practice of counter-surveillance:

> After a big demo, the phone rings off the hook with demonstrators who need shots of their arrests. After we stormed the National Institutes of Health in Bethesda, Maryland, one ACT UPer faced a trial for assaulting an officer. He was acquitted after showing the judge footage of himself passively resisting arrests (that is, refusing to stand up for the cop, which is resisting arrest, not assaulting an officer). We've got an image bank of cops

bending people's wrists to the breaking point, of cops slamming protestors on the back and the shoulders with billy clubs, . . . of cops threatening non-violent protesters with trumped-up charges of assault.

(Ibid.: 29–30)

Whereas previously there had, of course, been journalistic imagery of police violence on demonstrations, the proliferation of cheap consumer video equipment meant that the imagery gathered at ACT UP and other demonstrations in the late 1980s and early 1990s was of an unprecedented comprehensiveness.

By the mid-1990s the incorporation of counter-surveillance video recording into political demonstrations was a given, and the increased use of consumer footage in general by television news pro-grammes – in particular, the huge effect of the Rodney King video in generating public response – has meant that the police cannot be at all sure that any act of brutality has not been recorded and passed on to broadcasters. There have been several cases (ranging in scale from the police storming of the Million Youth Rally in New York, 1998, to incidents of police patrols beating up individuals in view of their own in-car video cameras) of police conduct being called into question because of recordings made on their own equipment.[1] While police in many countries, including the UK, still attempt to intimidate activists by recording them on video, in Western democracies at least, political demonstrations are undoubtedly an arena in which the omnipresence of surveillance has largely worked in favour of citizen freedom and against oppressive policing.[2] (An inverse example is provided by the Chinese government's use of footage caught on traffic cameras to track down protestors who participated in the Tiananmen Square demonstrations; Levin et al., 2002: 579.)

As Saalfield points out, however, the surveillance of activism creates effects beyond its original intent of monitoring policing. The videos also become records of the beauty, vanity, pain and humour of demonstrations. ACT UP members, who held the continued celebra-tion of queer sexuality during the AIDS crisis as central to their phi-losophy, used the video documents of their work not only as sources of evidence, but also as means of sexual display, memorialization (few peace-time movements can have had such a death rate) and celebration. Saalfield (1993: 33) describes the process of creating a memorial tape for her friend Roy Navarro:

199

For two days we were there, exorcising, purging, processing crying, giggling, and longing for an image to last forever, or better, to come back to life. We scoured the raw material of many videographers. Looking through footage of that Thanksgiving dinner before he got sick and the demo at the FDA, pausing for Ray's wide grin at a midnight gathering in his studio, trying to identify him at the takeover of the Sixth International AIDS Conference in Montreal, searching everywhere to find even the back of his head or his elbow, we plotted to preserve and to persevere. The finished tape was ultimately for the people who would crowd into his memorial service the next day. But for us it was a defense, our last work about losing a collaborator, a lover, a friend.

Perhaps the omnipresence of counter-surveillance in political activism coincided only by chance with the moment, in the USA at least, when gay and lesbian-led political movements were the most visible and troubling to the state, but it was at least a significant coincidence. For these self-consciously sexual and image-aware activists were quick to see the productivity of counter-surveillance imagery, and to explore such imagery's crossovers into and effects upon other fields of image production. DIVA TV produced a variety of work during the years that it was active, and its legacy in terms of how gay and lesbian people are seen by and portrayed in the media has been lasting. From its early days, the counter-surveillance use of video imagery exceeded its own apparent representational references of policing the police, and reflected also on the image of those who held the counter-surveying cameras.

Alongside such activist use of counter-surveillance video, there has long been a political critique of institutional misuse of surveillance. However, even this misuse can have surprising effects. Artist/activist John Greyson made a movie, *Urinal*, which specifically attacks police use of video to entrap gay men cruising for sex in public restrooms. Greyson's movie involves a complex aesthetic critique of surveillance; however, Greyson records his own surprise at how apparently abusive footage may be viewed. He describes an interview, featured in the movie, with a social worker in his fifties who, having had his life seriously affected by a video surveillance arrest, decided to fight the case in court, where the video footage of him engaged in sex with another man was shown:

I asked him to describe his response, assuming this further violation of his privacy would have been a horribly traumatizing experience. His answer caught me completely off guard:

> 'I didn't expect to see myself behaving sexually on tape. It was a very self-affirming experience. I was rather surprised by how good I felt, even given the anxiety-provoking circumstances, even given that, it was a very self-affirming experience to have to watch yourself behaving sexually on tape. I was delighted by how human and how physical and how sexual and how beautiful I was, and I was surprised.'

> During this monologue, audiences are often extremely quiet, anticipating, as I had done, a tale of degradation, of visual victimization. When he finishes speaking, having reclaimed this surveillance in such a graceful and surprising way, audiences often burst into spontaneous applause.
>
> (Greyson, 1993: 387–8)

Counter-surveillance then becomes not only about reversing the gaze but about opening a space for all sorts of reversals in relation to how the gaze and its imagery may be experienced.

## Outside

Such counter-surveillance reversals can take place on a popular level as well as via activism. A crossover of Greyson's political issues into the entertainment sphere took place in April 1998, when pop star George Michael was arrested in the public toilets at Will Rogers Memorial Park, Los Angeles, by a undercover police officer, on charges of exposing himself. In his subsequent single and video released later that year, Michael took on the subject of sex 'outside'. The *Outside* of the song's title became both a public coming out and a celebration of sex in non-conventional locations. Most notably, the video, featuring couples embracing in view of surveillance cameras and cops dancing and having sex with each other, implied that the libidinal energy released by Michael's own public coming out had allowed a revelation of the truth behind both the apparent covertness of gay cruising and the apparent disinterestedness of police activity.

201

Once, the video seemed to say, everyone has, like Michael, admitted to their desires, we will see an ecstatic orgy of public sexuality. The video is rife with a pop star's megalomania – Michael's long-delayed coming out releases everyone else from repression, and his interest in sex 'outside' is assumed to be universal – but it is also a fairly bold attempt to push through humiliation via self-ridicule into a transformation of the terms of judgement. Like participants on talk shows such as *The Jerry Springer Show* and *The Ricki Lake Show* (see Chapter 5 and below), Michael understands on some level that auto-representation is crucial in any attempt to counter a marginalization, a pathologizing, that has already been enforced. The ground of purity, of the judging eye, is not available – to appear is to be judged – but perhaps by asserting an excess in that appearance, the terms of judgement can be transformed. (That most famous, if indirect, subject of surveillance entrapment, Bill Clinton, discovered – in the wake of the humiliation arising from Linda Tripp's secret taping of her conversation with Monica Lewinsky about Lewinsky's affair with Clinton – that self-abasement rather than any appeal to privacy or understanding was the most effective way to public sympathy.)

In the months following Michael's high-profile arrest, there was almost a war of surveillances in the USA in relation to gay male public sex. With police upping the level of arrests for homosexual activity in public toilets, activists responded in at least one case by putting their own surveillance systems in the toilets and creating a documentary, which when run by local public service television led to the local police chief calling a halt to his officers' activities.[3] However, a third form of surveillance also increased in popularity; over forty American television stations ran late-night shows featuring sex scenes in public toilets. Like the police, the television stations found out about popular sex haunts through specialist sites on the World Wide Web. The late-night showings were, apparently, popular ratings boosters.[4]

In these competing surveillances we undoubtedly see a battle over meaning – illegality versus persecution versus entertainment. Bearing in mind the response of Greyson's interviewee and our earlier discussion of Benjamin's assertion of 'modern man's legitimate claim to being reproduced', we may also see, in the surveillances of both activists and television stations, an attempt to explore the nature of a sexual encounter undertaken not in the public eye, but not in a private place. As the activist recording indicates, the secrecy which has characterized the sexual activity of many homosexual men – particularly closeted homosexuals engaged in public cruising – is no longer the primary issue. Instead, it is the behaviour of police in creating an artificial public event – soliciting homosexual response and then prosecuting it as 'public' – which is up for judgement. In the activist videos, hiding the identity of the homosexual becomes secondary to revealing the behaviour of the police; exposure becomes a protection rather than a threat. In the late-night television showings, the legal considerations of both police and participants are sidelined in the pursuit of an entertainment which, however it may cloak itself in disapproval, undoubtedly receives an erotic charge from the assumption that the participants in the sex act are unaware of the viewing and yet have surrendered any claims to privacy. In the case of the surveillance by police, there is an attempt to reassert an ideology of public/private as a means to entrap homosexuals and raise arrest statistics. In the case of both activists and the cable television shows, however, there is an assertion of the otherness of surveillance space.

## Counter-talk

I would go so far as to argue that talk shows and reality television can themselves function as a kind of counter-surveillance. There are, of course, many negative aspects to these formats. In his book *Voyeur Nation*, Clay Calvert (2000) critiques what he describes as a culture of 'mediated voyeurism', in which, for reasons largely to do with media company profits, our worst voyeuristic instincts are being sanctioned and fed. While he cites research showing that 'despite their seemingly sordid subjects, the shows provide marginalized people with rare access to the means of mass communication to get their message out' (ibid.: 85), Calvert nonetheless believes that the reality television and talk show formats are deeply damaging – and primarily not to the participant, but to the viewer. In his essay 'Telemorphosis', Baudrillard more than concurs. Writing of *Loft Story* (the French version of the *Big Brother* television format) he asserts: '. . . the immersion in banality is the equivalent to a suicide of the species' (Baudrillard in Levin et al., 2002: 484).

We saw in Chapter 5, however, that there is an argument suggesting that the self-insertion of the ordinary individual (and this ordinariness, this banality, appears to be the great sin to Baudrillard) into the televisual realm via talk and reality shows is not simply a prostration before the consumerist logic of media exposure-as-value, but can be read, via Benjamin, as an existentially appropriate strategy in developing a complex bodily, spatial relationship to televisual products. Peter Weibel suggests that shows such as *Big Brother* are simply a way of immunizing the viewer to the surveillance future: 'Observation is not a menace. Observation is entertaining' (ibid.: 215). However, the surveillance future arrived before television's *Big Brother* did; it is equally plausible to suggest that, having realized we live in a surveillance-saturated society, *Big Brother* is one of the ways in which we are exploring what to do about it.

Calvert is appalled by the extremity of much of what is revealed on 'voyeur television'; Baudrillard is appalled by the banality. What is undoubtedly rare in either talk show or *Big Brother* format is a truly competent television performance, though the occasional participants who display this talent often get snapped up as ready-made celebrities (Brian Dowling, winner of *UK Big Brother 2*, is an example). But perhaps televisual performance skills are not what either participants or audiences want form reality shows. Perhaps the very qualities of grotesquerie and banality that so dismay Calvert and Baudrillard are, in fact, not dissimilar in their effects to the performances of surveillance enacted by the Surveillance Camera Players. By inserting ordinary life in all its unpreparedness into the televisual field, reality show participants are revealing to us, the monitor watchers, the system within which we watch – so easy to forget in the bombardment of highly produced tele-fare. And part of what we watch is television's complete inability to represent life. The participants in *The Jerry Springer Show* talk and talk but we do not really get to see their lives, their personalities or their relationships. The participants in *Big Brother* talk and talk, but at the end we feel as though we know almost nothing about them – about what the really think and feel – and, of course, every ejected contestant explains to us as he or she emerges that inside the house they were 'never really myself'.

There are two counter-surveillant delights in watching reality television. One is seeing nothing happen – not just no events, but no character, no life, no revelation. The (usually middle-class) participants who claim that the other housemates in *Big Brother* are boring because their conversation is trivial are missing the point. These people are supposed to be boring, banal, petty, inconsequential. We all suspect that we would be equally banal if we appeared on *Big Brother*. Who would take such an inappropriate opportunity to discuss Nietzsche or learn t'ai chi, and, if they did, would they become less boring? The banality of reality television reveals to us that, however much the various systems surveying us may see, however many times they may catch us picking our nose or failing to pay our credit card bills, they know nothing about us, and the more they survey us the less they know. The superficial nature of *Big Brother* is, contrary to Baudrillard's argument, its triumph for us. It reveals how free we are.

The other delight of these formats is related to, though in some ways also seemingly contradictory to, this banality. There is always a sense that the participants may in fact be performing. When guests on shows such as *The Jerry Springer Show* are revealed to be fakes looking for television exposure, or, in more ambivalent cases, to have exaggerated their dilemmas, the format does not collapse. Rather, we enjoy the frisson of undecideability that a few such cases introduce to our viewing. We take pleasure in judging whether or not the guests are 'for real'. Likewise, on *Big Brother*, contestants will complain loudly if they consider that one of the other participants is 'acting up for the camera'. At home, we enjoy discussing whether or not someone is 'really' as they seem. We particularly enjoy (and the editors of the show undoubtedly exploit) any instances where there is a gap between how a contestant is seen by the other 'housemates' and how we see them. (*Big Brother* in the UK rose to fame on the back of 'Nasty Nick' – adored by his fellow participants for much of the first series, but loathed, in a stage villain way, by the public for being two-faced and scheming.) It might be argued that the public engagement in such performances indicates a tendency to believe that the cameras will reveal what people are 'really' like, but in fact it is the contradiction between the ways of seeing an individual that seems to be enjoyed. It is the uncertainty, the undecideability, which, like the banality of these shows, fascinates.

As counter-surveillances, reality television and talk shows provide a space – albeit a commercially exploited and distorted space – in which the mass-surveyed public can enjoy the gap between the surveyed world in which most of us live and the narrativized, morally resolved world of film and television production, which might seem initially to provide a language by which to understand our captured imagery. In this sense reality television is in direct opposition to the shows such as *Crimewatch UK* analysed in Chapter 1, which work so hard to tie our surveillances back into television narratives. As suggested in the art works discussed in Chapter 5, *Big Brother* and its relations allow us to fantasize the multiplicity of selves we may unleash into the surveillance world, while also reminding us of the uncontrollable ways in which those selves will be distorted and exploited by the consumer–corporate system. In terms of talk show and reality television participants themselves, we may also see that – consistent with the prosthetic, distorted doubles produced in Julia Scher's art works – the grotesque self-parodies that participants often display are precisely the most appropriate way of dealing with self-reproduction in televisual society. It is in producing doubled, distorted bodies and circulating them that we undercut surveillance control, and what better way to do this than in front of millions on *Big Brother* or *The Jerry Springer Show*?

Of course, there is a big gap between *Big Brother* and counter-surveillance activism when it comes to the means of image production and distribution. Television show participants are not in control of the cameras that watch them, nor of the editing that to a great degree guides our responses to them. Questions of technological control are important to discussion of counter-surveillance precisely because surveillance technology can be so advanced. Even on the art-activist level there can be huge disparities in technological access. The Surveillance Camera Players make do with placards and props, while Steve Mann uses some of the most sophisticated portable imaging technology available. Mann comments that he is attempting to create commercially useful versions of his Wear-Cam so that it will become a common consumer product. Commercial availability for other purposes will have the side-effect of making it commonplace for stores to be under surveillance by their customers (Levin et al., 2002: 543). Such use of surveillance proliferation will probably reflect the ongoing battles for control on the web. It seems that such proliferation is a more likely outcome than the kinds of restrictions that some privacy activists hope for.

## Enemies in the state?

The issue of technological control and counter-surveillance is explored (and exploited) in movies such as *Enemy of the State* (Tony Scott, 1988). Scott's movie is probably the most commercially successful treatment in recent years of the theme of government surveillance. It portrays an America in which the National Security Agency (NSA) has developed its surveillance capabilities to the point that any individual can be tracked 100 per cent of the time. This is not a science fiction movie. While the utter amorality with which the agency pursues its agenda of inscribing its powers in law may or may not equate with fact, the technology depicted, from global satellite imagery to minute sensors and microphones, is no more than state of the art. The movie's declared politics is humanistic: pro-ACLU and the right to privacy in the home. Its aesthetics, however, involve an orgy of surveillance techno-fetishism, from the surveillance camera images of the opening credits, through the shots of satellites pinpointing action hundreds of miles below, to the closing scene in which hero Will Smith finds that his living room has been re-bugged by his counter-surveillance mentor, Gene Hackman, allowing them to exchange greetings and insults over an unknown distance. This techno-fetishism is, in fact, embodied in Gene Hackman's character, a former NSA operative, who loves the agency but, after being abandoned by it due to an aborted mission, can continue to engage in its culture only via illegal uses of the technology. Hackman's character has no discernible politics – he engages in Smith's struggle partly because he just gets caught up in the challenge and partly because of the NSA's murder of a woman who he thinks of as a daughter – but he engages passionately. He lives in a post-private world, an excessive version of Hackman's character in Coppola's 1974 *The Conversation*, whose obsession with secrecy is matched only by his conviction that real privacy is unobtainable. However, whereas Smith's ACLU lawyer wife is powerless to stop the destruction of their lives by the NSA, Hackman teaches Smith the realities of surveillance, and the key les-

sons of how to use 'your weaknesses as your strength' and turn the
surveillance network against itself. (Smith eventually manages to pit
NSA, Mafia and FBI systems against each other, leading to a shoot-
out in which he simply stands and watches.)

True to its genre as a Hollywood action movie, *Enemy of the State*
involves much jumping out of moving cars and scaling the sides of
buildings by Smith's labour lawyer character. On one level, we are
left feeling fairly hopeless as regards our own chances of successfully employing Hackman's counter-surveillance advice. On the other
hand, the movie demonstrates just how susceptible the government
system is to the omnipresence of surveillance. The action of the
movie is generated from the fact that the murder by the NSA of a
senator in a deserted park is caught on cameras installed to study the
park's birds; Hackman's counter-surveillance is made possible with
the use of equipment easily purchased in a commercial surveillance
store. However uncomfortably it may sit with the film's emotional
base in happy, private home life, it is the proliferation, the excess, of
surveillance technology which carries the hopes of the film. The film
suggests that, whatever our emotional longings, an effective strategy
of counter-surveillance necessarily involves the perpetual use of
surveillance technology to open up and revisualize the world and
work of its originators.

## Invisible cops

Like Peter Weir's *The Truman Show* (1998), *Enemy of the State* generates much of its audience's pleasure from allowing us to see the
highly sophisticated technical and organizational systems that keep
the protagonist under constant surveillance, while the protagonist
himself becomes only slowly aware of this surveillance. In this way,
these movies repeat the ideological structuring of surveillance crime
shows, in which the audience is placed in the position of surveyor, not
surveyed. (In contrast to these crime shows, however, the audience is
encouraged to identify with the object of surveillance.) The positioning of audience viewpoint at the point of surveillance omniscience is,
of course, counter to lived experience, which is closer to the situation
hauntingly figured in the conclusion to Coppola's *The Conversation*,
in which the surveillance expert Hackman tears his own apartment

apart, unsure whether or how he is being bugged, unsure as to the boundaries of his own paranoia. As this earlier example points out in fact, and as the emergence of the counter-surveillance scenes in the later part of *Enemy of the State* also suggest, there is no point of surveillance omniscience. However much we may see, we can never know that we are not also being seen and overheard.

The invisible cops who may or may not be watching us are susceptible to opposition not because counter-surveillance limits the reach of their surveillance capabilities, but because it proliferates the effects of surveillance beyond the control of any one system. An engagement in counter-surveillance involves a knowledgeable interaction with and use of intrusive technologies (though this knowledge may be as low-tech as the Surveillance Camera Players with their cardboard signs). As Julia Scher suggests in her work, it is in ignoring surveillance, in allowing it to record and reproduce us invisibly, that the greatest danger lies. Sher's installations insist that we engage productively, creatively, libidinally, with the systems of surveillance. A realization that the bodies created in the surveillance web are linked to our own bodies – are not simple representations or straightforward falsifications, but hybrid versions of our selves, susceptible to our interventions – moves us towards a strategic relationship to these surveillance bodies.

Not all of these counter-surveillances need involve 'real-life' situations. Orwell's story of Big Brother has been one of the most influential of all interventions into the public understanding and even the practice of surveillance. For all its Hollywood faults, *Enemy of the State* provided grounds for a range of popular journalistic investigations into state security systems, and other movies with related themes, such as *Gattaca* and *Minority Report*, have had similar effects.[5] The stories that we tell about surveillance will be important factors in how we counter, and encounter, it.

## Love in surveillance space

Perhaps some of these narratives will be love stories. In the conclusion to the last chapter I suggested that the multiple desires and identifications that arise within surveillance space can sometimes coalesce into feelings of love. When we 'uptake' the possibility that

the surveillance matrix creates not simply a parade of representations, but a lived space in which we experience our bodies and their
relationships differently from previously, we inevitably accept that
the emotions and needs intrinsic to human life will likewise be recon-
figured in this new space. An example of such a narrative is developed in Wim Wenders' morally and structurally complex 1997 movie
*The End of Violence*. Here, in one of the plots, a scientist in charge of
implementing a total street surveillance system for Los Angeles lives
in the dome of an observatory, his housekeeping needs seen to by a
Central American refugee. (As in *Enemy of the State* much of the plot
drive is provided by the government surveillance agency's attempt to
ensure that the legislature supports its work.) A love affair develops
between the scientist, who is increasingly troubled by his work, and
the 'housekeeper'. However, when the scientist attempts to alert an
investigator to illegalities being pursued in support of the system,
the housekeeper kills him. She has been keeping the scientist under
surveillance. The twist in the story, however, is not as simple as this
single turn. The suggestion is that the love between the two is real.
In a final scene between the housekeeper and the head of the security
agency, we learn that the woman has accepted the assignment in
order to pay a real debt to the agency for saving the lives of her
and her daughter in their home country. We also see the head of the
agency talk eloquently and with belief of the system's potential (for
now, at least, delayed by the public knowledge generated through the
narrative's developments) to increase safety and quality of life in Los
Angeles – to bring about the end of violence.

We have seen in detail in this study how spurious the claims to
equate surveillance with crime elimination can be; what is notable
in Wenders' movie, however, is the degree to which he allows a passion and romance to his various characters, his various surveyors.
He allows us to imagine that it is, in considerable part, this very
passion, this passionate surveillance, that creates and allows for the
love enacted in the movie. In one of the movie's most moving scenes,
the scientist bonds with the housekeeper's daughter as they stare up
into the skies through the observatory's old telescope, developing a
new familial relationship through the shared longing to see, to know.
Moreover, the movie also embodies a radical uncertainty in the status
of the surveyor. The scientist believes that he is falling for a subaltern

woman, ignorant of more than a few words of English. In fact, he is falling for his surveyor and assassin. There again, it is the woman's subaltern position in the wider geopolitical system that places her in this surveyor role.

## Mourning and meaning

The title of Wenders' movie points us to a key dilemma in relation to stories and actions of counter-surveillance as well as surveillance. The arguments can be made passionately that a particular surveillance system, or counter-surveillance action, will end violence by exposing it. However, we have seen that our engagement in surveillance is structured in a profound way by death, and, as Wenders' story indicates, there is sufficient ambivalence on either side of any surveillance binary to make it possible that a passion to prevent violence may have unexpected and even deadly consequences.

In analysing the early counter-surveillance of ACT UP, we saw footage taken on demonstrations being used to create memorials. Given the nature of ACT UP, such memorial tapes were all too frequent secondary uses of counter-surveillance footage, but this use of the tapes points not to an exception, but to a logic in the use of counter-surveillance footage – because if cameras are recording real or potential violence against us, they are also always potentially filming our deaths. Much of the emotion and urgency that surrounds the discourse of counter-surveillance and its activists undoubtedly arises from the profound structural relationship of surveillance to death. We saw in Chapter 3, in the case or Kevin Narey's death, that a sense of political outrage at the death among friends and family centred itself, uselessly, on the failure of surveillance cameras to record Narey's end – to protect him from a dying that in fact the cameras could only have witnessed. Similarly, if inversely, anti-surveillance activists tend to sense a very deep-running threat to life and livelihood in these passive recording instruments. Our relationship to death's aporia in the structures of surveillance is far from rational, rather it is traumatic – our surveillance images bring a bodily response that is closely linked to the suggestion in surveillance systems that our own deaths may appear at any time. As such, any appearance of ourselves on surveillance footage can carry traces of this trauma-in-waiting, the ultimate surveillance scene that we, of course, will never, ourselves, see.

The insertion of selves under the camera's gaze by reality and talk show participants is also structured by this trauma. When guests go on *The Jerry Springer Show*, they know full well that they will be presented as freaks. They also know that they will walk away safe, and perhaps with a bit of usable fame. The display that the guests enact is surely partly an attempt to control their trauma by exposing it. By presenting – performing – their personal conflicts and obsessions in the most extreme way they can, talk show participants externalize their traumatized selves, create, in the sense indicated in our analysis of Julia Scher's work, other bodies, separate from their physical bodies, which can exist in the televisual, ultra-surveyed realm. The more extreme these bodies are, the more they will separate themselves from the real lives and bodies that originated them. These talk show bodies can have effects of their own – disgusting, enticing, politicizing public discourse on a range of issues, and the guests can walk away, leaving these trauma bodies to circulate. Such a pact with the televisual realm and its self-abasements is fundamentally related to ways in which death structures our surveillance viewings – because the more separated from us the bodies appearing in the image realm are, the more the potential death haunting the realm is also separated from us. While not necessarily suggesting that an appearance on *The Jerry Springer Show* has any real positive effect in an individual's life, we might nonetheless say that, in a compulsive way, structured by surveillance culture, talk show guests present their traumatized selves on television to kill them off.

On reality television shows such as *Big Brother*, the relationship to self-presentation is far more cautious. As Baudrillard and many other commentators have noted, what surprises about these shows is the lack of anything interesting emerging – and our interest in this lack. We have discussed above why and how this engagement in 'banality' makes sense for viewers of *Big Brother*; for contestants, the basic structures are perhaps not dissimilar to those processed very differently by talk show participants. *Big Brother* contestants tend to construct their surveillance selves very carefully; unlike talk show guests, they will probably be called on to re-enact these selves for the public for anything from a few weeks to several years after the show has ended. We discussed above how little we get to know about these participants, for all our viewing, and the revelations that contestants make are often carefully judged for their impact. (Interestingly, different versions of the participants' selves, based on rumour and exposé of their pasts, are often living far more excessive, scurrilous lives in the tabloid press while the real bodies are locked inside the house.) When they do come, *Big Brother* revelations are hardly in the *The Jerry Springer Show*'s league – usually involving confessions of sexual orientation or of slightly risqué behaviour in younger days. Clearly, participants in the programme are partly attracted to it through the prospect of fame or, perhaps more accurately, of access, for a while at least, to the celebrity lifestyle that we are all supposed to covet. However, once under the twenty-four-hour cameras, they do not behave like celebrities (who would, of course, typically wear sunglasses and shield themselves from prying lenses in any non-controlled television studio or film set environment). Instead, the contestants find themselves making versions of themselves – the versions which can perhaps become celebrities once they leave the house. (In second-generation formats such as *Celebrity Big Brother*, this formula is used to recreate or reinvigorate declining celebrity status.) Like the extreme performances of the talk show guests, these newly created versions of self are separate from the 'real' people making them – they are constructed, carefully, in a pact with the cameras. As such, the *Big Brother* contestants engage with a desire deeper than the need for celebrity (and perhaps informing it) – the desire to create selves separate from our day-to-day identities, selves which will work and, eventually, die on our behalf.

In the seemingly protective gaze of activist counter-surveillance, the trauma of a pact between surveillance and death will inevitably cut deep. If the encounter with death structures our experience of surveillance imagery, its relation to counter-surveillance is particularly significant, and it is through an aesthetics of counter-surveillance that we register its full traumatic force. Whereas the policing gaze of surveillance, however much it may be eroticized and subverted, has an association with a disapproving and potentially destructive power at its core, the process of counter-surveillance is presumed to be one of protection. A policing surveillance, and the ideology of crime which structures its acceptance, implies a violence against those who are caught 'doing wrong'; counter-surveillance, by contrast, is imagined as a gaze which restores the integrity of the body, disproves rumours of its misbehaviour, restores its coherence in the face of its systematic misinterpretation. For this protective gaze also to carry an implication of our death is deeply disturbing. And if, following the arguments of this study, we see this counter-surveillance death not as an extreme, limit situation, but as the basic expectation informing all of our recorded appearances, we will begin to understand how emotional and upsetting our counter-surveillance appearances can be. As Saalfield indicates throughout her article, reactions by activists to the appearance of themselves and loved ones in counter-surveillance videos, or other compilations based on counter-surveillance footage, could be extreme. Such images show us selves cut off from our interiority; they allow us to appear to ourselves as we might appear to others.

In our encounters with ourselves under surveillance and under counter-surveillance, we are presented with an image of the self unframed, unnarrativized, unattached to our lives – an image of a self separated from our consciousness. This encounter is also based on the deep-seated assumption that an unexpected appearance of our image as news, as surveillance footage, implies a harm to ourselves, a fatality. This assumption is only strengthened in the case of counter-surveillance, the very purpose of which is to reveal wrongs that have been done to us. Watching ourselves re-presented, for whatever reason, on footage gathered for protective counter-surveillance purposes, we are shocked into a confrontation with the impossible possibility – with the ultimate separation from ourselves.

Under surveillance, I re-encounter my body as other, and discover that it is already dead.[6]

However, this discovery is not located in the realm of consciousness, where death can register only as an aporia; it is recognized instead somatically – evoking the body's responses to the desires for and fears of its death, summoning that trauma in the guise of elation or nausea.

## Encountering death

The idea that the image that counter-surveillance preserves is of a body which is 'already dead' would seem at first glance to be contradictory to its protective character. However, the recognition of the body as already dead, while it may inevitably be traumatic, is not necessarily horrific. Rather, the expression of that trauma, and its separation from the violence of the state, may become an act of liberation. As the memorial tapes of AIDS activists were a forum to reclaim meaning from the senseless death of loved ones, and to reclaim mourning from the unwanted religious ceremonies and silences of unsympathetic relatives, so the counter-surveillance image's traumatic conjuring of our deaths allows us to feel, if not think, the possibility that we are other than, or as well as, our consciousness, that we exist also in another's lust, another's mourning, and that the separation from self feared in death has already happened.

The surveillance encounter with the already dead body is profoundly disruptive of time and sequence. Again and again in analysing surveillance space, we have seen how the introduction of the recording device disrupts the expectation of presence – of a scene which is present to itself and in the present. Engaging in counter-surveillance, we attempt to protect our present selves by inserting into the event the possibility of future viewings, but we also make the event a scene of memorialization, a scene which expects its own recall and becomes other than its apparent actions. Whereas our holiday videos are a constructed attempt to tell the story of ourselves, to create sequence and make sense, to erase the difference between one moment of our consciousness and the next, our counter-surveillances are not made in the knowledge of how they will be used, and they do not centralize us or narrate us. Rather, they are made as means of negotiating a very Benjaminian world in which the events of the past are continually battled over. In this to-be-argued-over past, our images will be edited out or in according to values having little to do with the sequence of our own consciousness. Enacting our actions in the counter-surveillance gaze, we accept a politics of editing which may use or erase our images. Subjects neither of the narratives of our own videos, nor of the objectification of an external media camera, we are, in relation to this protecting counter-surveillance gaze, surrendering the meaning of our bodies to future interpretation, unpredictable but in line with the intent of our current actions.

In a strange but more than metaphorical way, activists who consent to counter-surveillance give up their lives for the cause.

## Open spaces

Surveillance culture is emerging and transitional. The framing ideology of crime prevention, which has, by and large, enabled the mass installation of surveillance systems in Western societies with an engrained attachment to privacy traditions, is no longer able to contain the innumerable manifestations of surveillance practice. In many ways, the job of the ideology is done. The surveillance systems are installed, they are not about to be dismantled. There is, in fact, no-one with the power to dismantle them. Despite its exhaustion, however, crime prevention continues to dominate public understanding of surveillance, alongside a nostalgia for privacy.

In this study, I have focused on the spatial characteristics of surveillance experience in order to achieve an understanding of the ways in which surveillance technologies actually function culturally, and to examine the possibilities of our agency within this culture. While spatial uptake of surveillance experience will eventually no doubt be encouraged in a commodified form, we have found that, fully experienced, surveillance space is radical in its discontinuity from given representational understandings.

Surveillance space reintroduces reference to death into our culture in surprising and important ways. The many characteristics of this space – the importance of its borders and obscurings, its temporal discontinuities, its separations of sound and image – cite the 'impossible possibility' of death, referring, ultimately, we have seen, to the image of an 'already dead' self. The existential possibilities opened by a full engagement in surveillance space are considerable. In particular, this space disrupts the boundary between concepts of public and private in a way which affects debates ranging from the legislation of homosexuality to the right of assembly in shopping malls. Whereas civil libertarians have sometimes fallen into a weary attempt to recreate privacy and public assembly absolutes within a relativistic culture, an understanding of surveillance space opens the possibility that these debates can be reframed around issues such as ownership of imagery and data selves, freedom of image/data circulation, the multiplicity and discontinuities of data experience and the emotional instability of security systems.

## Agency and suspense

However, the questions of surveillance cannot be resolved in a controlling discourse. We have found, rather, that there is a suspense in relation to surveillance space, a suspense at the point when the spatial experience has been uptaken, a suspense as to how we will be affected, how we will respond within this space. It is at the point of this suspense, not at a programmatic level, that the radical possibilities of surveillance space open up.

This does not deny the possibility of agency, even at the level of spatial production. For example, on a politically oppositional level, there are undoubtedly many activists and artists who create representational spaces using surveillance-related technology with the intention of having specific counter-hegemonic effects upon their audience. Indeed, without such counter-surveillance intentionality our capacities, our tools, for responding to surveillance society in general would be much limited. Such works of art and activism with very specific political messages cannot simply be surrendered to an indeterminacy in relation to the effect they have. Rather, the message of such work enters into the lexicon of surveillance, becomes part of the emotional experience which informs and determines our response to each surveillance incident. The 'force' of such work exists alongside the suspense of our responses to surveillance space, a necessary counter to hegemonic surveillance ideologies. However, this work does not produce a counter-ideology, and it has been the argument throughout this book that we should not be looking for one. Its force-as-message exists alongside, doubled with the weakness that acknowledges, traumatically, that this is all and only a field of representations.

The agency of counter-surveillance produces excess. It draws attention to the suspense in surveillance space, it demands that we pause there. And once we have paused, the self-evidence of surveillance will open into a multifaceted 'lived space'.

The art and performance works (including several of the examples of popular culture) discussed in this study may or may not have discursive intentions in terms of a counter-hegemonic engagement with surveillance practice. However, each example helps us to comprehend, to experience the possibilities for, the openness of, response in surveillance space. Not that this response is volitional; rather it is complex, traumatic, personal. These works help us to understand the degree to which discontinuity and excess define surveillance space, undercutting the simplifications of commodification.

## Secret codes in surveillance space

A key means of introducing the indeterminacy, the excess of lived space, into government and corporate surveillance spaces will be the use of code. The sound of surveillance has been found to be radically separate from the images and data worlds of surveillance. The relation of audio surveillance to code has been seen to grow out of the need to make sense of, to bring into representation, the emotions conjured by surveillance sound. This encodedness has, however, in turn produced its own excess, for example in Benjamin Zephaniah's language, which cannot be contained by representational equivalence. The sound of the voice under surveillance continues to conjure not some pre-deconstructive chimera of presence, but a sense of secrecy, mystery even – of a space that perpetually needs to be travelled into further, which has not revealed itself fully. The most surveyed areas of our cities (for example Newham, in London, which pioneered use of the Visionics face recognition system, and where Zephaniah lives) will often be the very areas where – through the cultural diversity of their inhabitants – the apparent self-evidence of the visual register will be daily undermined by the variety of languages and dialects spoken (Newham is the most multicultural of London's boroughs). The challenge of communication under surveillance is to develop a continual proliferation of codes, beyond any one authority's translation skills. In the face of such encodedness and its promises of realms beyond direct representation, the discontinuities of surveillance space will always win out over apparent ideological unities, and the troubling, troublesome edges of surveillance, the complexities of death, sexuality, race, will emerge as surveillance's true material. Artists, musicians and writers such as Zephaniah are creating the codes with which the multiplicity of surveillance space can be negotiated. Whereas the privilege of privacy stood in a binary with the concept of social space, such encodedness will wind through the web of surveillance. It will be in this encodedness that any state or corporate claim to *know* through surveillance will be revealed as false. Encodedness (not only of sound, but by extension of all surveillance media – and perhaps particularly of data) will be a key to counter-hegemonic surveillance practise. In Lefebvre's term, it will help maintain the promise of surveillance space as 'differential space'.

## Surveillance consciousness

The struggle over surveillance space is, then, a struggle between conceptual self-evidence and lived complexity. Excessive, productive surveillance space is both a current practice and a future hope. If, however, it is not to be reduced to a simplified and ultimately repressive equivalence between concept and effect, we will need to surrender an attachment to certain spatial notions – notably privacy – which work counter to an engagement in surveillance productivity. Data access, freedom of information and politicized counter-surveillance can all be tools of this productivity if they are undertaken on the understanding that the goal can never be to close down surveillance, but rather to multiply its effects, to deconstruct its power structures. (Encodedness – secret language, cultural specificity – has an association with struggle and minority status that the privilege of privacy could never match.) The proliferation of bodies and codes in surveillance space will weave suspense and indeterminacy through that space, subverting any tyranny of meaning.

The emergence of surveillance culture is nothing less than a challenge to our consciousnesses As Julia Scher warns, we ignore the circulating, multiple, hybrid versions of ourselves at our peril. If we deny their relation to us in an attempt to maintain the integrity of a unified self – rooted in rights of privacy – we risk surrendering any control, any agency, in relation to our lives and society. To embrace these other, hybrid selves, to incorporate them into a radically changed consciousness, is not an easy task. It involves, at its root, an engagement with the trauma of our own deaths. However, the art work and cultural practices discussed in this study demonstrate the numerous ways in which initial suspense-filled steps can be taken into the complex, spatial experience of surveillance.

Foucault, the arch-theorist of surveillance and disciplinarity, was infamous for predicting the death of 'man', the humanist invention. He could not, perhaps, know the degree to which the systems of surveillance which contributed to the formation of humanist ideology would, in their technological proliferation, help to instigate its collapse. Emerging into surveillance culture, reading through and beyond Foucault, we perhaps find a hint of the self which may replace 'man', not in the immortal cyborg of so much scientific propaganda, but in a disjointed, prostheticized, hybrid, multiple body, appearing and disappearing in the irregular, contradictory landscape of surveillance space.

# Notes

## Introduction: thinking surveillance

1  In *The Simulation of Surveillance*, William Bogard (1996: 24) makes a strong case for a description of contemporary 'telematic society' in which surveillance and simulation, while different processes, are two sides of the panoptic coin:

> a picture emerges of an 'observation-machine' that fashions its own images for its own consumption, for which an 'outside' no longer exists, where nothing is left to control because everything is under control from the very beginning.

His book:

> is not, or at least not only, an empirical description of telematic societies as they exist today. It is an account of a delusion of those societies, which today appear ever more willing to sacrifice themselves to simulation in order to push surveillance to its absolute limits.
>
> (Ibid.: 24)

However, the argument itself seems to become as hermetic as the society it describes and, although a long and complex journey is taken in the book, the conclusion seems ultimately to be a reiteration of the usual Baudrillardian world-view, with the activity of surveillance subsumed into the generic image circulation of the hyper-real, and exhaustion offered as the only way out:

> The high-tech gloss of electronics, the screen, the rush of hypercontrol, the fascination with decoding: the time is coming, perhaps sooner than we think, when all this will be excruciatingly boring, the endlessly dull fantasy, the simulated pleasures of virtual systems. Only then, perhaps, will the cyborg run out of time.
>
> (Ibid.: 183)

2  William Staples, in *Everyday Surveillance* (Staples, 2000), provides an enjoyable overview of surveillance in the USA, arguing largely from a Foucauldian perspective of disciplinarity throughout. See also *The Maximum Surveillance Society* by Norris and Armstrong:

There is no single 'Big Brother' who is watching over us but lots of little brothers each with their own agendas. This is where Foucault's conception of the dispersal of discipline is especially apposite.

For Foucault, the power of disciplinary social control lay not with its centralisation in a totalitarian state regime but in its dispersal from its idealised form in the prison throughout the myriad of public an private institutions that make up the social fabric. Thus, the deployment of CCTV is not to enable the enforcement of some singular disciplinary norms, but the situational norms relevant to particular sectional interests.

(Norris and Armstrong, 1999: 7)

3 In September 2002, the *Guardian* produced a series of three Saturday supplements specifically on surveillance, titled 'Big Brother', exhaustively chronicling the range of contemporary surveillance and framing the whole in a campaign for stronger civil liberties protections. Marx is also a prolific producer of articles himself (see Bibliography).

# 1 An ideology of crime

1 Cambell in Levin et al. (2002: 158–69). See also Davies (1996) and Parker (2000).
2 Ford, M. (1999) *Surveillance and Privacy at Work*, Institute of Employment Rights, London. 'Call to regulate growth in workplace spying', *Guardian*, 18 February 1999. 'Yes there is someone watching over you – the boss', *The Times*, 15 June 1998. Marx, G.T. and Sherizen, S. (1986) 'Monitoring on the job', *Technology Review*, November/December.
3 'Yours for £100; satellite pictures of the neighbours', *Sunday Telegraph*, 27 September 1997.
4 'All-seeing robodog set to become the NYPD's best friend', *Guardian*, 10 September 1996.
5 Norris and Armstrong (1999: 40–2) give an outline of one average man's day, counting his encounters with over 300 cameras and thirty separate CCTV systems.
6 'Data from the intercepts taken from international telecommunications systems can be collated and stored and run past the dictionaries. Any matches, however insignificant, can be plucked out and fed through two further filtering operations before being forwarded to analysts for human evaluation' (Parker, 2001: 116). 'In its most up-to-date form, Echelon can detect matches from interceptions of telexes, faxes, e-mails, and Internet documents, in fact all forms of modern communications, virtually without exception' (ibid.: 117).
7 In June 2002, the *Guardian* ran a series of articles exposing the UK government's plans to extend the Regulation of Investigatory Powers Act, 2000 in a way that would have allowed access to records of individuals' emails and phone calls. A range of bodies, such as local councils, the Food

Standards Agency and the National Health Service, would have been able to access these records without needing permission from the courts. The government withdrew the proposed amendment ('Blunkett shelves access to data plans', *Guardian*, 19 June 2002), although under the original act these powers remain available to the police, customs, the intelligence services and the Inland Revenue.

8    Perri 6 (1998) argues forcefully that privacy has been redefined rather than lost, developing to become no longer a question of limiting what organizations know about us, but rather of defining what it is permissible for them to do with that knowledge (ibid.: 13). However, it is questionable from a semantic viewpoint whether Perri 6's new definition retains sufficient connection to the generally accepted meaning of the word 'privacy' to make it viable.

9    The Police and Criminal Evidence Act, 1984. Norris et al. (1998: 270) note that, although police use of 'sus' may have been moderated in the 1990s, the 1994 Criminal Justice and Public Order Act in fact removed the requirement for 'individualized suspicion' before a stop and search could be carried out, in effect allowing the police to stop and search not only those exhibiting suspicious personal behaviour, but also any member of a group acting 'suspiciously'. In practice, this could justify stop and search on the basis of skin colour alone.

10    It is true that automatic heat or light sensors cannot discriminate on the basis of social class, race or gender, however intelligent image processing systems suffer from no such limitations. The same algorithmic techniques that can differentiate faces can also be used to differentiate between black and white and, with time, may also be able to distinguish between young and old and male and female. Again, rather than removing discrimination, the new automated technologies may intensify it. It is here that the regulatory context becomes crucial. And yet there are no laws banning, or even regulating, the use of discriminatory algorithms

(Norris et al., 1998: 270).

11    Britain is still probably the most heavily surveyed country in the world, with an estimated 2.5 million CCTV cameras, 10 per cent of the world's total (Meek, J., 'Robo Cop', *Guardian*, G2, 13 June 2002).

12    Norris and Armstrong (1999: 47) provide details of the massive deployment of surveillance cameras on the London Underground.

13    In the official inquiry, Lord Justice Taylor found that the officer in charge, Chief Superintendent David Duckenfield, had 'failed to take effective control', in 'a blunder of the first order'. What was never agreed upon was the degree of police culpability. Here the issue of surveillance was central. In the inquiry, the police maintained that a surveillance camera showing images of the overcrowded pens was faulty. Subsequently, the camera technician who installed and maintained the cameras claimed that they were working and that he himself could see on the day that the pens were over-full ('Controversial drama-documentary leads to calls for fresh investigation

into Hillsborough soccer disaster,' *Daily Telegraph,* 7 December 1996; 'Police "were aware of crush" at fatal match,' *Guardian,* 11 November 1996; 'Hillsborough TV drama revives fight for enquiry,' *Guardian,* 7 December 1996). In 1997, the case was reopened by the Crown Prosecution Service, after the tape taken by the camera in question was found in the archives of Yorkshire TV. The police had claimed that the tape had 'gone missing' (Hillsborough case reopened', *Guardian* 1 April, 1997).

14 The *Crimewatch* genre is closely linked to the police 'reality television' programme. This format, typified by the US Fox TV show *Cops,* follows police officers in their cars, a camera riding in the front passenger seat, Starsky to the driver's Hutch. Examples in the UK include *X Cars* (a *Cops*-type programme that makes direct reference in its name to a ground-breaking British fictional television cop programme, *Z Cars,* a show which, in the 1970s, was considered to have introduced a new level of 'realism' to British television).

15 A particularly interesting convolution of police surveillance and television occurred in the BBC series *Mersey Blues* (again located in Liverpool). In this 'fly on the wall' documentary series, the production team followed Merseyside Police squads involved in drug, firearms and murder cases. During the filming, one of the primary 'characters' to emerge as a subject of the documentary was Detective Chief Inspector Elmore Davies, who provided the sort of individuality upon which such documentaries thrive. While shooting, however, the production crew were not aware that Davies was under surveillance by Merseyside's anti-corruption unit. In the final episode of *Mersey Blues,* the documentary team watch as the anti-corruption surveillance team catch their man. Davies was subsequently sentenced to five years in jail ('Mersey police star in their own horror show', *Observer,* 10 January 1999; *Mersey Blues,* Episode 5, BBC).

16 In Žižek's reading of Lacan,' the symbolic realm into which the subject is brought through the imposition of phallic law is not only the sphere of language/signification in general, it is also the sphere of ideologies – the systems of understanding which, through language, have historically naturalized the development of power relations. In Žižek's work, a certain prima facie sense of the symbolic found in standard readings of Lacan is replaced by an ideological realm structured according to Lacanian principles but in a constant state of historical flux under the influence of pogroms, colonial ambitions and Hollywood fashions.

17 There is a mass of contradictory evidence as to the actual effect of surveillance cameras on crime rates. Studies carried out by the British Home Office in Newcastle and Birmingham were inconclusive:

> In Newcastle, cameras were installed in some parts of the city centre, but not other bits. Six months later, there had been no significant change in mugging, which CCTV is primarily aimed at preventing. Burglary, criminal damage and car theft had all fallen faster in the area with CCTV than in the Northumbria police district as a whole; but they had fallen nearly as fast

in the non-CCTV area of central Newcastle. .... In Birmingham, mugging, assault, car theft and burglary all fell significantly over two and a half years in the areas where CCTV was installed, compared with other areas. Theft from vehicles, however, rose four-fold over the same period. .... Odder still, a survey in the London borough of Sutton carried out last year by South Bank University found that, a year after the introduction of CCTV, crime had dropped by 13 per cent in the area covered by camera – and by 30 per cent in the rest of the borough.

(*The Economist*, 13 April 1996)

The survey also suggested that sometimes CCTV displaces crime into other areas ('TV cameras have limited effect on town centre crime', *Telegraph*, 2 January 1996). The primary evidence of success comes from police-compiled statistics and press releases ('Video cameras have cut mugging', *The Times*, 29 March 1998). King's Lynn, the English town which led the move towards street surveillance, never had a serious crime problem:

This town of 30,000 has 60 cameras linked to its central surveillance command, most of which can be pivoted and zoomed by remote-control operators. Plans are afoot to expand the system even further. Yet King's Lynn doesn't have a serious crime problem in comparison to elsewhere in Britain. Street muggings have always been rare here, murders rarer, and rapes virtually unheard of. 'What it comes down to is, there's a perception of crime, a fear of crime, rather than actual crime' [project director Barry] Loftus conceded. The surveillance system has grown because of a 'feel-good' factor it creates among the public, he said.

(*Washington Post*, 8 August 1994)

Norris et al. (1998) contains four separate studies (Chapters 7 to 10) of the effects of CCTV on crime in differing environments. In each case the evidence is complex and the results difficult to quantify. There is some evidence that some crimes are reduced when CCTV systems are introduced. Other crimes seem to be displaced into other areas while still others can increase.

In July 2002, British crime-prevention charity NACRO released a study demonstrating that better street lighting was consistently more effective than CCTV in reducing street crime ('Report says CCTV is overrated', *Guardian*, 28 June 2002).

18  This slippage continues to occur in media treatment of linked cases. When Holly Wells and Jessica Chapman were abducted in Soham, England, in August 2002, newspapers inevitably splashed their front pages with the last CCTV images of the girls, even though these images were never going to be of any use and the police already had reports from witnesses who had seen the girls much closer to the time of the abduction. (One of these witnesses was subsequently charged with the girls' murder.) A few days later, the *Guardian* carried a report asserting that the girls could have been saved

if plans to install video cameras on other streets had not suffered delays. The article presented no argument or evidence as to what these cameras would have done to prevent the crime, rather continuing to circulate the assumption that city centre cameras installed to prevent street crime and robbery somehow intervene in cases of abduction ('CCTV plan could have foiled snatch', *Guardian*, 12 August 2002).

19 The report of the inquiry by Sir William Macpherson into the Metropolitan Police's handling of the Stephen Lawrence case was published by the British Home Office on 24 February 1999.

20 The recordings were actually combined audio/video recordings. Visual aspects of the tapes, including the brandishing of knives by the suspects, also provided a link to the crime itself. Here, however, I want to concentrate on the importance of the sound of the racist words.

21 The private prosecution collapsed after the judge ruled key eyewitness evidence inadmissible and the covert footage was never presented in the courtroom ('Anger after race case collapse', *Guardian,* 26 April 1996).

22 Hate speech legislation bans the public use of certain words on the basis of the effect they have – a legislative practice justified by reference to the concept of 'fighting words', which are unprotected by the First Amendment (Butler, 1995: 206).

23 In July 2002, police in Los Angeles were caught on video camera beating Donovan Jackson, a young black man they had arrested in a petrol station forecourt. A decade after the Rodney King incident, police dealt with the imagery and its interpretation with a great deal more sophistication. Police representatives immediately pointed to the exclusions of the tape – indicating that the victim had attacked the policeman involved immediately before the moments recorded. They also made every effort to isolate the case, to indicate the degree to which the police department distanced itself from any such actions – ensuring that the tape was not 'uptaken' as an public experience of the police department's behaviour. The tape was carefully reattached to the specifics of the case, even as its evidential qualities were questioned.

## 2 Perverting privacy

1 Indeed, Freud's identification of the click of the imagined camera with the throbbing of the clitoris supports an association between the camera and pleasure (Freud, 1963a: 104).

2 Neither Lacan nor Irigaray repeats this conflation, though in both theorists' work the emphasis on sexual difference perhaps glosses over much that is interesting in Freud's analysis of the position of the male homosexual.

3 The case of *Bowers* v. *Hardwick* (the Georgia sodomy case) is the most notorious example of the failure of the US supreme court to extend constitutional privacy rights to homosexual acts.

4 The phrase is synonymous in this essay of Freud's with the 'ideal ego'. I have limited myself in this analysis to a use of the concept of the ego-

ideal as articulated in 'On narcissism'. In later work, Freud develops the concept of the super-ego in a far more complex manner. Here my focus is on the structural relation between the ideal ego and the sexualization of the law/the public space. However, it is worth noting in particular the degree to which Freud later emphasizes the directness of the relationship between super-ego and shared morality. In 'The ego and the id', he writes: 'Social feelings rest on identifications with other people on the basis of having the same ego ideal' (Freud, 1991: 377). He also stresses the closeness, even the interchangeability, of desire and hostility as the impulses over which the super-ego asserts a controlling force:

> Even today the social feelings arise in the individual as a superstructure built upon the impulses of jealous rivalry against brothers and sisters. Since hostility cannot be satisfied, an identification with the former rival develops. The study of mild cases of homosexuality confirms the suspicion that in this instance, too, the identification is a substitute for an affectionate object-choice which has *taken* the place of the aggressive, hostile attitude.
>
> (Ibid.: 377)

5  We should not underestimate the violence that may also attend this transgression. The narcissistic libido directs an aggressive force against objects that disrupt its self-completion, and the confusion evoked by the surveillance shower scene may also generate a sexualized destructiveness towards the bodies it displays. The violence implied in narcissism is an inevitable aspect of sexualized surveillance and reminds us of the misguidedness of any implication that alternative sexual practices under surveillance point towards a utopian potentiality.

6  The term also avoids the reproduction-centred concept of 'womb-envy' (see Spivak, 1996: 53–74).

7  Silverman sets great store by the feminine man (Silverman, 1992).

8  Indeed, the first movie that Silverman examines in detail in her study is Michael Powell's 1959 movie *Peeping Tom* (Silverman, 1988: 32–41). In this movie, the central character, Mark Lewis (Carl Boehm), has been permanently traumatized by his psychoanalyst father's decision to film his childhood as a scientific record of childhood development. As an adult, Mark uses a special camera to simultaneously film and kill women. The camera has a knife which emerges to stab Mark's victims in the throat, and a mirror, so that they can see themselves dying. Mark's movie then shows the woman's face as she watches herself die. Silverman develops an illuminating analysis of both *Peeping Tom* and the critical reaction to it (so negative that it more or less destroyed Powell's career). She emphasizes the fact that Mark's movie lacks a soundtrack: 'Hollywood's sound regime is present in it only as a structuring absence' (ibid.: 39). Whereas, Silverman argues, Hollywood is at greatest pains to evoke the sound of the female cry, Mark ultimately, in the moment of his suicide, adds to his movie the sounds

of his own childhood screams. Meanwhile, a discursive sense is developed by the character of Helen, daughter of Mark's landlady. Helen develops her romantic interest in Mark into the decision to write about the case. Silverman here suggests, specifically in the context of the psychic traumas associated with surveillance, that the silence of the surveillance image can open the possibility of feminine discursivity.

9  Of course, the disabled person may also occupy the positions of gay male or female, and my analysis is limited by its failure to examine the differing experiences of 'erasure of sexuality' for disabled people in differing subject positions. While the erasure undoubtedly occurs under the single social sign 'disabled person', attempts to counter this erasure must allow for the complexity of group and individual experiences within the social and political identities of disabled people.

10  Paul Virilio (1997: 21) displays an intensely phobic response to the process of prostheticization:

> Though none of us would dispute the inalienable right of the disabled to live the same way as everyone else, and therefore with everyone else, it is not the less revealing to note the convergences that now exist between the reduced mobility of the well-equipped disabled person and the growing inertia of the overequipped able-bodied person, as though the transmission revolution always yielded an identical result, no matter what the bodily condition of the patient, the terminal citizen of a teletopical City that is going up faster and faster.
>
> At the end of the century, there will not be much left of the expanse of a planet that is not only polluted, but also shrunk, reduced to nothing, by the teletechnologies of generalized interactivity.

Virilio's reliance, in his recent work, on an association of value with a concept of the natural body leads his critique of corporate/imperialist technophilia into a disturbingly conservative insistence upon the inherent destructiveness of prosthetics: 'Having no graphic or videographic outputs, the automatic-perception prosthesis will function like a kind of mechanized imaginary from which, this time, we would be totally excluded' (Virilio, 1994: 60). Unlike a politicized critique of prosthesis from disabled people, emphasizing the ways in which prosthesis is often used to reiterate society's fantasy of the whole healthy body (for example through the realistic artificial limb), Virilio's response to prosthesis seems determined by a fear that the prostheticization of the 'natural' body reduces it to equivalence with the disabled body, and ultimately destroys a subjectivity inextricably tied to the natural and whole.

11  See also, for example, *Observer*, 27 October 2002, special supplement on 'Sex uncovered'.

12  In *Everyday Surveillance: Vigilance and Visibility in Postmodern Life*, William G. Staples (2000) traces the development of webcam sites, initiated by college junior Jennifer Ringley, who set up the first twenty-four-hour

webcam site, JenniCam.org, displaying daily life in her apartment in all its detail. The site started as a hobby but quickly became a money-making operation, leading to thousands of similar, and often more explicitly sexual webcam sites, both amateur and profit-making. Interviewed online, Ringley maintains that her site does not affect her privacy 'as long as what goes on inside my head is still private' (ibid.: 145). However, the eagerness with which she and many other women have introduced cameras into the domestic sphere indicates a desire to change the terms of the domestic–private equation.

## 3   Accidental death

1   There are, increasingly, conscious uses of video recording by killers of self and others which could be analysed in relation to the earlier discussion of 'home-made' pornography. (One example is the Bjork 'fan' who mailed a bomb to the singer and then recorded his own suicide.) However, the connections of such scenes to the erotic structures of pornography are not straightforward and, in particular, the reception of the recording by the viewer is less likely to involve an acceptance (or understanding) of the terms on which the subject would have created this structure to incorporate subsequent viewing into the present act. Deaths staged for cameras known to be watching also manipulate the structures of surveillance in interesting ways, for example the case of the American who staged his suicide for watching news helicopters in a bizarre protest against health maintenance organizations ('Americans see suicide live on television', *Evening Standard*, London, May 1998; see also Calvert, 2002: 9).

2   A corollary phenomenon is the bringing of lawsuits by individuals who have survived near-death experiences that have been broadcast on television ('Man who attempted suicide can sue over film "invasion of privacy"', *Guardian*, 19 October 1996; 'Crash victim sues over secret TV film', *Guardian*, 4 March 1998).

3   For a good analysis of how a Derridean reading of Levinas can contribute to a notion of 'ethical alterity' in areas of justice/jurisprudence, and by implication wider social systems, see Cornell (1992: Ch. 3).

4   The missed, edited out moment in Joslin's film can also be related to the inevitable gap between the experience of death by the subject and its experience by the witness. In his essay 'Reading, mourning, and the death of the author', Ross Chambers (1997) analyses the functioning of this gap in works of 'AIDS witness', the diaries, texts and cultural products which record the death of their author. Chambers examines the impossibility of the phrase 'I am dead', which is the message of these texts, and the way in which it is approached by the possible enunciations of the subject, 'I am dying', and of the witness '"I" is dead'. Chambers suggests that the sense of loss evoked by this gap is a site where we can begin to address the experience of AIDS and other sites of devastation. Importantly, Chambers emphasizes

that to accept this functioning of loss in the reception of works of AIDS witnessing is to accept it in relation to all reading and cultural reception – only via such an epistemological shift will we begin to address the pain to which this loss relates. Chambers includes in his essay a detailed analysis of Laurie Lynd's movie, *RSVP* (ibid.: 71–4), an evocation of the silences and half-communications via which a man's death from AIDS is mourned and communicated by his lover and family. Central to the narrative of the movie is the fact that the dead man has requested a favourite Berlioz aria to be played on national radio, and that this aria is played and heard by his lover after his death. Because of time zone differences in Canada, where the movie is set, the lover communicates, via awkward networks, to the family that they should tune in to the radio to listen to the aria. Chambers uses this example to illustrate both the communication and loss that inevitably figure when a private message becomes a cultural statement:

> Each retransmitted message will be in some sense continuous with the message to which it responds but also, and inescapably, discontinuous with it. But the film seems to assure us that that is what is meant by broadcasting and that it is by virtue of such broadcasting, through which messages are socially (and not just privately) received, and of the responsibility of responsiveness jointly shouldered, that texts whose authors are dead – ultimately all texts – acquire an authority 'borrowed from death' and are able to exert their effects.
>
> (Ibid.: 74)

Chambers' argument is convincing and important. However, I find *RSVP* a far less evocative movie than he does, and not only because of my relative insensitivity to Berlioz. As a highly structured fiction, the movie takes loss, the awkward transmission of messages about loss, as its theme. It is a movie constructed from the viewpoint of the witness, the sufferer of loss. It does not, like *Silverlake Life*, attempt to grapple in its intent and structure with the impossible statement 'I am dead'. Chambers' analysis emphasizes the position of the reader, the witness, in the very structure, the conceptualization of the cultural works under discussion. In the surveillance-like works discussed in this chapter, a performative moment is emphasized, in which neither subject nor witness take precedence, but in which the aporia, 'I am dead' is approached. I would agree with Chambers, however, that the works of witness created in response to the AIDS crisis are a significant challenge to understand the importance of social, not just private, messages about death, and to recognize the effects of such a social message on all cultural communications.

5  Phelan takes this last point from Judith Halberstam (unpublished manuscript, 1995: 18; quoted in Phelan, 1997a: 165). Phelan notes that shot/counter-shot 'is the primary grammar of documentary'. I would question the degree to which *Silverlake Life* as a 'video diary' actually sets up any expectation

of such documentary conventions, while agreeing that some of the most powerful scenes in the film, such as the death bed scenes analysed above, derive much of their impact from the one-way gaze of the camera. Surveillance cameras, of course, never produce shot/counter-shot sequences. I think that video diaries are, in this as well as other ways, closer generically to surveillance than to documentary.

6  Similarities with *Silverlake Life* occur in the film *Sick: The Life and Death of Bob Flanagan Supermasochist* (directed by Kirby Dick, 1997). Flanagan, a visual and performance artist, cooperated closely with Dick on this documentary about his life and work. During filming, Flanagan was in the late stages of cystic fibrosis, a disease that had influenced much of his artistic output and which he knew would kill him sooner rather than later. While the film is more of a conventional documentary than *Silverlake Life* (in its structure; its imagery and subject matter are far from conventional), and as such the death scene itself does not have the radical effects of Joslin's (it comes at a point in the film when Flanagan as artist and sexual experimenter is marginalized and the scene becomes narrativized as a hospital death bed drama), in earlier moments in the film Flanagan addresses the theme of his death with extraordinary originality. At one point he proposes an art work, *Video Coffin*, in which a surveillance camera placed in his coffin will transmit images of his body's decay to an audience. This ultimate surveillance of death, of its effects on the body, while realized only as a concept, provides a resonant commentary on the relation between surveillance video imagery and death, on the camera's capacity to reconfigure our culture's processing of death.

7  This reading can be linked to Benjamin's notion of 'distracted viewing' (Benjamin, 1969: 239–41), which will be explored in some detail in Chapter 5.

8  The thousands of New Yorkers who experienced or to some degree saw the attacks directly have a very different context for these events, and the complexity of responses in that most complex of cities is very different to that of the rest of the world.

## 4  Dimensions, doubles and data: producing surveillance space

1  A series of such interviews are presented in the BBC documentary *Children of Crime: A Riddle Wrapped Inside an Enigma* (BBC, 7 April 1998).

2  ... conceptualized space, the space of scientists, planners, urbanists, technocratic subdividers and social engineers, as of a certain type of artist with a scientific bent – all of whom identify what is lived and what is perceived with what is conceived ... This is the dominant space in any society (or mode of production). Conceptual space tends ... toward a system of verbal (and therefore intellectually worked out) signs.

(Lefebvre, 1991: 38–9)

3 ... and hence, the space of 'inhabitants' and 'users', but also of some artists and perhaps of those, such as a few writers and philosophers, who describe, and aspire to do no more than describe. This is the dominated – and hence passively experienced – space which the imagination seeks to change and appropriate. It overlays physical experience, making symbolic use of its objects.

(Ibid.: 39)

While Lefebvre's implicit endorsement of artists, writers and philosophers 'who describe and aspire to do no more than describe' might initially seem unpleasantly reminiscent of a Lukácsian realism, it plays out in his work more as an endorsement of abstract and body-related arts (with a particular emphasis on rhythmic music), as opposed to the conceptually systematized.

4 Images of Hatoum's exterior organs, including her eye, are included in the loop, periodically inverting the viewing dynamic and further complexifying the experience of the work. However, the vast majority of the footage is of the internal organs, and most audiences experience this aspect of the installation.

5 In 1999, Paul Schmidt also died of AIDS. Though less of a public figure than Vawter, Schmidt's importance as a writer and translator (particularly of Chekhov and Rimbaud) stretched far beyond his association with The Wooster Group. As both on-stage translator (sometimes providing footnotes) and performer of the role of Chebutykin in *Brace Up*, his playful yet professorly presence added a new tone to The Wooster Group's work. His upbeat reading of the character, at the same time as the video technologies of the show reduced him to an image on a particularly small television screen, in a way emblematized his situation at this point in life: a respected professor who knew that he was dying, he had run away to join the theatre.

6 *Fish Story*, though not one of the company's most successful works, is a poignant howl of loss in response to Vawter's death. The performance opens with a raucous soundtrack sampling Vawter's version of Versinin's final speech: 'I have to go.' The later part of the piece focuses quite simply on the monologue shown at the memorial service.

7 Lacoue-Labarthe's concept of weak writing is a reference point here:

... perhaps, not writing exactly what we wanted to write, we experience a weakness, a powerlessness that is no longer the effect of an excess of power, but rather like the obscure work of a force that is foreign to what we say.

(Lacoue-Labarthe, 1993: 11)

8 Though note Cindy Patton's analysis of the dangerous performativities of epidemiology (Parker and Sedgwick, 1995: 173–96).

9 'Autobiography as self-surveillance' Stanley's keynote address at Surveillance: An Interdisciplinary Conference, at Liverpool John Moores University, June 1998.

## 5 Staging the spectator

1  In a decision on the so-called 'Spanner' case (the name was that of the sado-masochistic group under prosecution), which was appealed unsuccessfully in the European Court of Human Rights in 1997, it was declared illegal under English law for a person to carry out injurious act on another, even with that other person's permission – a decision with considerable consequences for practitioners of consensual sado-masochism. This decision was a specific reference point for Blast Theory.

2  The effect is produced simply by having a camera send an image to a monitor diagonally opposite. Viewers can see themselves in the monitor only as they are turning the corner because only then are they both in view of the camera behind them and able to see the monitor around the corner in front.

3  An earlier version of this essay appeared in 1988 ('Brechtian theory/feminist theory: toward a gestic feminist criticism', The *Drama Review* 32:1, spring 1988: 82–94). Some of the work discussed in Diamond's later version was undoubtedly influenced by the ideas she put forward in the earlier version.

4  Writer Patricia Spears Jones placed the title word in quotation marks to indicate that this was a label, a name spoken by others.

5  Spivak retranslates Foucault to emphasize the aspect of speech.

6  Armstrong, S. 'The theatre of cruelty', *Sunday Telegraph Magazine*, 5 July 1998; Gardner, L. 'This pair are going to take two people hostage and film the results and they call it theatre,' *Guardian*, 1 May 1998; Stratton, K. 'Cyberbondage', *Time Out*, 8 July 1998.

## 6 Encountering surveillance

1  In one example in Britain, two black youths under attack by racists were sprayed with CS gas by police, arrested and charged with violent disorder. After CCTV cameras revealed evidence of what had actually happened, the police were forced to withdraw the charges and were put under investigation themselves ('Beaten by skinheads, gassed by police', *Observer*, 26 April 1998).

2  Of course, government attempts to redress the balance in favour of the police are ongoing. In Britain, the 1998 Crime Prevention and Disorder Act gives police powers to remove and take away balaclavas and other headgear when they stop and search demonstrators – regardless of whether the individual is under any criminal suspicion. An article in the *Big Issue* indicates the variety of discourses of privacy and surveillance that such a change in law provokes:

> Other activists are accusing the police of double standards: 'I was at a demonstration about five or six weeks ago when the police had balaclavas on, and we have video footage where they're not showing their numbers

as they're meant to. So its one law for us and one law for them,' said a spokesman for the Hillgrove Cats animal rights campaign group. Officers attending demonstrations now routinely take long-lens video and still camera, to record the day's events and to build up a national database of protestors' faces. This surveillance was until recently a covert activity, but now officers carry and use equipment regularly.

... Announcing the new clause on 'face-coverings' in May last year the then Home Office minister Alun Michael, said: 'For too long, cowardly thugs have been allowed to hide behind masks to inflict terror and violence on innocent members of the public.'

('The men in the masks face a new balaclava ban', *Big Issue*, 18 January 1999)

On the other hand, the video taping of police continues to have results. Again, the *Big Issue* reports:

A black media student who filmed officers form Greater Manchester Police during a stormy encounter which led to his arrest and conviction for public order offences has used his own video footage to get the conviction squashed.

('Black student freed after filming his own arrest', *Big Issue*, 29 March 1999)

3 'Cottaging guerrillas turn cameras on US police', *Pink Paper*, London, 11 December 1998.
4 Ibid. The article reported:

No fewer than 40 towns and cities have started video-recording sexual encounters between men in public locations for broadcast late at night. The sensational broadcasts have been transmitted across America, including Philadelphia, Oklahoma, New York, Las Vegas, Cincinnati, San Diego and Houston. Phylis Kariss of the University of Pennsylvania explained how the television stations operate. 'They go to the cruising-for-sex web sites, find the locations of tearooms in their area and then bring in the hidden cameras.' She added: 'If public sex is such a social problem, then you have to ask why these programmes tend to go out when the stations' audience ratings are due to be audited.'

5 For example, the *Guardian* 27 August 2002 ('US city where you can be guilty until proven innocent'), which bases an exploration of policing in Wilmington, Delaware (where police arrest on the basis of photographic evidence showing that the suspect – usually a black male – regularly congregates where the crime took place), on a comparison with Spielberg's *Minority Report*.
6 In her essay 'Not surviving reading' (Phelan, 1997b), which is written as a response to Ross Chambers' essay 'Reading, mourning, and the death of

the author' (Chambers, 1997), Peggy Phelan develops the idea of the reader, and the subject in general, who is 'already dead'. She notes that certain subject positions, for example the queer adolescent, necessitate a death to 'the Law of the Social'. Consequently, such subjects have personal narrative experience of the statement: 'I am dead.' Going on to analyse Artaud's identification with (the dead) Van Gogh, she writes:

> For Artaud, death was precisely not in 'the beyond'; death happened continually, constantly, endlessly in the past. Artaud did not mean, as so many people do, that dying is ongoing; he meant that in terms of the infinite towards which all art aspires, death is always already in the past tense. Choosing, as far as he was able, to be 'already dead', Artaud was freed from looking for and dreading death.
>
> (Phelan, 1997b: 84)

Phelan's arguments usefully indicate how we might begin to process and make use of the traumatic realization through surveillance that we are 'already dead'.

# Bibliography

Althusser, Louis (1984) *Essays on Ideology*, London: Verso.

Archer, M. and Hilty, G. (1997) *Material Culture: The Object in British Art of the 1980s and '90s*, London: South Bank Centre.

Artaud, A. (1958) *The Theater and its Double*, New York: Grove.

— (1988) *Selected Writings* (ed. Susan Sontag), Berkeley, Calif.: University of California.

Austin, J.L. (1976) *How To Do Things With Words*, Oxford: Oxford University Press.

Baudrillard, Jean (1983) *Simulations*, New York: Semiotexte.

— (1993) *The Transparency of Evil*, London: Verso.

— (1996) *The Perfect Crime*, London: Verso.

Beckett, Andy (1997) 'An end to the struggle', *Guardian Magazine,* 18 October 1997.

Benjamin, Walter (1969) *Illuminations*, New York: Schocken.

Bentham, Jeremy (1843) *Jeremy Bentham: Collected Works* (ed. J. Bowring), London.

Betsky, Aaron (1997) *Queer Space. Architecture and Same-Sex Desire*, New York: William Morrow.

Bogard, William (1996) *The Simulation of Surveillance in Telematic Society: Social Control in the 1990s*, Cambridge: Cambridge University Press.

Brecht, Bertolt (1957) *Brecht on Theatre* (ed. John Willet), New York: Hill and Wang.

Bugliosi, Vincent (1996) *Outrage, The Five Reasons OJ Simpson Got Away With Murder*, New York: W.W. Norton.

Butler, Judith (1990) *Gender Trouble*, New York: Routledge.

— (1993) *Bodies That Matter*, New York: Routledge.

— (1995) 'Burning acts - injurious speech', in *Performance and Performativity* (eds Andrew Parker and Kosofsky Sedgwick), pp. 197–227, New York: Routledge.

— (1997) *Excitable Speech: A Politics of the Performative*, New York: Routledge.

Califia, Pat (1994) *Public Sex,* Pittsburgh, Penn.: Cleis Press.

Calvert, Clay (2002) *Voyeur Nation,* Boulder, Colo.: Westview Press.

Cameron, Don (1997) *Mona Hatoum* (programme for the exhibition at the New Museum of Contemporary Art), New York: New Museum of Contemporary Art.

Chambers, Ross (1997) 'Reading, mourning and the death of the author', *Narrative* 5(1), 67–76.

# Bibliography

Chekhov, Anton (1979) *Three Sisters* (trans. Jean-Claude van Itallie), New York: Dramatists Play Service.

Cohen, Stanley and Taylor, Laurie (1992) *Escape Attempts: The Theory and Practice of Resistance to Everyday Life*, London: Routledge.

Cooper, Dennis (1991) *Frisk*, New York: Grove Weidenfeld.

Cornell, Drucilla (1992) *The Philosophy of the Limit*, New York: Routledge.

Cummings, Dolan (1997) *Surveillance and the City*, London: Urban Research Group.

Davies, Simon (1996) *Big Brother: Britain's Web of Surveillance and the New Technological Order,* London: Pan.

Davis, Mike (1988) *City of Quartz*, Verso: London.

Debord, Guy (1995) *Society of the Spectacle*, New York: Zone Books.

Deleuze, Gilles and Guattari, Félix (1983) *Anti-Oedipus*, Minneapolis, Minn.: University of Minnesota.

Derrida, Jacques (1977) 'Signature/Event/Context', *Glyph*, Vol. 1, pp. 172–97, Baltimore: Johns Hopkins University

— (1982) *Writing and Difference*, Chicago, Ill.: Chicago University Press.

— (1993) *Aporias*, Stanford, Calif.: Stanford University Press.

Diamond, Elin (1988) 'Brechtian theory/feminist theory: toward a gestic feminist criticism', *The Drama Review*, 32, 1, 88–94.

— (1997) *Unmaking Mimesis*, New York: Routledge,

Druckrey, Timothy (1996) 'Julia Scher: telephobic modernity and the ecologies of surveillance', *Art and Text*, May, 50–3.

Dworkin, Andrea (1979) *Pornography: Men Possessing Women*, New York: Perigee Books.

Dyer, Richard (1981) 'Entertainment and Utopia', in *Genre: The Musical – A Reader* (ed. Rich Altman), pp. 175–89, London: Routledge.

Foucault, Michel (1973) *The Order of Things*, New York: Vintage.

— (1977) 'Intellectuals and power', in *Language, Counter-Memory, Practice* (ed. Donald Bouchard), pp. 205–17, Ithaca, N.Y.: Cornell University Press.

— (1978) *The History of Sexuality*, Vol. 1, *An Introduction*, New York: Random House.

— (1980) *Power/Knowledge*, New York: Pantheon.

— (1986) 'Of other spaces', *Diacritics*, 16, 22–7.

— (1991) *Discipline and Punish*, London: Penguin.

Freud, Sigmund (1961) *Beyond the Pleasure Principle,* New York: W.W. Norton.

— (1963a) *Sexuality and the Psychology of Love*, New York: Macmillan.

— (1963b) *General Psychological Theory*, New York: Macmillan.

— (1975) *Three Essays on the Theory of Sexuality*, New York: HarperCollins.

Friedlander, Jennifer (1998) *Moving Pictures: Where the Police, the Press and the Art Image Meet,* Sheffield: Sheffield Hallam University Press.

Garfinkel, Simson (2001) *Database Nation: The Death of Privacy in the 21st Century,* Cambridge, Mass.: O'Reilly Associates.

Garland, D. (1990) *Punishment and Modern Society,* Oxford: Clarendon Press.

Genet, Jean (1990) *Prisoner of Love*, London: Pan.

# Bibliography

Gever, Martha, Greyson, John and Parmar, Prathibha (eds) (1993) *Queer Looks: Perspectives on Lesbian and Gay Film and Video*, New York: Routledge.

Goodin-Williams, Robert (ed.) (1993) *Reading Rodney King, Reading Urban Uprising*, Routledge: New York.

Gould, Timothy (1995) 'The unhappy performative', in *Performance and Performativity* (eds Andrew Parker and Eve Kosofsky Sedgwick), pp. 19–44, New York: Routledge.

Greyson, John (1993) 'Security blankets: sex, video and the police,' in *Queer Looks: Perspectives on Lesbian and Gay Film and Video* (eds Martha Gever, John Greyson, and Prathibha Parmar), pp. 383–94, New York: Routledge.

Habermas, Jurgen (1987*)* *The Philosophical Discourse of Modernity: Twelve Lectures*, Cambridge: Polity Press.

Heidegger, Martin (1977) *Basic Writings* (ed. David Farrell Krell), New York: Harper & Row.

Hevey, David (1992) *The Creatures That Time Forgot*, London: Routledge.

Hope, Tim and Sparks, Richard (eds) (2000) *Crime, Risk and Insecurity: Law and Order in Everyday Life and Political Discourse,* London: Routledge.

Irigaray, Luce (1985) *Speculum of the Other Woman*, Ithaca, N.Y.: Cornell University Press.

Kant, Immanuel (1987) *Critique of Judgment* (trans. Werner S. Pluhar), Indianapolis, Ind: Hackett.

—— (1993) *Critique of Pure Reason*, London: Everyman.

King, John (1996) *The Football Factory*, London: Jonathan Cape.

Koon, Stacey (1992) *Presumed Guilty: The Tragedy of the Rodney King Affair*, Washington, D.C.: Regenery Gateway.

Lacan, Jacques (1977) *Ecrits: A Selection* (trans. Alan Sheridan), New York: W.W. Norton.

—— (1981) *The Four Fundamental Concepts of Psychoanalysis* (trans. Alan Sheridan, ed. Jacques-Alain Miller), New York: W.W. Norton.

—— (1985) *Feminine Sexuality* (trans. and eds Juliet Mitchell and Jacqueline Rose), New York: W.W. Norton.

Lacoue-Labarthe, Philippe (1993) *The Subject of Philosophy*, Minneapolis, Minn.: University of Minnesota Press.

Lefebvre, Henri (1991) *The Production of Space*, Oxford: Blackwell.

Levin, Thomas Y., Frohne, Ursula and Weibel, Peter (2002) *CTRL [SPACE]: Rhetorics of Surveillance from Bentham to Big Brother*, Cambridge, Mass.: MIT Press.

Lyon, David (1994) *The Electronic Eye: The Rise of Surveillance Society*, Minneapolis, Minn.: University of Minnesota Press.

—— (2001) *Surveillance Society: Monitoring Everyday Life,* Buckingham: Open University Press.

Lyon, David and Zureik, Elia (eds) (1996) *Computers, Surveillance and Privacy*, Minneapolis, Minn.: University of Minnesota Press.

Marx, Gary T. (1986) 'The iron fist and the velvet glove: totalitarian potentials within democratic structures', in *The Social Fabric: Dimensions and Issues* (ed. James E. Short), Beverly Hills, Calif.: Sage Publications,.

# Bibliography

—— (1988) *Undercover: Police Surveillance in America*, Berkeley, Calif.: University of California Press.

Meyrowitz, Joshua (1985) *No Sense of Place: The Impact of Electronic Media on Social Behaviour*, Oxford: Oxford University Press.

Morrison, Blake (1997) *As If*, London: Granta.

Mulvey, Laura (1975) 'Visual pleasure and narrative cinema', *Screen*, 16(3), 8–18.

Norris, Clive and Armstrong, Gary (1999) *The Maximum Surveillance Society*, Oxford: Berg.

Norris, Clive, Moran, Jade and Armstrong, Gary (eds) (1998) *Surveillance, Closed Circuit Television and Social Control*, Aldershot: Ashgate.

Parker, Andrew and Sedgwick, Eve Kosofsky (eds) (1995) *Performance and Performativity*, New York: Routledge.

Parker, John (2000) *Total Surveillance: Investigating the Big Brother World of E-Spies, Eavesdropping and CCTV*, London: Piatkus.

Patton, Cindy (1995) 'Performativity and spatial distinction: the end of AIDS epidemiology', in *Performance and Performativity* (eds Andrew Parker and Eve Kosofsky Sedgwick), pp. 173–96, New York: Routledge.

Penley, Constance and Ross, Andrew (eds) (1991) *Technoculture*, Minneapolis, Minn.: University of Minnesota.

Perri 6 (1998) *The Future of Privacy*, London: Demos.

Phelan, Peggy (1993) *Unmarked: The Politics of Performance*, London: Routledge.

—— (1997a) *Mourning Sex: Performing Public Memories*, London: Routledge.

—— (1997b) 'Not surviving reading', *Narrative*, 5(1), 77–87.

Poster, Mark (1990) *The Mode of Information*, Cambridge: Polity Press.

—— (1995) *The Second Media Age*, Cambridge: Polity Press.

Ravenhill, Mark (1996) *Shopping and Fucking*, London, Methuen.

Regazonni, Carlos, Fabri, Gianni and Vernazza, Gianni (eds) (1999) *Advanced Video-based Surveillance Systems*, London: Kluwer.

Ritchie, Jean (2001) *Big Brother 2: The Official Unseen Story*, London: Channel 4 Books.

Rule, James (1973) *Private Lives, Public Surveillance*, London: Allen Lane.

Saalfield, Catherine (1993) 'On the make: activist video collectives', in *Queer Looks: Perspectives on Lesbian and Gay Film and Video* (eds Martha Gever, John Greyson and Prathibha Parmar), pp. 21–37, New York: Routledge.

Scher, Julia (1995) 'The institutional state', in *Els Limits Del Museu*, a catalogue which accompanied an exhibition at the Antoni Tapies Foundation of Barcelona.

Sennet, Richard (1977) *The Fall of Public Man*, London: Alfred Knopf.

—— (1991) *Conscience of the Eye*, London: Faber & Faber.

Shearing, Clifford D. and Stenning, Philip C. (eds) (1987) *Private Policing*, Thousand Oaks, Calif.: Sage.

Silverman, Kaja (1988) *The Acoustic Mirror: The Female Voice in Psychoanalysis and Cinema*, Bloomington, Ind.: University of Indiana Press.

—— (1992) *Male Subjectivity on the Margins*, New York: Routledge.

# Bibliography

Smith, David James (1994) *The Sleep of Reason: The James Bulger Case*, London: Century.

Soja, Edward (1989) *Postmodern Geographies: The Reassertion of Space in Critical Social Theory*, London: Verso.

Sparks, Richard (1992) *Television and the Drama of Crime*, Buckingham: Open University Press.

Spivak, Gayatri (1988) 'Can the subaltern speak?', in *Marxism and the Interpretation of Culture* (eds C. Nelson and L. Grosshery), Basingstoke: Macmillan Education.

—— (1996) *The Spivak Reader* (eds. Donna Landry and Gerald MacLean), New York: Routledge.

Staples, William G. (2000) *Everyday Surveillance: Vigilance and Visibility in Postmodern Life*, New York: Rowman and Littlefield.

Storr, Robert (1997) *On the Edge: Contemporary Art From the Werner and Elaine Danheisser Collection*, New York: Museum of Modern Art.

Thomas, Douglas and Loader, Brian D. (eds) (2000) *Cybercrime*, Routledge: London.

Thomson, T. (1998) 'Identity crisis', *Time Out*, 24 June 1998.

Virilio, Paul (1989) *War and Cinema*, London: Verso.

—— (1994) *The Vision Machine,* Bloomingto, Ind.: Indiana University Press.

—— (1997) *Open Skies*, London: Verso.

Whitaker, Reg (2000) *The End of Privacy: How Total Surveillance is Becoming a Reality*, New York: The New Press.

Williams, Linda (1989) *Hard Core: Power, Pleasure, and the 'Frenzy of the Visible'*, Berkeley, Calif.: University of California Press.

Zephaniah, Benjamin (1996) *Propa Propaganda*, Newcastle upon Tyne: Bloodaxe Books.

Žižek, Slavoj (1989) *The Sublime Object of Ideology*, London: Verso.

—— (1992) *Enjoy Your Symptom/Jacques Lacan In Hollywood and Out*, New York: Routledge.

—— (1993) *Tarrying With the Negative: Kant, Hegel and the Critique of Ideology*, Durham, N.C.: Duke University Press.

# Index

241

# Index

# Index

# Index

# Index